Patrick Harpur is a long-time stud
tradition. He has published two nov
fiction, including a study of alchemy, *Mercurius: or, The Marriage of Heaven and Earth*; a study of visions and apparitions, *Daimonic Reality: A Field Guide to the Otherworld*; and a history of the imagination, *The Philosophers' Secret Fire*. He lives in west Dorset, England.

Other books by Patrick Harpur:

The Philosophers' Secret Fire: A History of the Imagination
Daimonic Reality: A Field Guide to the Otherworld
Mercurius: or, the Marriage of Heaven and Earth

Novels:
The Serpent's Circle
The Rapture

A Complete Guide to the Soul

Patrick Harpur

RIDER

LONDON · SYDNEY · AUCKLAND · JOHANNESBURG

1 3 5 7 9 10 8 6 4 2

First published in 2010 by Rider, an imprint of Ebury Publishing

Ebury Publishing is a Random House Group company

The Random House Group Limited Reg. No. 954009

Addresses for companies within the Random House Group can be found at www.rbooks.co.uk

A CIP catalogue record for this book is available from the British Library

The Random House Group Limited supports The Forest Stewardship Council (FSC), the leading international forest certification organisation. All our titles that are printed on Greenpeace approved FSC certified paper carry the FSC logo. Our paper procurement policy can be found at www.rbooks.co.uk/environment

Printed and bound in Great Britain by Clays Ltd, St Ives plc

ISBN 9781846041860

Copies are available at special rates for bulk orders. Contact the sales development team on 020 7840 8487 for more information.

To buy books by your favourite authors and register for offers, visit www.rbooks.co.uk

To my aunts, Cicely and Boobela

Contents

Introduction

I t is notoriously difficult to talk about the soul. If we believe that we have a soul, we tend to picture it vaguely – as some essence of ourselves, some core of our being which constitutes our 'real' selves or our 'higher selves'. Even if we are not specifically religious we can all still resonate with the notion that there is some part of us which should not be sold, betrayed or lost at any cost. We can understand the idea that we can 'lose our souls' and still go on living, just as we can lose our lives but retain our souls. We still use the word 'soul' to mean something real or authentic. Whenever music, dance, architecture, food is said to have soul, we mean that it is the real thing, that it speaks to the deepest part of ourselves. It is not a tangible reality, of course, but it is understood to be more real than ordinary life. So the first attribute of soul is as a symbol of depth and authenticity. Wherever it slips in, it stirs in us a sense that there is more to this world than meets the eye, something behind mundane events that is more than human. It stirs, in other words, a religious feeling, regardless of any religious denomination.

The notion of soul is also oriented towards death. If we believe that some part of ourselves lives on after death, that part is the soul. Despite what modern materialists tell us – that we are only our bodies – we persist in feeling that we do in fact inhabit our bodies. We persist in feeling that the most real moments of our lives occur when we – perhaps our souls –

temporarily leave our bodies, whether in joyful or in agonized passion. For example, we are 'outside' of ourselves when we are deeply engaged with a landscape or a lover, when we are 'lost' in a piece of music or dance. Conversely, when we are in heightened states of rage or fear, we spontaneously say: 'I wasn't myself!', 'I was beside myself!', 'I was out of my head!' The Greek root of the word 'ecstasy' means to 'stand outside (oneself)'. Such feelings enable us to experience the reality of what most, if not all, cultures have always asserted: that when we step outside ourselves for the last time, at death, the body rots – but this essential, detachable part of ourselves, our soul, goes on.

While the soul is obviously connected with our sense of depth, of religion and of death, it is also connected with the question of life, and of life's purpose. 'Where am I? Who am I? How did I come to be here . . . ?' asked the philosopher and 'father of existentialism' Søren Kierkegaard. 'How did I come into the world? Why was I not consulted? . . . And if I am compelled to take part in it, where is the manager? I would like to see him.'[1] There are times when we have all echoed Kierkegaard's indignation with our own questions to the manager – 'What is my purpose in life? What am I for? Where do I go when I die?'

Whoever is lucky enough to have found their purpose on Earth knows that they have done so because they feel fulfilled. They may have found their purpose in some job or in some person – a 'soul-mate' – but they are convinced that it is 'meant'. Their lives are not necessarily free of suffering, but they are full of *meaning*. Those of us who are not so lucky nevertheless feel that we should search for a purpose, as if for our own souls. It might be that the search itself is our purpose.

The poet John Keats considered such questions too, suggesting that although people have 'sparks of divinity' in them, they are not 'souls' till they acquire an identity – 'till each one is personally itself'. 'Call the world if you please "The vale of Soul-making," ' he wrote in a letter to his siblings. 'Then you will find out the use of the world.'[2] The question of our paradoxical condition – that we are born with souls yet also, in another sense, have to 'make' them – is at the centre of this book about the soul, its nature and destiny.

This book is therefore for people who are wondering what we consist of – what our essential nature is – and what happens to us when we die. It is for people who are sceptical of materialistic claims that we consist only of our bodies; sceptical of rationalist claims that the only reality is one that is subject to narrow empirical definitions. It is also for people who are disenchanted with the major religions – and especially Christianity – for squabbling over liturgy, gender issues and so forth, and neglecting the one thing religion is founded on: knowledge of the individual soul and its relationship with God. It is for people whose supernatural longing leads them to the East – to Buddhism and Taoism, for instance – only to be downcast by the difficulty of entering wholeheartedly into an alien culture and language. It is a book, too, for people who are drawn to New Age-style 'spirituality', only to find that this is at best abstract and diffuse, at worst, woolly and embarrassing. In short, our souls long for meaning and belief just as much as they ever have, yet they can find no lasting nourishment in modern offerings of philosophy and science. We are like starving people who are given cookbooks instead of food.

Fortunately, help and sustenance lie to hand – not from some outlandish belief system or foreign land, but from a secret tradition within our own culture. It is a kind of 'perennial philosophy' which remains true no matter how radically times appear to change. Why then do we not all embrace it today? Because it is difficult and demanding. However, it is not difficult because it is, for example, in German or in academic jargon. It is difficult because it is subtle and elusive, more an imaginative vision of how things are than a system of thought. Neither is it demanding because it requires tremendous effort, willpower and work; it is demanding because it wants us to turn our whole world-view upside down, forbidding us to fall back on the ideologies, whether of religious dogma or scientistic literalism, that we use simplistically to try to settle the matter of reality once and for all.

Instead, we are talking about a tradition of thinking or, better, seeing, which asks us to see through our own suppositions about the world, to dissolve our certainties, to read many levels into the world as if it were a great poem, and, in changing our perception, to transform our lives.

Although this tradition is secret, coursing through Western culture like an underground stream for the last eighteen hundred years, it occasionally wells up into the mainstream at times of crisis and transition – times, in fact, like our own. I have documented the extraordinary and fertility-bearing floods which inaugurated those great flowerings of culture amongst the Renaissance magi, the Romantic poets and the depth psychologists in my book *The Philosophers' Secret Fire*. Now I want to describe the personal implications of this secret tradition for us as individuals. More, I want to initiate the reader into this brilliant and creative world-view in a language no longer alchemical and arcane but as straightforward as possible. For we all have to rediscover the ancient truths and retell the old myths in a way that speaks to our own generation.

Although its shape constantly changes to suit the age, the central tenets of the secret tradition remain the same. The idea, for example, that *psyche*, soul, constitutes the very fabric of reality; that humans are individual manifestations of a collective Soul of the World which interconnects all things; that imagination, not reason, is the chief faculty of the soul – though not the pale imitation of imagination as we now know it; that there is another world whence the soul comes at birth and to which it returns at death; and that the idea of *gnosis*, of a personal and transforming experience of divinity, is of the essence.

These are the sorts of notions I hope to unpack in the course of this book. Together they add up to a world-view very different from the one to which we in twenty-first-century Western culture are accustomed. It is a sacred outlook, so to speak, which is rich in meaning but neither dogmatic nor agnostic. Nor is it against other systems of thought, such as science, but simply gives us the perceptual tools to look through science's assumptions and to relate its hypotheses back to their mythic origins. Nor is it against religion. It merely enables us to dissolve the sclerotic ideologies which have hardened the heart of religion, letting it beat again. It particularly does not require new-fangled ideas or jargon, but tries to apply new insight to old ideas in order to present them afresh.

To this end, I begin with a survey of the way the soul is understood in tribal cultures very different from ours. I contrast their ideas with the sophisticated notion of soul developed by the Greek founders of our culture, and especially its apotheosis among the Neoplatonists. They best expounded the traditional view that soul is the flagstone of reality, underlying both us and the world, and forming a bond between the two which modern dualism has mistakenly severed. By re-introducing soul to the world we re-enchant the environment and reconnect with our own experiences of the divine which we have been encouraged to ignore or forget, just as Western culture has suffered a collective loss of memory concerning soul itself.

I also re-introduce the soul's traditional spokesman – that guide, guardian angel, Muse or daimon of which Socrates spoke so eloquently – and show how it transforms chance to fate, and fate to a Providence in which whatever randomly occurs is seen to have been forever ordained.

I describe the strengths of our historically recent and culturally unique consciousness, centred on an indomitable ego – and also its weaknesses, not least our own fond belief that it is the highest form of consciousness there is. Central to this deconstruction is the role of initiation in dismantling our tendency to be over-conscious, over-rational – and over-literal. And I shall stress the necessity of reviving those rites of initiation which, though lost to us, are still informally and unconsciously enacted, especially by teenagers, in a desperate bid to keep us in touch with soul, our authentic selves and the world at large.

Lastly, I describe what happens to the soul when it leaves the body, both during life and after death. Part of the impetus behind this book was provided by an eminent English novelist who, in reviewing *Everyman* by the renowned US novelist Philip Roth, praised Roth's view of death as an exchange of 'our fullness for that endless nothing.' He further congratulated Roth on 'casting such a cold crystalline eye on the unfairness of death, and concluding that there are no answers: just the terror of nothingness that we all share.'[3] But, on the contrary, we do not all share such an impoverished view, and as exponents of imagination these novelists should know this – and know better.

Anyone with even a modicum of initiatory experience knows that death is a portal into that greater reality which can already be glimpsed in this world as an imaginative experience of the Otherworld. Whatever physical pain members of traditional cultures may suffer, they do not suffer the mental anguish of eminent modern novelists because they know that they will pass seamlessly into an afterlife where, gathered up by rejoicing ancestors, they will live forever in an ideal version of their beloved homeland, free of sickness and want. Many, perhaps most, people in Western culture – particularly those who are uncontaminated by scientistic and existential nihilism – believe much the same thing. As the Greeks maintained, death is not the opposite of life but of birth – life is a continuous realm out of which we are born; which (as Plato says) we can dimly remember during our existence; and to which we return when we die – return to that totality of life compared to which mortal existence seems but a dream-like fragment.

At the same time, there is no doubt the Afterlife can appear, at worst, as hellish and, at best, as a Hades-like realm of shades which, according to old Irish laments for example, are pale by comparison with the richness and colour of life in this world. The Afterlife is paradoxical, in other words; and I shall explain how it tends to mirror our own souls so that we get the Afterlife we deserve – the Afterlife we already, in a sense, inhabit without being aware of it.

It is a purely modern affectation to claim that we can know nothing of life after death. It means ignoring the accounts of mystics, poets, mediums, medicine-men, shamans, prophets and so-called Near-Death Experiencers, to say nothing of those who have crossed the narrow sword-bridge during moments of love or rapture, during heightened states of illness or drug-taking, in visions or dreams. Such experiences may last only moments, but they can outweigh in importance years of mundane existence. 'Strange as it may seem,' wrote the most famous of all humanists, Erasmus, in 1519, 'there are even men among us who think, like Epicurus, that the soul dies with the body. Mankind are great fools, and will believe anything.'

ONE

Soul and body

All cultures, apart from sections of our own, agree that humans are made of a body and a soul. For Christians, the uniqueness of the soul and its equivalence in each of us guarantee our individuality and our equal rights, the two basic principles of modern liberalism. Moreover, we are used to thinking of body and soul as being divided, the one mortal and the other immortal. This was a Western development, promoted by the ancient Greeks and adopted by Christianity: Plato had a decisive influence on the theology of St Augustine, while Aristotle's thought pervades that of St Thomas Aquinas – still the pre-eminent theologian of Roman Catholicism. However, the division between soul and body is by no means universal. Nor is the singularity of the soul. Pre-literate tribal cultures – which I shall be calling 'traditional' – usually subscribe to more than one soul; and all agree that, although it is distinct from the body, it retains a certain identity with it.

In Africa, for instance, the Basutos are wary of walking along a river bank because if their shadow falls on the water it might be seized by a crocodile – and the owner of the shadow killed.[1] One of the earliest anthropologists, E. B. Tylor, noticed[2] that many tribal cultures, from Tasmania to North America, from Malaysia to Africa, use the word 'shadow' – or a word like it, such as reflection, image, echo, double, dream-body – to signify that part of a human which can detach itself from the body, notably at death. It was natural therefore that anthropologists, who, whether Christian or not, all came from a culture grounded in Christendom, should call this 'shadow' the *soul* – and begin to puzzle over it.

Tylor found that as well as surviving bodily death, the shadow was believed to appear to others separately from its body. It could be placed elsewhere, hidden in a secret place; for it is vulnerable to attack and can even be eaten. Moreover, this shadow or soul was located in, or identified with, various parts of the body: for the Caribs of South America and for the Tongans it is the heart; for the Australian Aboriginals of Victoria the 'kidney fat'; for others, the blood or the liver.[3] The breath is also a common synonym for the shadow or 'breath-body', whether in Western Australia or in Greenland. This was also true of the earliest period of Western culture. 'Breath' is the original meaning of the Greek word *pneuma*, spirit, and a connotation of *psyche*, soul. The notion that the soul leaves the body with the dying person's last breath was a Roman belief – both *animus* and *spiritus* in Latin imply 'breath' – which persisted into Elizabethan times and beyond. But since soul has long since ceased to be linked to anything concrete in our culture, we are struck by how materialistic traditional cultures seem to be in their spiritual ideas.

To compound the puzzle of soul, traditional cultures also often claim that we have more than one. We might have one that is mortal, for example, and another that is immortal. Or a third which is really the soul of a dead ancestor that becomes attached to us as a guide. In North America the Algonquins believe that one soul can leave the body while the other remains behind, so that at death the first departs for the land of the dead while the second is plied with offerings of food, and the Dakotas claim four souls: one stays with the corpse, one stays in the village, one goes into the air and one goes to the land of the spirits.[4]

Were-leopards

If this were not enough to confuse Western anthropologists, they found among many African peoples the idea that humans have 'bush souls' in the form of an animal counterpart. This is a ubiquitous theme – the Korichi Malays of Sumatra, for instance, describe killing a tiger which turned out to be in fact a were-tiger (from the Old English *wer*, 'man'), for they found it had the same gold-plated teeth as its human counterpart![5] The same idea crops up among the Naga people of North-Eastern India, where, J. H. Hutton tells us, a man called Sakhuto was suddenly afflicted by a wound in his back, appearing out of nowhere. He had been shot, he said, while he was in the form of leopard.[6]

And yet similar beliefs were current in Europe until recent times. There are numerous variants of the tale of the hare hunt in Elizabethan England, when a hare was shot and wounded in the leg and the hunters followed its trail of blood to a remote cottage where, inside, an old woman was found, dressing a wound on her leg . . . . The old woman is, of course, a witch; and witches have always been credited with the power of shape-shifting, taking on the form of certain animals such as hares or cats. Isobel Gowdie, who was accused of witchcraft in sixteenth-century Scotland, gave the following charm as her means of transmuting herself into a hare: 'I shall go into a hare / With sorrow and sych and meickle care; / And I shall go in the Devil's name,/ Ay while I come home again.'[7]

Among the Naga such transformations were not confined to sorcerers or witches: cases of were-leopards were common among ordinary men, such as Sakhuto, who when in leopard form suffered pains in their joints and moved convulsively in their sleep. If they were being hunted (in leopard form) they threw themselves about in their efforts to escape. However, the Naga do not claim to *turn into* leopards; they say that their soul (*ahonga*, shadow) is projected into the leopard, which can be recognized as 'human' by the fact that it has five claws on each paw.[8] When the animal dies, its human counterpart is not long for this world; and indeed, Sakhuto died nineteen days after his leopard was killed.

While amongst some societies ordinary people may have 'bush souls', shape-changing is typically – and universally – attributed to the shamans of the tribe, the sorcerers and medicine-men. However, there is a range of subtle distinctions in the way they do it. They can, as we have seen, project their souls into an animal, such as a crocodile or tiger[9] – or they can simply change their *body* into the shape of such an animal. Among the Dowayos of the Cameroons, however, a sorcerer becomes a leopard at night by turning inside out – that is, he has the skin of a man during the day and that of a leopard by night.[10]

There is also a sense in which a shaman takes on the identity of a sacred animal by dressing up in its skin or feathers – an image we find in Norse myth where Sigmund finds a wolfskin and, putting it on, becomes a wolf for nine days. We remember too the widespread legend of the Scottish and Irish seaboards about the seal-woman – a seal which, conversely, casts off its skin and becomes a beautiful maiden.

In other words, traditional cultures are either vague about the means by which a man changes into an animal, or else they have different theories. They assert a duality of soul and body, but they deny the dual*ism* which marks our theology. They insist that soul and body are separable – at death, for example – but deny that they are separate. The anthropologist Lucien Lévy-Bruhl goes even further when he says that even the term duality is misleading, because in the case of were-leopards, were-crocodiles, etc. duality is actually 'bi-presence':[11] the sorcerer is both man and leopard at the same time but in two different places.[12]

The Inuit of the Bering Strait give us a striking image of

dual existence: they believe that in the beginning all animate beings could take on each other's form at will. If an animal wished to become a man, it simply pushed up its muzzle or beak like a mask and it became *inua*, man-like, the thinking part of the creature and, at death, its spirit. Shamans had the ability to see through these masks to the *inua* behind.[13] Analogously, for a man to wear an animal mask is to become the creature it represents.

Humans, it seems, are convinced of their dual nature, their two-foldness, whether it is expressed as soul/body, mind/brain, energy/matter – or human/animal. The many ways we depict our two-foldness shows how intensely we are engaged in the attempt to imagine our paradoxical nature. The way in which traditional cultures are untroubled by contradictions may suggest that our attempts always to *resolve* them one way or another is simply the result of our modern outlook, and may not be desirable or even possible.

Captured souls

It is almost universally agreed, then, that the soul can detach itself from the body. It can wander off on its own, during sleep for example. Sometimes it becomes lost, cannot find its way back to its owner and has to be retrieved by a shaman, who flies into the Otherworld of dreams to fetch it back. Sometimes the soul is held in the Otherworld by spirits of disease whom the shaman has to persuade or overcome to release the soul. Sometimes it is not so much lost as stolen – by witches, super-natural animals or the dead. In such cases the body that is left behind is but a husk which wastes away, and sometimes dies if its soul is not returned to it.

In Irish folklore, for instance, it is said that when a young man or woman is taken by the fairies they leave behind a 'log', or else 'the likeness of their body or a body in their likeness'.[14] What remains, in other words, is not human but a kind of 'living dead', like the Haitians whose souls, they say, can be locked up in jars by sorcerers while their bodily remains are abducted – as zombies – to work as slaves.[15] There is always this unwillingness to allow the body to become too material and the soul too spiritual. Each remains tied to the other and bears the other's attributes. Such ideas invite us to picture the body as fluid, insubstantial and liable to shape-shift as the soul is concrete, substantial and liable to remain fixed in the body. What happens to one happens to the other, no matter how far apart they have drifted. There is the merest membrane, what the legend of the seal-woman describes as a skin 'softer than mist to the touch',[16] between body and soul.

Even in death, when the soul might be thought to have finally separated from its body, they remain close. As many Africans say: 'The dead are still living.'[17] Thus, if you want to strike out at a dead man whose 'shadow' is remote and invisible, you have only to act on his bodily remains. The Aboriginals of the Brisbane district were known to mutilate a dead man's genitals to prevent his having sex with the living, while those of the district of Victoria might tie his toes together to stop him 'walking'. In West Africa the Ogowe used for the same reason to break all the bones in a corpse and hang it in a bag from a tree. In *The People of the North*, Knut Rasmussen noted a similar custom among the Inuit regarding those who had committed murder: they cut up the victim's body, ate the heart and covered the remains with stones or threw them in the sea – all to render the dead person incapable of post-mortem revenge.[18]

Often if misfortunes do occur after a death, the body of the dead person will be exhumed. Sometimes it is found to be intact, with a blush still in its cheeks, and an appearance more of being asleep than dead – a clear sign that the dead person was during life a witch or sorcerer who had gone undetected.[19] Such a belief is not only found in places as far apart as Nigeria and Burma, it is also found in Europe. There, however, it is usually reversed: the intact corpse is held to be that of a saint rather than a sorcerer. When the coffin of St Cuthbert, for instance, was opened some four hundred years after his death in 687, his body was found to be unchanged and undecayed. These signs of sanctity can also be read in an opposite way: unnaturally healthy-looking corpses in Eastern Europe used to be re-buried with a precautionary stake through the heart.

The human race, it seems, has always been anxious about the powers of the dead, whether for good or ill. In so far as a dead person is one with its corpse we can attempt to neutralize it by burying, dismembering or mutilating it. Yet in so far as the deceased can apparently be in two places at once, like the were-tiger, they can also return as troublesome spirits or 'hungry ghosts', as the Chinese say, in order to plague us.

Fact and fiction

In Western culture we are particularly confused by traditional views of the relationship of body to soul for, I think, two reasons:

Firstly, traditional beliefs about body and soul are analogous to the difficulty we have with the literal and the metaphorical. Because we live in a highly literal-minded society, where something is either a fact or a fiction, true or false, we think that traditional societies are the same, and that therefore they take their (to us) absurd beliefs about the soul and the body literally. In fact their beliefs are more like what we call metaphors. They do not believe that men and leopards are interchangeable. Such a view is a metaphor for our double nature. But the moment I say this, I have to contradict myself: there is a sense in which all traditional beliefs are very much held in a literal fashion. The truth of the matter is that traditional peoples just do not make the distinctions that we do. Their thinking precedes any division between the literal and the metaphorical. They are not bothered by apparent contradictions. The shadow is both an optical phenomenon and a soul. The sorcerer in his hut and the leopard in the forest are the same being in different shapes. Their reality is exactly that combination of fact and fiction which is called *myth* — a word which, unfortunately, is identified by us with something untrue. It is a reality in which soul and body exist as different manifestations of each other. We, too, can enter this reality by thinking in a traditional way. Except that for us it is not thinking so much as *imagining*.

Secondly, we have tended to polarize body and soul to such an extent that, as a tribesperson might say, we have allowed our souls to stray so far from our bodies that we are in danger of losing our souls altogether. Our bodies are therefore left to wander the Earth like zombies, who tell themselves that there never was such a thing as a soul; that we must simply face up to our inanimate condition, and grin and bear it.

Soul and psyche

The roots of our Western thinking about the soul are buried in ancient Greek culture. It is difficult for us to imagine how the Greeks saw themselves at the time of Homer (about 800 BC). Like the tribal cultures we have been looking at, they did not have our modern sense of not being identical with our bodies. Whereas we feel that we have a personality, an essence – a soul – somehow located inside, or carried by, our bodies, they felt that their soul was dispersed throughout their bodies; or, that each part of their bodies expressed a different function of their soul. Indeed, they did not have a word for a living body. They usually referred to it as 'limbs'.[1] The word *soma* (body) referred to a corpse. Only gradually did the idea of the soul withdraw itself from the parts of the body to one central point. And only gradually was that point deemed capable of separating itself permanently from the body.

Homeric Greeks thought we had two souls, *psyche* and *thymos*. Modern scholars at first associated psyche with the breath and thymos with the blood. But in his book *The Origins of European Thought* . . . R. B. Onians shows that the 'breath-soul' is actually more appropriate to thymos, which is spoken of as feeling and thinking, as being active in the chest and lungs (*phrenes*) as well as the heart.[2] Psyche, on the other hand, was associated with the head and acted as a sort of life-principle, the force that keeps us alive.[3] When we die, psyche leaves the body and lives on in Hades, the Underworld of death. Thymos also leaves the body at death but it does not live on.

Later Greek thinkers differed about the location of the soul in the body as much as did our tribal cultures. Epicurus placed it in the chest; Aristotle, in the heart; Plato, in the head.[4] But, more and more, psyche began to take precedence over thymos, so that by the fifth century BC it had come to include thymos, which was still vaguely located in the chest but no longer identified with the 'breath-soul'. At the same time, psyche was thought of as more diffuse, mainly – but no longer exclusively – associated with the head.[5] Already we begin to suspect that the soul is so difficult to pin down precisely because its own nature is to present us with differing pictures of itself.

There was disagreement, too, about psyche's fate after death. Some said that it was a breath that dispersed in the air on the death of the body, while others thought that Empedocles was right: that the soul is a daimon which is reborn in other people.[6] Most, however, believed that the soul went to Hades where it flitted about in the form of an *eidolon*, a 'shade' or image, 'the visible but impalpable semblance of the once living'.[7]

Even in Homeric times there was no sense in which psyche is responsible, as thymos is, for thinking and feeling. It is not concerned, that is, with consciousness either in life or death. At least, it is not concerned with what we think of as ordinary daylight consciousness. Psyche has its own consciousness, not thymos' 'life-consciousness', infused with warmth and feeling, but a colder, more impersonal 'death-consciousness'. Psyche's home is Hades, whose ruler (also called Hades, god of the dead) possessed a famous helmet. Enclosing the head – that is, the psyche[8] – it made the wearer invisible. This is a metaphor for the way the invisible soul hides a death-consciousness within life. Psyche is the perspective of death concealed within all living things, where death is not extinction but another, more profound kind of life.

According to Heraclitus (535–475 BC), we can take this insight a step farther. Whatever thymos wishes for, he said, it purchases at the cost of psyche.[9] There is a reciprocal, even antagonistic, relationship between our warm, waking, desiring conscious life and the life of psyche – which comes into its own in the dark, while we sleep, during dreams, after life. And just as our conscious wishes and desires sap the vitality of the unconscious psyche and cost the soul dear, so conversely psyche wants to draw our conscious life downwards, towards the deeper perspective of Hades. In fact it was Heraclitus who first drew attention to that defining feature of soul which most concerns us here: depth.

'You could not find the ends of the soul,' he wrote, 'though you travelled every way, so deep is its measure [*logos*]'.[10]

The revolutionary idea that the soul is somehow at odds with the body, even opposed to it, was attributed to the followers of the legendary figure of Orpheus. No tribal member – no Homeric Greek – would have entirely separated soul from body. Even after death they remain tenuously linked. But the Orphics held that the soul was able to detach itself from the body and exist entirely independently. But where on earth did they get such an idea?

Shamans and Egyptians

In *The Greeks and the Irrational*, Professor E. R. Dodds thought it most likely that they got the idea from the Scythians, who lived to the west of the Black Sea, and the Thracians, who lived on the East Balkan peninsula. These tribes had in turn been influenced by the horse-cultures of Central Asia and, even farther north, by the reindeer-cultures of Siberia. They were influenced, in other words, by shamanistic cultures whose most striking feature is that the shaman enters a trance state and 'flies' into the Otherworld, often carried Pegasus-like by a spirit horse or reindeer.[11] He is no mere eidolon, or shadowy image, but his real self.

Orpheus, who was traditionally connected with Thrace, travelled into the underworld of Hades, armed only with a lyre and his songs. Like the shaman's sacred chants, they could charm the dangerous denizens of the underworld and persuade them to release souls they had abducted. Orpheus sought the release of Eurydice, his wife, who had died of a snakebite. She symbolizes his own soul – which he retrieved from Hades, only to lose her at the last minute when he fatally looked back to make sure she was following him. (However, the earliest versions of this myth relate that he was successful in retrieving her from death.)[12]

Orpheus was the first Western shaman; and Orphism had a profound influence on Pythagoras, whom Dodds also calls the Greek equivalent of a shaman. His teachings and practices were in turn given philosophical expression by Plato, who thus combined the tradition of reason and logic with magical and religious ideas from, ultimately, central Asia and Siberia. So real was the experience of the soul when out of the body that for the Orphics and the Pythagoreans the impermanent and corruptible body came to be seen as the 'prison-house' or even the 'tomb' of the immortal soul.[13] This became one of Plato's key doctrines. At the same time, the underworld became less a shadowy grave of eidola than a realm more real than the everyday world.

However, the distinguished Egyptologist Jeremy Naydler takes a different view of how the Greeks arrived at this doctrine of the soul. He acknowledges Plato's debt to the Pythagoreans but reminds us that it is by no means certain that Pythagoras was influenced by northern shamanic cultures. There is no tradition of his having visited there, for example. But there is a tradition of his having visited Egypt (for twenty-two years, according to Iamblichus), where he was said to have mastered hieroglyphs and to have been initiated into the mysteries of the gods.[14] Pythagoras subsequently settled in southern Italy in the mid- to late- sixth-century BC, a region which had had links to Egypt for at least two hundred years. Plato established his own strong links with the Pythagoreans in this region, making three journeys there between 388 and 361 BC. He is also said to have visited Egypt once, or even twice, according to Diogenes Laertius and Cicero; while an earlier source, Strabo, was shown by Egyptian locals the place where Plato stayed in Heliopolis.[15] Thus Plato could well have derived his doctrine of the soul from the Egyptians, who had their own shamanistic tradition in which the soul existed independently of the body and was able to travel through the Otherworld.[16]

The Ba

The Egyptians held a psycho-physical view of the soul similar to that of the Homeric Greeks. The heart was their chief centre of consciousness, while the belly was the centre of 'hot' or 'cold' instinctive impulses. The limbs were the bearers of the will: strong arms or legs indicated the capacity to carry out one's wishes effectively. While the head was not the centre of consciousness, it was most closely identified with the whole person. Just as the head, according to the Homeric view, carried the psyche as it travelled into the Underworld, so in Egypt the head winged its way through the Dwat – the Egyptian Otherworld – attached to the body of a bird. A human-headed bird is the hieroglyph for the *ba*, or soul.[17]

Like the psyche, the ba only came into its own when a person was asleep or dead – or in between, for example in a trance state during initiation. The main thing was that the components of the body – heart, belly, limbs – be 'stilled' so that the 'soul-forces' which were normally distributed throughout the body 'could be gathered into a unity and concentrated into the form of the winged ba.'[18] According to Dodds, this is exactly what the Orphics did: they concentrated their psychic power to forge a unity of soul absent among the Homeric

Greeks, for whom the soul was similarly distributed throughout the body. In this way they were able to experience the soul as an entity separate from the body. In Plato's dialogue *Phaedo*, Socrates confirms Dodds' view when he says that the practice of true philosophy demands *katharsis*, or purification, which 'consists in separating the soul from the body and teaching the soul the habit of collecting and bringing itself together from all parts of the body, and living so far as it can, both now and hereafter, alone and by itself, freed from the body as from fetters.'[19]

It has to be said that not everyone was a 'true philosopher'. To become one required a high degree of initiation, just as it does for any shaman. This was also true of Egyptian religion: the operations of the ba took place in an esoteric, priestly context.[20] Moreover, since the ba is usually depicted hovering over the inert body or loitering around the tomb of a dead person, its prime function might have been to see the body as inert or dead in order to know itself as independent of it. It provides us with first-hand proof, as it were, that while our bodies are subject to death and decay, some essential part of ourselves lives on.[21] But the ba — it literally means 'manifestation' — is not perhaps what we would understand by the word 'soul' in its fullest sense since it seems reluctant to leave the body's vicinity.[22]

The ba is only severed completely from the body when it becomes an *akh*, 'which may be understood as the *ba* divinised.'[23] The word 'akh' has connotations of light, shining, illumination and intelligence. It is like the inner core or higher manifestation of the ba. It is very like Plato's idea that there is an immortal core to the psyche, which he variously calls *logistikon*, *daimon*, or *nous*.[24] It is what I shall be calling 'spirit'. We tend to use the terms 'spirit' and 'soul' interchangeably, but I shall be making a strong distinction between them. I will also be resisting the idea that spirit — like akh or nous — is 'higher' than soul, and explaining that it is a characteristic of spirit always to project itself as 'higher'.

We can only attain wisdom through the transformation of the ba into the akh because wisdom can only come by crossing the threshold of death and entering a state remote from the body. Plato agreed with the Egyptians: wisdom comes to one whose soul is free of the body's opacity and can see into the reality of the Otherworld.[25] This can be achieved by philosophers who 'grow wings' and can fly up to 'the immortal region of the gods and, standing on the back of the universe, behold what lies beyond – the colourless, formless and intangible reality that only the *nous* is capable of perceiving.'[26]

The division of soul and body enabled a new kind of knowledge or, as Plato prefers, wisdom, through a mystical participation in a transcendent reality which paved the way for all subsequent mystical experience. Yet, paradoxically, the same division also led to an opposite kind of knowledge. By detaching us from the material world, it enabled us to develop that dualism out of which our modern scientific world-view was born.

The Christian soul

Christianity adopted the Greek division between soul and body. For Christians the soul is our most treasured possession. It determines us as individuals. It is immortal. We are made in the image of God, and if we truly repent of our sins, our souls will go to Heaven. We have Christ's assurance for this when he tells the repentant thief who is crucified next to Him that he will go to Heaven that very day. Christ, however, was not a theologian. We learn from Him no technical details about the soul. He prefers to talk in parables and to describe the Ground of Being – God – in personal terms: we are in the same relation to God, He says, as children are to an exacting but always loving father. No one can come to that Father in Heaven except through Him, Jesus Christ, who is 'the Way, the Truth, the Life.' Our task is to have faith in that fact, and to love God, our neighbours and even our enemies.

I am not going to linger over Christian doctrine. This is not a book about theology but about psychology in its original meaning, as the logos of psyche; and whatever is most profound in Christian thinking about the soul comes from the Greeks. The early Church Fathers, such as Clement, Origen and Augustine, were all Platonists. Further, as a monotheistic religion, Christianity has a tendency to concentrate on spirit at the expense of soul. The first theologian, St Paul, whose epistles are the earliest writings in the New Testament, mentions spirit (*pneuma*) countless times, but soul (*psyche*) only four times. This foreshadowed the official declaration of the Church Council of 869 that we are composed of a material and an immaterial part; but that the immaterial part is spirit, which thereafter subsumed soul, losing that essential distinction I will be insisting on later.[27]

When soul re-established itself it was not in the pre-eminent position it had held among the Platonist Church Fathers; it was through the work of St Thomas Aquinas, whose theology is still pretty much that of official Roman Catholicism today. He did not derive his view of the soul from the Platonic tradition, but from Plato's pupil (but not his follower) Aristotle: the soul was the *entelechy* or 'form' of the body. For Aristotle, this meant that the soul is inseparable from the body and therefore mortal. While Aquinas agreed that the soul is indeed the form of the body he thought that it did not depend on the body for its existence and that it survived death. A body without a soul, he reasoned, would be formless, not a proper body at all; and that is why the body disintegrates after death.[28] Conversely, although the soul survives death, it is not properly a human soul without a body. Therefore some sort of body has to accompany the soul into the afterlife. In other words, Aquinas did not finally resolve the problem of the soul's relationship to the body. Even the doctrine of the immortality of the soul did not become Church dogma until the Lateran Council of 1513.

Aquinas also took on Aristotle's belief that plants and animals have souls. The way the soul was pictured from the Middle Ages onward was as a three-fold substance. We contained both the 'vegetable soul' of plants and the 'animal' soul, but we also had our own unique kind of soul – a 'rational soul'. That is, we did not have three souls but, rather, the rational soul managed in some way to embrace the 'lower' forms of the soul and to remain a unity. It was this rational soul which, after the scientific revolution in the seventeenth century, enabled philosophers to quietly begin doing away with the word 'soul' and to promulgate instead the idea that our highest faculty is merely rational. Indeed, their elevation of Reason during the eighteenth-century Enlightenment not only dropped the old association with soul; it also led to that rationalism which denies soul altogether.

The tradition of soul

Meanwhile, the great Platonic tradition that centred on the soul – to anticipate the next chapter – had also been excluded from Christendom. In my book *The Philosophers' Secret Fire* I describe how it had flourished among the Neoplatonist and Hermetic philosophers who lived alongside Gnostics, Epicureans, Stoics, Sceptics – and Christians – in that melting-pot of cultures and religions based around the Hellenic city of Alexandria. Then, when in 330 the emperor Constantine declared that Christianity was to be the empire's official religion, this 'soul' tradition became suspect, even heretical, and either disappeared or was forced underground. Most of its writings, including much of Plato and Plotinus, were lost until the Renaissance a thousand years later. Indeed, their rediscovery provided the impetus behind the Renaissance, which was a rebirth of classical learning. So exciting and fruitful was this rebirth of the 'soul tradition' that Marsilio Ficino, the Florentine who translated so many of the rediscovered texts, began to think of synthesizing a whole new religion out of Hermetic philosophy, Neoplatonism, alchemy and the Jewish Kabbalah, with the aim of overcoming the destructive schism in Christianity between the Catholics and the new Protestants. His scheme was taken up with missionary zeal by his pupil Pico della Mirandola and by Giordano Bruno; and, in England, by the intelligentsia who surrounded Sir Philip Sidney – not least the Renaissance magus *par excellence*, John Dee.

When this project was defeated by the rise of the new scientific method in the seventeenth century, our tradition was once again pushed underground, only to resurface in a different guise – as the Romantic world-view which sprang up among such German thinkers as Fichte, Schiller, Schelling and Goethe and was eagerly espoused by English poets, especially William Blake, William Wordsworth and Samuel Taylor Coleridge. Submerged once again by the weight of nineteenth-century Christian fundamentalism and, equally, scientistic materialism, its latest incarnation was another exercise in shape-shifting: the depth psychology initiated by Sigmund Freud and elaborated by the great Swiss psychologist C. G. Jung.

So what are the basic tenets and beliefs about the 'soul' of this tradition? To answer this question I will take a representative figure: the leading Neoplatonist, Plotinus (AD 204–270), whose works opened the way for St Augustine – that great lover of the soul – to be converted to Christianity.

THREE

Soul and world-soul

According to his pupil Porphyry, Plotinus 'was caught by a passion for philosophy' and studied in Alexandria before moving at the age of forty to Rome. During his life there he went to fight for the Romans in Persia, where he took the opportunity of studying what the 'magi and the Brahmans' believed.[1]

Plotinus was a Neoplatonist. That is, he took the dialogues of Plato as his starting-point, and elaborated on them. We must remember that for Plato, reality consisted of an ideal world of eternal Forms. This was the 'intelligible' world known as *nous*. The Forms are the blueprints for everything that exists in this world. Every tree or animal, for example, is determined by, and participates in, the Form of the Tree or the Form of the Animal, which in turn contain the Form of the Oak, say, or the Form of the Mouse. Abstract concepts, too, have their Forms. We know that something is good, true or beautiful to the extent that it participates in the Forms of the Good, the True and the Beautiful. Indeed Plato sometimes calls this trio the ultimate reality; at other times he prefers a kind of monotheism whereby everything aspires to the Form of the Good alone.

Our world is not created by an all-powerful Judaeo-Christian type of God, producing the universe out of nothing. It is made by a creator-god whom Plato calls the Demiurge and who is more like an artisan: he looks into the intelligible world of the Forms and copies – crafts, moulds, sculpts and cobbles together – the whole of our universe from what he sees therein. Thus the world we call reality is in fact a replica, shadow or mirror-image of reality.

Having made the world the Demiurge brings it alive, as if it were a great organism, by weaving throughout its fabric a *soul*. Plato called it *psyche tou kosmou*, the psyche of the cosmos. But we know it better – after the Latin Anima Mundi – as the Soul of the World.

Plotinus sometimes follows his Platonist predecessors in holding the view that reality consists of two worlds, the ideal world of the Forms (or nous) and the world of disorganized matter (our sensory world). The two are linked by soul, which also organizes the world of matter according to the Forms to make the orderly universe we inhabit.

At other times, he prefers the theory, adopted from Plato's dialogue *Parmenides*, that soul does not so much bring together the two worlds but is the product of one – nous – and produces the other, our world. Each level of reality emanates from the one above as light emanates from the sun or heat from fire. All three levels ultimately emanate from a fourth: a God-like entity he calls the One.

Plotinus was not altogether satisfied with this hierarchical model of the cosmos. He sensed, perhaps, that hierarchies are always exactly that – models – and, as such, useful for picturing reality but also liable to distort it by being taken too literally and thus becoming rigid.

A more fluid, more dynamic – more realistic – way of envisaging the cosmos is to say that it consists of soul alone.[2] Plotinus was the first philosopher to seize upon Plato's world-soul and make it 'the cosmic force that unifies, organizes, sustains and controls every aspect of the world.'[3] He even compares the motion of soul to a Shiva-like cosmic dance, in which everything is patterned, meaningful and self-delighting. According to this model, soul is not generated by nous, generating our world in turn. Instead, the intelligible world of nous is simply a sort of refined, spiritual aspect of soul, while our sensory world is its material aspect – and the One is the unity of soul even as it manifests in all its multiplicity. Or, to put it another way, it is as if the whole cosmos is a single oceanic flow composed of soul-stuff. It is no longer seen as having four levels, each *transcending* the next, but as different images enfolded or *immanent* in each other, like a set of Russian dolls. For example, the Form of the Tree is no longer transcendent, existing outside this world, but immanent in it as the inner ideal tree – its *numen* or spirit, as the Romans would say: its dryad.

The daimons

Dryads are one example of what the Greeks called daimons. They were held to inhabit the Soul of the World. They have some remarkable characteristics: for a start, they are always ambiguous, if not downright contradictory. They are both material and immaterial, for example, which is why anthropologists mislead us when they refer to the daimons as 'spirits'. They are highly elusive, only caught in glimpses from the corner of the eye, if at all. They are shape-shifters. Fleeting, marginal creatures, they prefer to appear in liminal zones (*limen* = 'threshold') such as bridges, crossroads and shorelines in the landscape; or, in time, at dusk, midnight, Midsummer's Eve or Hallowe'en; or, in the mind, between consciousness and the unconscious, waking and sleeping. In fact, there's no boundary the daimons do not straddle, including the boundary between fact and fiction, literal and metaphorical.[4]

Every culture has always had its daimons, from the Greek naiads, nymphs, dryads and fauns to the Roman *genii loci*, who inhabit Nature, and the *lares* and *penates* who inhabit households; from the pan-European fairies and elves, hulderfolk and land-spirits, to the Chinese kwei-shins and the Arab jinns.[5] All of these are as likely to be mischievous as benign. The fairies are as famous for leading us astray or blighting our crops as they are for healing us or leading us to treasure – it may depend on how we treat them; for all cultures agree that while we must keep a proper distance from the daimons, we must also pay them proper respect and attention, leaving food out for them and remembering them in our rituals. Much the same could be said of our relationship with soul. Christianity, unhappy as it is with ambiguity, divided and polarized the daimons into angels and devils. The act of polarizing made them literal beings, which daimons are not. They are real, and even, at times, physical – but, like soul itself, cannot be taken literally. Where it did not divide the daimons, Christianity tried either to cast them out – armies of friars were sent to exorcize the fairies from farms and dairies, woods and streams, as Geoffrey Chaucer describes in 'The Tale of the Wife of Bath';[6] or else to tame them – many a daimon of stream and rock and well was 'christened' with the name of a saint or of the Blessed Virgin Mary.

Paradoxical, elusive, borderline, shape-shifting creatures – we see how the daimons provide us with an outstanding metaphor for the nature of the soul (or, as we might now say, the unconscious psyche) which, as the Neoplatonists pointed out, they personified.

Perhaps their most crucial function was to act as intermediaries between this world and the Otherworld of the Forms. Socrates, Plato's mentor, puts this vividly in the *Symposium*: we can have no contact with God or the gods, he says, except through the daimons who 'interpret and convey the wishes of men to the gods and the will of gods to men . . . . Only through the daimons is there conversation between men and gods, whether in the waking state or during sleep.'[7] Anyone, he adds, who is an expert in such intercourse – we would call such people shamans, mediums, mystics, visionaries, poets and even psychotherapists – is 'a daimonic man' or woman. It is worth noting that the arch-daimon is Eros: Love.

The Neoplatonist Iamblichus (d. AD 326), who attempted a whole system of daimonic classification, recognized that soul itself does not relish hierarchical schemes of either the cosmos or the psyche, but prefers concrete images and, especially, personifications. He saw the intelligible world of the Forms, therefore, as the realm of the gods and the Soul of the World as that of the daimons. Just as we can never know the Forms in themselves but only as the images or objects they are the Forms *of*, so we cannot see the gods except through the appearance they take on. The daimons are exactly these appearances – the faces which the transcendent gods show to us. Proclus (?410–485) tells us that they are a kind of 'preceding retinue'[8] of the gods: the aspects of the gods we encounter before we meet the gods themselves. This has important implications for depth psychology, as I hope to show. For now, I merely want to emphasize the crucial role of daimons as Eros-like intermediaries without whom we cannot know the shining reality that lies behind this shadow world. 'He who denies the daimons', wrote Plutarch, 'breaks the chain that unites men to the gods.'[9]

The Soul of the World has been banished from religion and philosophy, but like the daimons who are said to inhabit it, it simply shape-shifts and reappears in another guise. For example, it can be discerned in the way that ecologists have commandeered James Lovelock's 'Gaia hypothesis' and made Gaia the animating principle, like a goddess, of an organic world. Its return can also be seen in Einstein's re-modelling of the universe, in which gravity is less like a force and more like a field. Not a field within space-time but a field which contains the whole universe including space-time:

'The cosmos is like a net which takes all its life, as far as it ever stretches, from being wet in the water; it is at the mercy of the sea which spreads out, taking the net with it just so far as it will go, for no mesh of it can strain beyond its set place.'[10]

In this metaphor, the sea can be read as the gravitational field in which our universe is extended like a net. But the image is not Einstein's; it comes from Plotinus, and he is describing the way the universe is extended in, and embraced by, the Soul of the World – the model from which Einstein's picture is unwittingly drawn. Nowadays, it is the World Wide Web which is an unconscious attempt to reproduce, but in a literal fashion, the deep global intelligence of the world-soul.

In the history of thought, however, the two most important re-workings of the Soul of the World are the Romantic concept of Imagination and the concept of the unconscious, notably C. G. Jung's collective unconscious, which I will be addressing shortly.

Imagination[11]

The idea that the chief faculty of the soul was not Reason but Imagination was vigorously promulgated in the second half of the fifteenth century by Ficino, who derived the notion from Plotinus. It was further expounded by Jacob Boehme in the early 1600s. He boldly asserted that Imagination was, like its root metaphor the world-soul, the principle that held everything together, but he added a Protestant spin: Imagination was the creative energy of God, by which He made the universe. Moreover it was this primordial Imagination which had been embodied – made flesh – by Jesus Christ. Nearly two hundred years later 'Jesus the Imagination' became central to the poetry and art of William Blake, who insisted that reality was above all imaginative – and not the grey, rational reality of orthodox mainstream thinkers such as Newton, Locke and Hume.

The primacy of Imagination was the defining feature of Romanticism. It took on particular force in the late eighteenth century, at the time of Blake, because the exaltation of Reason

during the Enlightenment was fast becoming an ideology –
rationalism – which denied and even demonized anything it
considered superstitious, murky, irrational or even ambiguous,
from dreams and daimons to soul and imagination itself. All the
English Romantic poets baulked at this, the second generation
of Keats, Shelley and Byron no less than Blake, Wordsworth and
Coleridge – who spoke for them all when he ringingly
declared:

'The Primary Imagination I hold to be the living power and
prime agent of all human perception, and is a repetition in the
finite mind of the eternal act of creation in the infinite
I AM . . . .'[12]

It is difficult for us, as children of the Enlightenment, to
grasp what he means. We think of imagination as something
desirable in children but less so in adults, who have to 'come
down to earth', 'face up to reality' and so forth. We think of it
either as the pictures which come to mind when we daydream
and fantasize, or as related to memory – the images of things we
recall when they are absent. Either way, imagination is generally
held to deal with things which are less than real and soon
dispersed like smoke upon the cold breeze of 'reality'.

But for everyone of a Romantic disposition, Imagination is
reality itself. Like another world it has its own laws and
denizens, its own spontaneous life quite different from ours,
even if we picture it as being inside us. It is dynamic, daimon-
ridden, and does not depend on us at all. On the contrary, it
underpins all our perceptions. It generates myths. The universal
stories which shape and govern our lives, as well as the lives of
cultures and economies, are all born in the thunder of the
Primary Imagination, of which our feeble imaginings are but
echoes. Every tale we tell, yarn we spin, theory we hypothesize,
has its roots in imagination. It is synonymous with soul, which
is nothing if not 'the imaginative possibility in our natures, the
experiencing through reflective speculation, dream, image and

fantasy that mode which recognizes all realities as primarily symbolic or metaphorical.'[13]

So jaded are we by an old materialism and an even older rationalism that we habitually denigrate imagination or damn it with faint praise, leaving it to excitable children, unrealistic poets or unreliable story-tellers. Yet its strangeness and beauty are still available to all of us, at every moment. For it is not only an Otherworld, but the reality behind this world. And because we participate in it willy-nilly, we can see into it, not only in poetic trance, visionary journey or lucid dream, but simply whenever we attend to the things of this world deeply, intensely and selflessly. Whenever, that is, we imagine. Every little effort of imagination is both supplied by Imagination itself and also a means by which we can begin to enter fully and creatively into it.

The individual soul

The relationship between the Soul of the World and the individual soul is easy to put into words but difficult to picture: our souls are microcosms, miniature versions of the cosmos. We consist of levels of being which extend from the material body, through soul, to the intelligible level (nous) and finally to the One. The task of the human soul is simply to return from its exile in our shadowy, less-than-real material world to an ecstatic union with the One Source of all reality. It is a return because everything emanated from the One in the first place.

We can imagine the soul's journey as upward through the vast architecture of the macrocosm. Alternatively we can picture the journey as downward, into our own depths where the ever-living Forms or gods dwell and, beyond them, the ultimate Unity. These journeys are of course not actual. They are metaphors for the transformation of the soul. They are not really 'up' or 'down' – these are only ways of speaking in order that we can produce images of the soul's transformation. Soul is non-spatial[14] but it always represents itself spatially, for example as 'inside' us or 'outside'. A concentric model of the soul might be more apt, perhaps. We can see the body as in soul, soul as in nous, nous as in the One. Soul is not, as we usually think, inside the body because, as Plotinus reminds us, the Greek meaning of the preposition 'in' does not so much refer to a place as to being in something's power. Body is 'in' soul because it depends on soul's power.[15]

So we have to make another leap of the imagination and picture the concentric model of the soul made dynamic and fluid, each of its levels co-inhering, to use an old theological word. Now we are no longer arranged hierarchically. We are all soul. It is just that each of us is an individual manifestation of the collective world-soul. Each of its levels is now a way that soul represents itself – now as an individual, now as collective.

When Marsilio Ficino began to translate the newly discovered Neoplatonist writings into Latin, making them available to fifteenth-century Western Europeans, he was struck by the grandeur of their conception of the human soul. As a model in miniature of the cosmos, it is 'the greatest of all miracles in nature,' he wrote. 'All other things beneath God are always one single being: but the soul is all things together . . . . Therefore it may be rightly called the centre of nature, the middle term of all things . . . the bond and juncture of the universe.'[16]

Ficino is contemplating with amazement how we contain the immensity of the world-soul, a whole 'inner' universe whose study would become depth psychology. But we must remember, too, that we are also and paradoxically contained *by* the world-soul, like droplets in the ocean. This is the vision of traditional cultures whose members see the world-soul 'outside' themselves as an ensouled Nature in which they are only one soul among many.

For Plotinus, 'the' soul does not always need the definite

article because it is at root the world-soul.[17] It is the source of life not just in the body, but in the whole universe. It goes without saying that it cannot die. By the same token it cannot come into being. Soul has always been, and always is, in its own timeless and non-spatial realm. The Neoplatonists thought it irrational of Christians – with whom they agreed about the omnipresence of the divine and the immortality of the individual soul – to believe that this soul exists after death without also believing that it exists before birth.[18] This discrepancy led to differing beliefs about how we acquire knowledge.

Aquinas followed Aristotle in thinking that we know nothing until experience informs us. Our souls come into the world like blank slates on which the data received through our senses writes. John Locke in his *Essay Concerning Human Understanding* (1689) made this doctrine central to the Enlightenment; and it remains, I suppose, pretty much the modern orthodox view. Plato and his followers, however, tell us that the soul carries into the world knowledge of the eternal Forms it had before birth. It is just that it forgets this knowledge in transit. However, by the exercise of what Plato calls *anamnesis*, or recollection, we know truth when we see it. Learning is less about cognition than recognition – something we hear or read about strikes us immediately as true, as if we had always known it but were only now remembering.

Soul and body revisited

Just as soul is both individual and collective, it is also paradoxical in relation to the body. It is both continuous with the body, yet also discontinuous, since it can leave the body and live separately from it. As we have seen, traditional cultures simply accept this contradiction. But Western culture has seen it as a problem which needs solving. For instance, in the Middle Ages, the rational soul was thought to be fixed to the body *gumphis subtilibus*, 'with subtle little nails' called 'spirits'. But this pictur-esque solution still falls foul of the perennial conundrum: if the 'spirits' are material at all then both ends of the bridge, as it were, rest on one side of the chasm; if they are not, then both rest on the other. No matter how finely you attenuate materi-ality it remains material until, at some point, it is not. Conversely, no matter how gradually spirit is made denser there is the same point of discontinuity.[19]

As I write, teams of subatomic physicists in an underground complex bigger than a cathedral are firing up the Large Hadron Collider (LHC) in the hope of discovering the legendary Higgs boson. This highly elusive particle will explain why the universe has mass. For what is missing from the scientific model of the universe is the thing that turns particles into matter; or, rather, that gives matter its mass – without mass there would only be radiation, only particles moving at light-speed. The Higgs boson (or 'God particle') is thought to be able to congeal these particles into the substantial bodies the universe seems to contain.

We have here the latest attempt to solve the problem of the relationship between the immaterial and the material – what was traditionally called spirit and matter. It is the same problem on the macrocosmic scale as, on the microcosmic, the problem of the relationship between soul and body. We may call the latter the mind/body or mind/brain problem, just as we might call the former the matter/energy problem, but it is the same old problem in modern dress.

We can of course 'solve' the problem by abolishing one side or the other of the equation. Philosophical materialists for example simply do away with soul: everything is only matter; we are only our bodies. On the other hand, those of a spiritu-alistic or theosophical disposition see the universe as a wholly spiritual phenomenon consisting of many 'planes' that 'vibrate' at different rates. The lower the rate of vibration, the denser the level until, at the lowest rate, the material world seamlessly appears. This is a metaphor essentially drawn from sound. A similar metaphor was favoured by the Orphic tradition and enthusiastically taken up by the Romantics: the material universe is a harmonious resonance of a prior spiritual Platonic world in the same way that certain strings on an instrument resonate in harmony with other strings which have been plucked. Plotinus used a similar analogy to explain how the changeless soul nevertheless effects changes in the body. Soul is like a perfect piece of music and the body is like a stringed instrument. When the music is played, it is not the music which moves but the strings – while the strings cannot move unless the music directs them.[20]

For his description of the macrocosm, however, Plotinus usually employed, as we have seen, a metaphor drawn from light. Light does not vibrate or resonate, but emanates. Thus the whole cosmos emanates from the One. Discontinuity between levels is brushed over by the continuity of emanation which somehow, at its farthest reaches, gives rise to the material world. These metaphors are not causes. They are imaginatively satisfying but not mechanically so.

The main trouble with the whole spirit/matter, soul/body problem is that it is not soluble. It is what used to be called a mystery. It is a modern error to take mysteries literally; that is, to turn them into problems which then have to be solved. We cannot solve mysteries – we can only enter into them; and then it is we who are solved or dissolved, transformed in such a way that we see the 'problem' quite differently, as a delightful paradox for instance, like the traditional cultures who are unworried by the contradiction between soul and body.

The attraction of the Christian treatment of the soul's relations with the body is that it recognizes the discontinuity between them, notably at death; but it also resists separating them. It insists that the soul passes into immortality accompanied by a resurrected body. 'It is sown a natural body; it is raised a spiritual body,' thought St Paul. But what is a 'spiritual body' if not a contradiction? To say it is pure spirit is to deny the body; and to say the body is literally resurrected is to lapse into absurdity, something which does not deter fundamentalist Christians. St Paul's spiritual body can only be something like the 'subtle body' proposed by many Neoplatonists. In one attempt to bridge the gap, Proclus for example suggested that we have two 'vehicles' of the soul, one of which is immortal while the other perishes.[21] But no matter how we multiply subtle bodies – some theosophists claim at least seven, including the etheric, astral and spectral bodies – discontinuity has to occur at some point.

It is easy to predict that the physicists will in fact detect the Higgs boson. But its nature will remain a mystery. It will be highly elusive, shape-changing, mediatory and, like all 'virtual particles', ambiguous – not quite matter, not really energy; sort of *there* but also *not-there*. It will be, in other words, a daimon which will retreat at the speed of light into mystery just as we seem able to pin it down.

Only connect

Western philosophy does not on the whole subscribe to metaphors of vibration, resonance and emanation – it remains steadfastly materialistic – but it does favour the principle of continuity, expressed in the old Scholastic doctrine that 'Nature makes no leaps'. There is to be no abrupt transition between different orders of reality, whether between the spiritual and the material, or between species and genera in our modern theory of evolution. There must always be a Higgs-boson-like intermediary. This principle is derived from Iamblichus, whose Law of Mean Terms emphasized the role of the middle term between two extremes. The example he gives is that of daimons. Indeed, soul itself – the realm of the daimonic – is such a term since it both links gods to men and sets them apart, at the proper distance from each other. In this way the transcendence of the divine was guaranteed while, at the same time, the gulf between us and the gods was prevented from becoming unbridgeable.[22]

Like the daimons, soul observes both continuity and discontinuity. It does not have to be either connected or opposed to the body because the body is its outward image. Like all images it is definite and concrete, but that does not mean it is literal. It is the peculiar perspective of modernity to identify the physical with the literal. This makes of the body an intransigent, opaque lump when really it is fluid, transparent and subtle. It can be imagined differently – as a rich storehouse of metaphors. All the body's moods, exaltations, sensations, ailments and symptoms can be read, not just physically or organically, but metaphorically as well. I can even imagine someone imaginative enough to deliteralize their own body altogether, to blur its borders, to make it transparent to soul and thus free of the literal constraints of our Newtonian world. Such a person would apparently defy the laws of space, matter, time and causality as we do in dreams. They would be able to levitate, for instance, or walk on water; see into the past or future; effect things acausally by healing the sick, or even feeding a multitude with a few loaves of bread. But, of course, all such marvels are routinely attributed to saints, sages and shamans, and even to ordinary people in heightened states, such as the distraught mother who lifted the bus off her crushed child.

On the other hand, it is part of soul's self-imagining also to present itself, not as an image of the body, but as separate from the body. We need not, however, take this literally either. Soul cannot be identified with *any* literal perspective. Its separateness from the body is a metaphor for its reluctance to be defined and pinned down in any single image. As the very thing which sees through everything else, soul is not itself anything. It takes on the coloration of whatever image is currently embodying it.

The very word 'soul' is an image for itself, which, in itself, is 'empty', like the Tao, drawing its substance from whatever forms it assumes. We do not have to choose between continuity and discontinuity because there is no contradiction which soul cannot, like its daimons, overcome simply by shifting our point of view.

Soul and mana

What might it be like to experience the Soul of the World? The Romantic poet William Wordsworth catches some of its flavour while describing his childhood in *The Prelude*:

To every natural form, rock, fruit, or flower,
Even the loose stones that cover the highway,
I gave a moral life: I saw them feel
Or linked them to some feeling: the great mass
Lay bedded in some quickening soul, and all
That I beheld respired with inward meaning.[1]

Perhaps most children catch a glimpse of such an ensouled world; but few adults, or even poets, recapture that vision. Yet for traditional societies it is the norm. In the nineteenth century, E. B. Tylor called it animism. It is a word which, unfortunately, writes off what it seeks to describe, because for traditional cultures there is no such thing as animism – nor any kind of -ism; there is only a world which presents itself to them in the first instance as animate, daimonic, respiring with inward meaning.

The reindeer-herders of Siberia, the Eveny, for example – a people who hunt as well as herd – recognize a principle which governs wild as opposed to domesticated animals; which governs, in fact, the whole landscape. It is pictured as an old man called

Bayanay. He is the master of all the animals as well as the forests, rocks and streams. But he is also acknowledged as the force or essence – that is, the soul – behind every visible surface, that which makes a thing what it really is. Every thing is a manifestation of Bayanay, yet he is also a continuous elemental animating power which, like the sea, 'can wax and wane, surge or retract at different moments, in different locations or for different hunters'; sometimes he works in your favour, at other times against you. Like his animals he is 'capricious and hard to fathom.'[2] You have to treat all his creatures properly, respecting both the body and soul of the animal you hunt so that, when it is reincarnated, it will again offer itself to you.

Everything imbued with Bayanay is a presence, like a consciousness, which has intention towards you. A place, a tree, even a tool, can look on you benignly or with hostility. You have to divine its mood with careful observation, adjusting your behaviour accordingly. You can be helped in your divination by paying minute attention to barely discernible signs: a crow's flight, the plash of a fish, the snort of your reindeer.

'I came to understand Bayanay', writes Piers Vitebsky, who lived among the Eveny, 'as a vast field of shared consciousness which encompassed the landscape as setting, as well as all the human and animal roles in the drama of stalking, killing and cooking. This state of super-consciousness was so delicate and precarious that when talking of hunting, especially in the forest, one could not refer to animals by their ordinary names.'[3] Thus *kyaga*, a bear – which contains the highest concentration of Bayanay – becomes *abaga*, grandfather, before the kill, as if in this heightened state when soul shows itself it is natural to assert the affinity of the animal with the human. After the kill, it is offensive to Bayanay if anyone is boastful or immodest. Delicacy and discretion are the order of the day when dealing with soul. No mention of killing is made; rather, the hunter says merely '*Kungan churam*', 'I have obtained a child'.[4]

Mana

Bayanay is synonymous with what Melanesian culture called *mana*, a term introduced to us by E. H. Codrington in the 1890s. It was taken up by other anthropologists who recognized the same phenomenon in the tribes they were studying. For everyone, it seems, has subscribed to something very like mana – a force present everywhere and in everything like a world-soul. It is always ambiguous, as intangible as air yet able to manifest its presence. It is impersonal, pervading the universe uniformly; yet also personal, showing itself most clearly in individuals, as their own power. It is benevolent at one moment, malign at the next, always paradoxical. It can be acquired by humans through their deeds or just through the accumulated experience of age. It radiates from them, so that the more mana they possess the wider their sphere of influence among the living and the longer their endurance after death. Mana also sticks to our possessions. The more intimate the possession – a spear, a hoe, a head-dress or bowl – the more of our mana inheres in the object so that it cannot be used by others when we die. Being imbued with a portion of our soul, it must be buried with us or else destroyed lest it contaminate others with misfortune.

We echo these beliefs whenever we venerate the relics of a saint or treasure the pen of a writer. We still feel that we are touching a part of them when we touch their accoutrements, just as we attribute special virtue to an heirloom, such as grandfather's watch, or even to our most precious belongings – the capricious old banger we coax down the motorway, or the new pair of trainers that gives us the power to outrun the wind. We would not be human if we were not all to some extent 'animists'.

Marrying bears

We can see how Bayanay, mana, soul, is what we now tend to

call the unconscious part of our psyches, the wilderness within. And just as our unconscious lives are completely other than us, they are also the substrate of our conscious lives. We can read the elaborate beliefs and rituals that surround the Eveny hunt as a guide to the way all relationships with the unconscious should be conducted. For like Bayanay, the unconscious is the unpredictable ground of our livelihood, as nourishing and as dangerous as a bear. The good hunter 'has Bayanay'. He has the soul, the contact with the unconscious, which attunes him to the Soul of the World, and especially its manifestation as prey. If he dreams of having sex with a young woman before a hunt, this is a good sign because she is Bayanay's daughter.[5] Relations with Bayanay are often erotic, especially in his chief manifestation as a bear. A skinned bear resembles a naked human. Women who become too close to the forest are said to be seduced by bears and to share their winter lair, later giving birth to mixed litters of cubs and babies.[6]

Stories of seduction or abduction by daimons are universal, whether they are the Irish *sidhe*, the desert *jinns* or, in modern times, little grey 'aliens'.[7] They are not to be taken literally, but nor are they laughable superstitions. They are *myths* – which, as I have tried to suggest, precede such distinctions in order to express a greater truth. 'These things never happened,' said Sallust sublimely; 'they are always'.[8] Our relations with soul, the unconscious, are as reciprocal, erotic and strange as marriage to a bear. They are not abstract or 'spiritual' but as concrete as a bear hunt – which in turn is as nightmarish or dreamlike as an Otherworld journey. You enter the shivering, sentient forest where you watch and wait for a long, long time. Even the tiniest sign is significant, portentous, laden with meaning. Then the sudden violent attack . . . . 'My friends', said Vitebsky, 'were transformed in some mysterious way so that they seemed almost afraid of themselves.' For, of course, the bear is also within. 'In this terrible blend of nourishment and murder, in which the animal both colluded and was angry, one had to honour one's prey and at the same time deceive it.'[9]

Always there is this ambiguity between the nourishing soul and the destructive, the friend and the enemy. Always the shudder of the alien, yet the recognition that the alien is also ourselves, with whom we must make exchanges and on whom we depend. As if there is a finite amount of mana in their environment, the Eveny believe that only so much game is allotted to each hunter in his lifetime, so that too much success means that he is not long for this world.[10] Moderation and equilibrium rule the reciprocal relations of man to animal, as well as ourselves to soul.

We can see how intensely, even religiously, these relations are lived yet how fragile they are in the face of Western culture's heavy-handed certainties, its black-and-white reality and its insistence on facts. How quickly indigenous peoples learn to awake from the enchantment of their own culture as if from a dream, to deny that they ever believed their women married bears or that they made love to Bayanay's beautiful daughter. Yet such a relationship with ourselves, with others and with the world is the background not only to traditional cultures, but to ours before the scientific revolution.

The invisible thread

Until about the early seventeenth century we had little sense of being a 'self' borne by a body, still less of a 'self' separate from a world 'outside' us. Instead we participated in the world as a microcosm within a macrocosm, a part which reflected the whole. As Owen Barfield put it in *Saving the Appearances*, pre-modern man 'did not feel himself isolated by his skin from the world outside him to quite the extent we do. He was integrated or mortised into it, each different part of him being united to a different part of it by some invisible thread.'[11] We were less like islands than embryos. We can see this, he says, in paintings where perspective was unnecessary because it was as if the artist was himself in the picture. The world was not extended away from us like a stage across which we moved; it was more like a garment we wore about us.[12] There is a big difference between a world we look out at through our eyes, and a world in which we participate, deeply implicated in every fibre of our being. But perhaps to make art, whether with perspective or not, is nothing other than to attune our souls in harmony with the Soul of the World.

The metaphor of resonance is particularly apt when we move from the reindeer-herders to the Pygmies of the African rain forest. Since visibility is poor in the jungle, the Pygmies are especially sensitive to sound. Their Soul of the World is called *molimo*, the Animal of the Forest; and it is never seen, only heard. In his book *The Forest People*, Colin Turnbull describes how the molimo is summoned.

First of all a special place is prepared and a special fire lit. Food and wood are collected from every member of the group because the molimo is a great hungry animal who must be fed and warmed. Above all he is only lured to the fireside by song, especially when someone has died or when the hunting is bad. On these occasions it is as if the forest is sleeping and must be woken by singing. It is a solemn occasion, and a dangerous one. All the men must sing; no one is exempt. Any woman or child who inadvertently runs into the molimo dies.

The singing may go on for nights on end. And every night the molimo responds. Its answering song is heard far off in the forest. As it approaches, its call is sometimes deep, gentle and loving – sometimes a hair-raising growl, like a leopard's. 'As the men sang their songs of praise to the forest,' writes Turnbull, 'the *molimo* answered them, first on this side, then on that, moving around so swiftly and silently that it seemed to be everywhere at once.

'Then, still unseen, it was right beside me, not more than two feet away, on the other side of a small but thick wall of leaves. As it replied to the song of the men, who continued to sing as though nothing were happening, it sounded sad and wistful, and immensely beautiful.'[13]

Double vision

The Nganga people of the Cameroons believe that we are born with four eyes: two open and two closed. The closed eyes open at death. If a child is born with all four eyes open he accordingly sees the invisible ancestors. This is disturbing; and two of the child's eyes have to be closed by rituals so that he does not 'go back' – that is, die. Conversely, for those people with a visionary vocation, the two closed eyes must be opened. A goat stands in for the person, and when it is sacrificed, gives its eyes to that person. One member of the Nganga, Eric de Rosnay – who was also a Jesuit priest – had his second set of eyes opened without his knowing it by a master called Din. Despite his ignorance of his own initiation, de Rosnay soon 'began to see differently'. His eyes 'were opened' to the hidden violence in people; and images came to him of what was in people's hearts.[14]

The opening of the 'goat's eyes', associated with death and the ancestors, is a potent metaphor for the power of intuition and insight. It is a concrete image of what William Blake called 'double vision'[15] – the power of seeing through the surface of things to what lies beneath. Shamans use this power to 'see into' people in order to diagnose what ails them. They can see, for example, a sorcerer battling with the ancestors for a patient's soul. Blake on the other hand used it to make poetry.

> This life's dim windows of the soul
> Distorts the Heavens from Pole to Pole
> And leads you to Believe a Lie
> When you see with, not thro', the eye.[16]

When we see *with* the eye alone, we are seeing the world as it appears; when we see *through* the eye, we see the world as it is. The first is literal eyesight, the second is metaphorical vision. Blake put it more succinctly:

> With my inward Eye 'tis an old Man grey;
> With my outward, a Thistle across my way.[17]

With his eye he sees a thistle; through his eye he sees an old man. To see only a thistle is literalism. But, equally, if we were *only* to see 'an old Man grey' we would be literalizing in another way, turning poetic vision into illusion or hallucination. The trick is to cultivate 'double vision', which sees the old man in the thistle or the dryad in the tree, but does not lose sight of thistle or tree. 'For double the vision my Eyes do see, / And a double vision is always with me.'[18] A sense of metaphor, of translation – of two worlds interpenetrating – must be maintained. But this is also the essential movement of the imagination. We see through the literal world to the shape-shifting Otherworld behind. Thus Nature herself is seen as the Otherworld. 'To the man of imagination,' wrote Blake, 'Nature is imagination itself.'[19] It is only our abrupt literalism which freezes the flow of Nature, stops it in its tracks, and insists on a single 'factual' reality.

All imaginative works re-introduce us to double vision. They show us another, deeper reality. No matter how prosaic the subject of a painting by Cézanne or van Gogh – a bowl of fruit or pair of boots – it glows with independent life. It is animate, like a person. It is a Presence. (It is a daimon.) 'The alternative to literalism,' wrote Norman O. Brown, 'is mystery.'[20] Art embodies the same 'double vision' required to see, read or hear it aright.

To see the soul as a shadow, as our traditional cultures so often do, is a compact image of double vision. A person is seen in the first instance as two-fold, as body and shadow, where 'shadow' is suggestive of a dark twin, the unconscious which is only visible when the overbearing light of consciousness is blocked. Yet although the shadow is completely concrete, it is also fleeting and ungraspable.

Sacred and profane

In defending soul I have had to be devoutly anti-literalistic. But, apart from the fact that it is always doubtful to be too devout about anything, I ought now to speak up for the literalism we all find it so difficult to escape. Indeed, the myths of a Fall may be exactly that: stories of a lapse from the daimonic Otherworld of imagination, symbolized by our Edens and Arcadias, into the cold grey world of facts. If there were no Fall, no lapse into literalism, soul would be everywhere manifest, as it was when God walked with Adam in the cool of the day. It would not be hidden, secret; a mystery. There would be no call for us to exert our imaginative powers of reflection, insight and mythologizing on which soul-making depends.[21] It seems that we need that very literalism which, if it is not seen through, is so deadening. We have to acquire the 'double vision' without which there would be no art or religion worth the name because there would be no reality behind this one, no depth.

We sense the presence of soul most, perhaps, whenever depth makes its appearance. Watching a play, dance or musical performance (it is a satire on us that we form audiences when, in traditional cultures, everyone participates) it sometimes happens that performers and audience become as one, the dancers dancing out of their skins and the hair of the audience lifting. Soul has made a mysterious entrance, and this is what we all hope for but can never engineer or predict. Soul deepens – and then connects. Or connects by deepening. She appears in a landscape and it is as if perspective were inventing itself before our eyes, everything coming alive like a presence. She appears in a casual conversation and suddenly we are no longer talking to an acquaintance but to a friend, connected at a deeper, unspoken level. Soul is what turns ordinary events into experiences; what imparts to the passing moment depth, connection and resonance. We cannot describe it but the effect is unmistakable: an experience of stillness in our heads, and in our hearts a fullness. It should be obvious that soul is what is transmitted and received in the experience, similarly unspeakable, which we call love.

When Colin Turnbull was allowed by his Pygmy friends to help 'bring the *molimo* out', he was surprised to find that it was a length of metal piping stolen from a roadside construction crew. The original molimo was made of bamboo, carefully carved and decorated; but, the men told him, this metal one was better because the old ones rotted and, besides, took a lot of hard work to make. Turnbull had trouble squaring such a profane object, and such a profane attitude, with the sacredness of a molimo ceremony. But the Pygmies had no such trouble. It was only a metal pipe as long as it was 'sleeping' in the tree they hid it in. As soon as it was 'brought out', it became the molimo. On the journey to the camp, for example, it had to be allowed to 'drink' at every stream. But it only truly became transformed into the molimo when it was blown into, and made to sing.[22]

We humans can make anything sacred. To the profane mind, nothing is sacred – the soul of the forest is only a metal pipe, the blood of Christ only sickly wine. Everything depends on the creative act of imagination. The more we imbue the world with imagination, the more the world is ensouled – and the more soul it returns to us, singing with meaning.

Soul and the unconscious

In October 1913, the Swiss psychologist C. G. Jung was alone on a journey when suddenly he was 'seized by an overpowering vision'. He saw a monstrous flood engulfing most of Europe, 'mighty yellow waves, the floating rubble of civilization, and the drowned bodies of the uncounted thousands. Then the whole sea turned to blood.' There followed three dreams of equal horror in which Europe was hit by a new Ice Age and everything froze.[1]

When the First World War broke out shortly afterwards, Jung was almost relieved. He had interpreted the dreams as meaning that his consciousness would be submerged by violent unconscious forces – that he was, in other words, on the brink of a psychosis. It looked instead as if the dreams had been prophetic. At the same time he began to try to understand the stream of fantasies which had started to assail him. 'I stood helpless before an alien world . . . I felt as if gigantic blocks of stone were tumbling down upon me. One thunderstorm followed another'. He survived these storms by 'brute strength'. He had no doubt that he must find the meaning of what he was experiencing in the fantasies. 'When I endured these assaults of the unconscious I had an unswerving conviction that I was obeying a higher will . . . .' He used yoga exercises as well as all the strength of his will to hold his emotions in check lest they completely shatter him. But as soon as he was calm again he rejoined the fray, allowing 'the images and inner voices to speak afresh'. One of the ways he coped was to translate the emotions into images – 'to find the images which were concealed in the emotions'. Had he left the images hidden in the emotions, he felt, they would have torn him to pieces.[2]

He wrote down the fantasies in the grating high-flown rhetorical style that the archetypes, as he was to call them, seem to favour. He submitted to emotions of which his normal self disapproved. He wrote down fantasies which seemed like nonsense. 'For as long as we do not understand their meaning, such fantasies are a diabolical mixture of the sublime and the ridiculous.' (This is another characteristic of soul we are not used to considering.)

He knew that sooner or later he would have to plummet down into them. He was terrified, and braced only by the thought that he could not expect his patients to do something he did not dare to do himself.[3]

On 12 December, he wrote, 'I was sitting at my desk, thinking over my fears. Then I let myself drop. Suddenly it was as though the ground literally gave way beneath my feet, and I plunged down into dark depths. I could not fend off a feeling of panic. But then . . . .'[4]

Well, I will go on with the story in a minute. First I ought to say that Jung's 'breakdown' was partly owing to his break with Sigmund Freud. He had been greatly excited by Freud's discovery that the psyche was not – as had been assumed for the previous three hundred years – confined to a conscious mind ruled by reason. Instead, below consciousness and its ability to say 'I' – its *ego* – lay the much larger realm of the subconscious 'it', or *id*. This was a seething cauldron of memories, emotions, wishes, desires and fantasies, which had all been forgotten or repressed but clamoured for expression. If they were not admitted into conscious life, they plagued us in other ways; for it is a law of the soul, as Freud said, that whatever is repressed changes shape to return in another guise. This meant that when Freud's patients appeared with outlandish physical or mental symptoms, such as hysterical fits, compulsions and obsessions, he had only to find out what repressed desire or wish lay at their root for them to disappear and the patient to be 'cured'. Often, it seemed, the root cause of the disturbing symptoms was sexual. The cure was not to be a physical or medical one, however; it was to be a 'talking cure'. Freud called it psycho-analysis. The telling of one's life story seemed to be therapeutic in itself. Language could connect the conscious mind up – or down – to the subconscious life hidden from it. Again and again it seemed that the unacknowledged wish of Freud's patients – no wonder it was repressed – was to have sex with their mother or father, depending on the gender of the patient. As for the other parent, the patient simply wanted them dead. Freud thought that he had stumbled across a universal pattern, as old as the myth of Oedipus, who unwittingly killed his father and married his mother. He called the pattern the Oedipus complex; and its counterpart in women, the Electra complex.

Freud was prepared for the stories which emerged from the subconscious to be different from the self-justifying tales we all tell ourselves in everyday life because he had attended some famous lectures given by Charcot in Paris.[5] They were as much like vaudeville shows as lectures because Charcot's party trick was to hypnotize young women and to question them about their symptoms while they were entranced. The results were startling: the women revealed a different personality, perhaps multiple personalities, beneath their everyday one; and these personalities spoke quite differently, usually more knowledge-ably – sometimes in a foreign language unknown to the unhypnotized patient – as if another person lived hitherto undetected inside them. These displays naturally had a profound influence on Freud, and on his hypothesis of an alternative subconscious life containing complexes that gave voice to the buried desires and wishes of the patient. The complexes were not really different personalities – as if the patient were possessed by autonomous spirits – but fragments of the patient's psyche which had become isolated through repression and so assumed the appearance of a separate person. They especially embodied parts of the patient which had become frozen in the past owing to some childhood trauma or cut off from consciousness because of the shameful nature of its desires.

In the early 1900s, Freud became friendly with Jung, whose brilliance he immediately recognized and in whose hands he wanted to place the future of psychoanalysis. Jung was enthusiastic to begin with, but as time wore on he began to have doubts about the details of Freud's model of the psyche. Rather foolishly, Freud did not try to overcome Jung's objections to his increasingly dogmatic system, but asserted his authority as Jung's mentor, more or less ordering him to toe the line. Jung wanted to – but could not. He broke with Freud, and the breach contributed to his mental breakdown which, ironically, led to his deepest insights into the nature of the soul.

Archetypes

When he let himself plunge into the depths, it was like dying or – even worse for a psychiatrist perhaps – like going mad. He more than half-expected to lose himself entirely: instead, at not too great a depth, he landed on his feet in a soft sticky mass. He entered a dark cave where there stood a dwarf with a leathery skin, as if mummified. He squeezed past the dwarf and waded through icy water to the other end of the cave where, on an outcrop of rock, there was a glowing red crystal. He lifted it up and found a hollow beneath. Within it he saw running water and the floating corpse of a blond youth with a wound in his head, followed by a huge black scarab, and then a red sun dawning out of the depths of the water. Dazzled, he was about to replace the crystal when, out of the opening, blood began to well up, then leap out in a thick jet. The blood spurted for a long time before ceasing. The vision ended.

'I was stunned by this vision', wrote Jung. 'I realized, of course, that it was a hero and solar myth, a drama of death and renewal, the rebirth symbolized by the Egyptian scarab. At the end, the dawn of the new day should have followed, but instead came that intolerable outpouring of blood . . . .'[6] Jung had braved the depths, travelling like a shaman into the daimonic realm of Imagination where he found, not the madness he feared, but . . . *myth*.

After this experience Jung practised more of these conscious descents. The way of soul, we notice, is downward rather than the upward flight of the mystic. He realized that beneath the little pool of light we call consciousness, governed by its ego, there is not just a subconscious full of personal history, forgotten or repressed, but a mythic realm full of teeming images which is common to us all. He verified this realm through the work he did with his patients. Unlike Freud, who worked with so-called neurotics – usually Jewish, well-to-do, middle-class Viennese citizens – Jung worked in a mental asylum where the patients were from all walks of life and, crucially, far more disturbed – psychotic rather than neurotic. He could do very little for most of them except talk to them and observe them. He began to notice that the stories they told, the mad fantasies they were gripped by, sometimes resembled myths. For instance, one patient told him that the sun had a penis which was where the wind came from. Four years later, Jung came across an obscure text in which the same belief was part of a Mithraic ritual his patient could not possibly have known about.[7]

Jung realized that not all mental disorders could be traced back to events in our early lives. He was forced to revise Freud's model of the psyche: beyond the subconscious, which Jung now renamed the personal unconscious, he postulated another, mythic level to the psyche. He called it the collective unconscious. He had rediscovered the Soul of the World, but, like the Romantic Imagination, he had discovered it within us. Moreover, during long observation of his patients' dreams and fantasies, he found that the collective unconscious contained what he called archetypes. As he acknowledged, they were very like Plato's Forms. But they were not abstract. They preferred to appear as personifications – that is, as daimons and gods. They formed narrative patterns – myths – which structured our unconscious psyches and determined our lives without our knowing it. Jung mentions a dozen or so archetypes in his pantheon, including the Great Mother, the Divine Child, the Helpful Animal, the Trickster, the Healer and the Wise Old Man. The ones that perhaps interested him most were those which all of us seem to encounter in the course of our psychic development: the Shadow, the Anima or Animus and the Self.

Jung realized that these archetypes, appearing as images, possessed a reality superordinate to everyday life. It is not we who personify them – rather the gods and daimons come to us as persons. We do not create them; if anything, they create us. So-called animism and polytheism, Jung began to see, are not the result of primitive anthropomorphism, as if we projected images onto an inanimate world, but the reverse: daimons and gods are the divine images of archetypes which come from outside us – that is, from an unconscious which is outside our conscious lives and which, moreover, cannot even be located with any certainty inside us. It might be, as the Neoplatonists thought, a property of the world itself, like an underlying soul.

When Jung said that the archetypes were unknowable, he was following Immanuel Kant, who held that behind every phenomenon was an unknown 'noumenon' – an idea which echoed Plato's view that behind our world lay a world of ideal

Forms. But paradoxically the archetypes *could* be known – through the images by which they represented themselves. They are 'endowed with personality at the outset', claimed Jung, and they 'manifest themselves as *daimones*, as personal agencies . . . felt as actual experiences.'[8] Plotinus had similarly maintained that just as soul connects us to the Forms, so the daimons in the Soul of the World connect us to the gods – two ways of saying the same thing. Proclus perhaps put it best: the gods who are in themselves 'formless and unfigured'[9] appear as daimons, many of whom are different images of the same god. Thus the daimons both link us to the gods yet, from another point of view, they are appearances of the gods.

There is part of us – I shall be calling it spirit – which always thinks that there is a greater reality, some abstract truth, Form or archetype, behind or beyond what is apparent. From soul's point of view the images and daimons *are* reality, and the sense of something deeper – beyond, behind or beneath – is really her way of pointing to her own depth, of leading us on into further insight, of keeping us always desirous and full of longing. Keeping us, in other words, in love; and keeping soul herself moved and moving.

Soul, in short, prefers to represent herself in myths rather than abstract schemes; and as personages rather than concepts. Even Freud dimly recognized this, creating a new mythology out of his Oedipus story and, later, his tale of two overriding principles, Eros and Thanatos, Love and Death. Jung went farther. He understood that all myths are alive and well in the depths of the psyche; that you could not explain mythology by recourse to psychology but, on the contrary, psychology was another form of mythologizing because myths are soul's preferred mode of self-expression. 'Mythology is a psychology of antiquity; psychology is a mythology of modernity'.[10]

Myth-blindness

Soul cannot be known objectively, only subjectively through reflections and insights. Whenever we talk about soul we are only recording what she says about herself through us. A psychology which thinks, for instance, that it is scientific is blind to the fantasy it is promulgating as objective truth. We cannot step outside soul to study her. She is a way of looking at all disciplines and thus hidden within every field of enquiry.

Whether we see soul as single or multiple, mortal or immortal, the source of life or the portal to death and so on, depends on the structure, archetype or god within soul herself through whose perspective we are seeing. Any attempt to describe the soul, including this book, is doomed unless we keep shifting our viewpoint.

This is an imaginative activity, and intrinsically good for the soul because it prevents us from identifying literally with any single perspective and so being trapped in it – we have to be able to see our own perspective, which means seeing *through* our own perspective (which itself means 'seeing through'). This imaginative effort in turn leads us to other archetypes, other gods, to other perspectives on the world – and to the world as a set of perspectives. For the gods are never isolated but are all implicated in each other, as their complicated kinship in mythology attests. Each changes its meaning depending on its relationship to the others. As Plotinus said of the Platonic Forms, 'All is in all.' Each Form experiences all the other Forms from its own outlook. This is a crucial idea because it tells us that the cosmos is not a fixed entity we can empirically know, but a fluid dynamic that shapes itself according to the Form, archetype or god through whom it is imagined.[11]

Most of us are, most of the time, blind to the gods who govern our lives. This is especially true of the archetype Jung called the Shadow. It is aptly named because it is projected out of the unconscious directly onto the world. In this way we do not realize that our sense of inferiority, weakness and failure which we hate and fear is projected onto blameless other people. It is our psychological and moral task, thought Jung, to open our eyes and bring our shadows to consciousness, dispelling our blind bigotries and ideologies. Only then can we begin to meet the challenge of the archetype which most concerns us here: the anima.

Anima

Jung was chary of using the word 'soul' because of its theological connotations. He used the word 'psyche' instead because it sounded more scientific to use a Greek word. But for Jung, psyche referred to both consciousness and the unconscious, the totality of the personality. His word 'anima', the Latin for 'soul', referred to the principal archetype of the unconscious. He identified the anima as being behind the sudden moods which possess us for better or worse, behind our reveries and inarticulate longings. In dreams and fantasies she appears as a myriad female figures: the girl on the bus, the show-jumper, waitress, call girl, French-teacher, orphan girl, holy virgin, voodoo priestess . . . there is no end to the anima's images. Through our lust or love, pity or terror, she keeps us emotionally connected to the unconscious, to soul. Like Sleeping Beauty she is herself the soul who must be awakened to her destiny with a kiss. Like Cinderella she is often overlooked, hidden in ashes, but in reality the radiant Princess. In dreams she can be an elusive, even faceless, but nevertheless alluring nymph whom we pursue through unknown streets or a party crowd, like Arthurian knights lost in a dark forest. But we lose ourselves in pursuit of the anima in order to find ourselves in a deeper sense, the Grail Chapel shining in the unexpected clearing. Whenever we are bowled over by the dazzling girl we must possess at all costs, the anima is at work. No wonder so many marriages go astray when the dazzle dims and we cannot square the goddess we glimpsed with the quotidian woman we are living with.

The anima is the personification of the unconscious, said Jung. She is also the mediatrix between consciousness and the unconscious. She is the 'feminine' side of the psyche. She is, we might say, the image of our souls within the world-soul. She is therefore paradoxical: as archetype she is the personification of the Soul of the World, but as archetypal image – the personal way she appears to us – she is the individual soul.

We think of the ego, our sense of 'I', as giving us our identity. But really it is given to the ego by the anima. She bestows on us that feeling of being unique and special. But at that very moment we are in fact – another paradox – at our least unique, our most collective. We have only to look at the behaviour of lovers to see the truth of this. For just when lovers feel that nobody has ever experienced such love before and that it is unique to themselves – this is the very moment when they manifest to everyone else the most stereotypical behaviour and language, common to lovers everywhere.

Anima teaches the ego – teaches us – that we are human but with inhuman depths; that we are persons with impersonal underpinnings; and that we are composed of more than one personality despite what our egos, desperate for unity, tell us.[12]

My experience of soul as 'my own' and as 'within' me now becomes something different. It no longer refers exclusively to an actual entity called 'me', because soul is more impersonal and inhuman than it is personal and human. Instead 'my' soul refers to soul's own privacy and interiority. Not a literal private and interior ownership, but the metaphorical 'in-ness' of soul in all events.[13] This is an essential part of the way soul imagines herself, *as if* she were within things, including us humans, because she wants to be contained, and cherished like a secret.

The unconscious is feminine in a man and personified by the anima, thought Jung. In a woman it is masculine and personified by the animus, which often appears as multiple male figures. But this opposition is to identify consciousness with biological sex. In fact, we all – men and women – can have a consciousness which is 'feminine' or 'masculine'. Likewise, we all have both an anima and animus. 'Anima phenomenology is not restricted to the male sex. Women have little girls in their dreams, and whores; they too are lured by mysterious and unknown women . . . . We say of a woman "she has soul", and we mean much the same as when we say this of a man.'[14] In other words, anima is not confined by gender. She is the feminine in all of us, as long as we do not take this 'femininity' literally.[15] After all, she does not have to appear to us as a woman. As the image which best represents the soul and its inchoate yearning, she can appear as anything, from a longed-for pony or steam engine to a mountain stream or lost landscape. We are all a complex interplay of anima and animus, the two complementary archetypes which I will be elaborating later on as soul and spirit.

What I have been calling, after Keats, soul-making, Jung called *individuation*. In the course of our lifelong quests and odysseys we encounter the archetypes of the unconscious and are initiated by them. We battle with our Shadows, try to accommodate and come to terms with our anima and animus, and, through them, begin to see what we might become: a Self.

The Self is Jung's ultimate archetype. It is foreshadowed by the figure of the Wise Old Man, which Jung called the archetype of meaning. The Self is the totality of the psyche, like a conjunction of anima and animus, masculine and feminine, consciousness and the unconscious. It is what we are individuating towards. Like all archetypes it is unknowable in itself, but the images by which it represents itself show a certain conformity. For example, it appears as a tree, notably the mythic World-Tree which connects Heaven and Earth. It appears in abstract form as a four-fold unity such as a mandala, a circle divided into four quarters. Jung also demonstrated at length that whoever Christ is, theologically or historically speaking, *psychologically* He is a symbol of the Self.[16] The Self is to the microcosm what the One is to the macrocosm. In myth it is often depicted as a union of wise old man and anima, such as blind old Oedipus and his daughter Antigone. In alchemy, the Self is symbolized by a hermaphrodite or androgyne ('man-woman'); or by, of all things, a stone.

Soul and alchemy

The Great Work of alchemy was, Jung discovered, not just a form of primitive chemistry but a science of the soul. 'I had stumbled', he wrote in his autobiography, 'upon the historical counterpart of my psychology of the unconscious.'[17] The transformation of metallic substances in the alchemists' cucurbits and retorts, collectively known as the 'Hermetic egg', mirrored the psychological transformation of the alchemist himself. Alchemy is soul-making. In the oft-repeated motto 'make that which is above like that which is below and that which is below like that which is above', Jung saw an injunction to bring consciousness to bear on the unconscious and vice versa. Analogously, the alchemist had 'to make the fixed volatile and the volatile fixed' – a concurrent operation which separated and purified the elements, both physical and psychic, before joining them again. In this process they began to interpenetrate in new ways. More important than the heat of a literal fire was the 'secret fire' of the imagination, which transformed and fused all the elements of the psyche in the impossible, miraculous 'Stone'. Only the uninitiated believed that the aim was to turn base metal to gold. True alchemists always said that their aim was a mysterious 'philosophical gold'.[18]

Alchemical recipes read like psychodramas that take place, like a waking dream, in the in-between world where what is inside us is outside and vice versa, very much like the making of art. Typically, the Work begins with the Prime Matter, symbolized by an ourobouros, a serpent biting its own tail, which is separated into the primordial principles, 'our sulphur' and 'our mercury'. These ingredients cannot be understood literally. They are dramatis personae, more often called Sol and Luna (Sun and Moon) or Rex and Regina (King and Queen). They are like constituents of the psyche – soul and spirit, spirit and body – which, obeying the command 'Solve et coagula!', have to be dissolved and coagulated, wrenched apart and recombined in the course of many distillatory 'circulations'. The Raven's Head appears, signalling the conjunction that is death and putrefaction, a sinking down into the 'black blacker than black' of the Blackness. As the watery 'body' of the conjoined King–Queen is further heated, its airy 'soul' ascends to the top of the Egg, or 'Heaven', where it condenses and returns as a 'dew' to consummate the marriage of the Above with the Below. Months, even years of circulations might be needed to cleanse 'our body' before the sudden iridescence of the Peacock's Tail heralds the soul's readiness to raise the 'body' up into the Whiteness, Luna rising in cold glory out of Sol's grave.

Whereas the resulting 'white stone' represents the preliminary marriage of certain opposed principles, such as soul and body, above and below, consciousness and the unconscious, the final conjunction is reserved for the Redness. Unlike the rebirth symbolized by the white stone, the marvellous reconciliation of the conjoined soul and spirit with a new body is like a resurrection, symbolized by the Philosophers' Stone, the 'Stone that is no Stone'.

It is impossible in the space available to give more than the merest flavour of alchemy's strange imagery and arcane complexity. Yet it may not be as alien as it seems. Artists probably understand it best – the years of struggle with intransigent materials, forever going over the same ground in the attempt to purify their self-expression or expression of self; the fusing of subject and object in the fire of imagination; the sympathetic mirroring of inner and outer worlds. But we are all prey to mercurial moods and sulphurous rages, to leaden despairs and the blackness of depressions, to blocks and fixities and manic volatilizations, to dreams of lacerating beasts, revelatory white Queens and a wise golden child, the 'son of the macrocosm', another synonym for the Stone.

The Great Work of alchemy tells us that soul-making is not at all the same as the movement favoured by most modern psychotherapies. They tend to emphasize *growth* and *progress* towards the *unity* of an integrated personality. This betrays a Christian, and more especially, a Protestant bias towards upward, linear ascent; or else the hidden influence of the Mother archetype in relation to whom we are eternally children who must grow and mature. But this biological metaphor is not appropriate to soul. Nor is the insistence on unity at all costs. It is the monotheistic tendency of our culture which holds up the oneness of soul as an ideal, and which psychotherapy imitates. But soul is intrinsically multifaceted and polycentric, resistant to being located in a single point. The idea of unity is not a property of soul but one of soul's perspectives. It does not refer literally to the soul as a single substance or a separate unit. Rather, it is a metaphor for the fact that all things are images of soul and connected to each other in soul. In other words, the unity we wish to pin on soul really refers to a unity of perspective that sees everything as primarily a reality of soul. The circulations of alchemy, always shifting levels and perspectives, dissolve its own literalisms.

Certainly alchemy acknowledges our desire for linear movement, which is archetypal and therefore unavoidable. For example, it divided itself into stages that varied in number from four to twelve and always subscribed to the three great symphonic movements, called the Blackness, Whiteness and Redness. But each stage comprised many 'circulations'. And so, while 'the goal of psychic development is the self,' wrote Jung, 'there is no linear evolution; there is only a circumambulation of the self. Uniform development exists, at most, only at the beginning; later, everything points towards the centre . . . .'[19]

His diagram of the self – the mandala – has to be pictured as dynamic and revolving. Its four-fold structure, like a squared circle, is less a unity than a wholeness: what Jung called 'a complex of opposites'. Sometimes the soul's dynamic is represented as a spiral where each loop recapitulates the one beneath it, but at another level, just as in life we so often seem to repeat the same pattern. Yet the pattern is not, on closer inspection, identical – our psychic lives are like a kaleidoscope, with every turn forming a new pattern out of the same elements and the same structure. At other times, individuation is imagined as a labyrinth or maze in which we wander as if lost. Just as we seem to reach the centre, we are whisked out to the periphery again; or, just as we seem most remote from our goal, we find that we are on a clear path towards it. Analogously, we know from our own experience that however much we wish the soul's path to be straight, upward and ascending, it is more likely to be meandering, full of regressions, downward turns and backward glances. The endless, wearisome circulations of the alchemists give us hope that the endless obsessive patterns and neuroses we are so often trapped in may be resolved by the simple act of repetition itself.

Jung was inclined to think that the self was a virtual centre, a synthesis we never achieve. The journey, it seems, is everything. We have to follow Hermes *psychopompos*, 'guide of the soul', who alone among the gods can travel freely between Mount Olympus and Hades, the Above and the Below. He guides our souls to the Underworld after death. He is Lord of the Crossroads, a foot in both the worlds he weaves together, like the serpents entwined on his thyrsus. Like him, soul needs no goal, centre or rest for it is always at home on the winding road.

Reflux distillation

Plotinus frequently mentioned that the motion of the soul is circular. And it is the circular process of reflux distillation which provides the best model of the dynamic psyche. Chemically speaking, a liquid is heated and evaporates to a gas which rises, cools and condenses into a liquid. This is the purifying process of distillation. Reflux (literally a 'flowing back') occurs when the distilled liquid is then fed back into the original liquid, so that the operation is circular. This simple chemical procedure provided a rich metaphorical template for the 'circulations' of the alchemist, who saw in the heated liquid 'our matter', and in the gas a 'volatile soul' which rises out of the body of the matter as if at death, only to return, purified, to the body – to become 'fixed' – while at the same time transforming the body to which it returns.

Jung read this in psychological terms: through the secret fire of imagination – the 'fire that does not burn' – consciousness differentiates itself from the unconscious, rising 'above' what is 'below'. It then condenses around an ego, which reflects – turns its light back onto the dark unconscious in order to differentiate further and to raise up unconscious contents into consciousness.

More simply, we can see in reflux distillation a metaphor for the whole self-reflecting and self-transforming nature of soul. Its movements, elusive and shape-changing, become visible when it is 'fixed' in matter, and then become invisible again as it is volatilized into spirit.

Essentially, alchemy is not about the literal freeing of soul from body, spirit from matter, but about freeing matter from its literalisms so that it can be once again 'subtle' and fluid, transparent to soul as soul is embodied in matter. We are constantly distilling our selves out of ourselves like fountains that gush from underground wellsprings, flash briefly in the sun and return to their source. With every looping movement we recollect the gods from the Underworld below consciousness, where recollection implies both remembering the gods and gathering them into ourselves.

SIX

Soul and myth

When I was five years old an enlightened primary-school teacher used to read us stories from Greek mythology. All us little boys liked the Greek heroes. We recognized the prototypes of our adventure-book heroes and comic-book superheroes: powerful Heracles rampaging through his twelve labours, Jason and his gang of specialists nabbing the Golden Fleece, Theseus negotiating the Cretan labyrinth with a ball of thread to kill the Minotaur, high-flying Bellerophon on his winged horse, hare-swift Achilles laying waste to the armies of Troy. Some of us admired the subtler heroes, such as Perseus, who out-manoeuvred the gorgon Medusa; the artistic Orpheus, who used music rather than brute force to master the Underworld; or wily, red-haired Odysseus, who thought up the Trojan Horse. I later came to realize that all our different styles of heroic stance towards the world find their archetypal blueprint in the myths.

Did the little girls similarly thrill to these tales? Or did they identify with neglected Deianeira, Heracles' wife; with poor Ariadne who teaches Theseus about the thread and is abandoned for her pains; or with powerful, witchy Medea without whose help Jason would have failed to procure the Fleece? I don't know. But I do remember that we were all affected by the story which, above all the others, stayed with me.

It is the story of an innocent girl called simply the Kore, or 'maiden', who is drowsily picking narcissi and poppies in a sunlit meadow when, suddenly, the earth opens and Hades, god of the Dead, flies out in his brazen chariot, snatches her up and carries her off into the Underworld. It is a violation, even a rape – as children we were not explicitly told this, of course, but we keenly felt how appalling the vivid opening scene was. I had a cosmic vision of the whole green Earth withering as the Kore's heart-broken mother, Demeter, goddess of crops and growing things, neglected her duties and wandered the blighted world in search of her daughter.

All would have perished from famine if Zeus had not sent Hermes into the Underworld to bring the Kore back. He was successful: Hades promised to let her rejoin her mother. But whether she had been unable to resist eating some pomegranate seeds, or whether Hades had secretly popped one into her mouth, she had eaten in the Underworld. And to eat Hades' food is to be condemned to stay there forever. However meagre the seeds, they doomed the Kore, now renamed Persephone, 'Bringer of Destruction', to spend one-third of the year below the earth.

At first I was quite pleased, when, years later, the myth was 'explained' to me as a primitive account of how the seasons came into being. The Kore was the part of Mother Nature which 'went underground' in winter and re-emerged in spring. The myth was made into an allegory, with a single meaning, satisfying my desire for facts. But I felt, too, a loss of depth and complexity in the myth. It continued to resonate in my mind far beyond the explanation I had been given. I began to see that the myth was about the loss of the Soul of the World, symbolized by the wasteland of the earth's surface, yet at the same time soul's continued existence in 'Death's dream kingdom'.[1] I also began to see, by the way the myth had gone on haunting me, that myth was operative in my life, and that it deepened its meaning over time and according to how much imagination I brought to it. Myth is, like great art, as bottomless as soul itself, capable of limitless readings and interpretations. I could see, in other words, that all the gods and their stories are still informing the stories we tell ourselves, including our scientific theories and hypotheses. For, as Karl Popper reminds us, 'scientific discovery is akin to explanatory story-telling, to myth-making, and to the poetic imagination.'[2]

We are all in the grip of a myth. We are all inhabiting an imaginative structure determined by the perspective and set of ideas we used to call a god. Proclus thought that myths are composed by the daimons and that the daimons shape our lives.[3] The idea that the daimons who inhabit myths also invented them is a remarkable metaphor for the way myths generate themselves out of Imagination. 'I have often had the fancy', wrote the Irish poet W. B. Yeats, 'that there is some one myth for every man, which, if we but knew it, would make us understand all he did and thought.'[4]

This is why the recounting of myths, especially to children, is intrinsically healthy for the soul and why we go on listening to, or reading, different versions of the same myths all our lives.

Gods

Because soul is occupied by – and the soul preoccupied with – the gods, it is religious. It is just that its religion is not denominational or dogmatic. Worse still, it is not monotheistic. This is why the Judaeo-Christian tradition has been on the whole inimical to soul. It rejects soul's natural animism and polytheism, and insists on one God. It is suspicious of icons, images, art and imagination. It tends to denounce all myths other than its own as untrue.

Soul on the other hand is tolerant of monotheism. It recognizes our need for unity, and so it embraces monotheism as one of its many points of view. What it tries to resist is the drive inherent in the monotheistic outlook to exclude all other gods, hence all other perspectives. Monotheism takes its one God literally, approaching Him with ritual, prayer, worship and belief. Soul does not believe in its gods so much as imagine them.[5] They may be powerful, supernatural, dazzling and awesome, as Pallas Athena is for Odysseus – but they are not literal beings. They do not require repentance or dispense forgiveness: what they require is attention and what they dispense is insight and meaning. Soul accommodates our desire for a single god by moving us to address one god at a time – while continuing to acknowledge all the others.

It is as if, whenever one god or archetype steps forward to be spotlit at centre stage, the others are all present in the background or waiting in the wings, ready to enter and interact. Meanwhile, however, we express the viewpoint appropriate to the ascendant deity through whose eyes we see the world without being aware of the fact – in fact the world we see is the creation of the god who is governing us. Each god carries a set of ideas and a mode of imagining which precedes our perception of things. In short, each god carries with it its own cosmos. Its presence in our lives is so dazzling that we are often blinded to any other god's point of view. We end up mistaking our ruling deity's perspective on the world as the world – end up mistaking, as is sometimes said, the map for the territory. As Jung said of the archetypes: 'All we know is that we seem unable to imagine without them . . . If we invent them, we invent them according to the patterns they lay down.'[6]

The god behind science is golden Apollo the 'Far-Seeing', the 'Wide-Awake'. He is the god of consciousness, clarity, order, purity, reason and progress. When he came to dominance in the sixteenth century, bringing with him the theory of a sun-centred cosmos, he brought the light of reason which would usher in the Enlightenment. The scientific world-view was not complete, however, until Apollo's rationalism had been underpinned by materialism – the eccentric doctrine that everything is only matter – whose begetter, we suspect, is the great Mother Hera, wife of Zeus (the Latin *mater*, 'mother' and 'matter' are cognates),[7] who keeps us grounded and mindful of matter.

Dionysus is the god of communal ecstasy. His devotees are Maenads, 'raging' women who celebrate his midwinter rites with the wine of which he is the god, and, thrashing their long hair about, with the dismemberment of a goat that stands in for the dismembered god. He is like the lord of misrule who is allowed to reign for short periods to prevent the orthodox order and rules from becoming too repressive. Whenever we submerge our individuality in collective out-pourings – political rallies, wild parties ('raves', for instance) or chanting football crowds – Dionysus is present.

Jung identified the god behind fascism as the northern, Germanic deity Wotan, whose wild hunt sweeps across Europe leaving slaughter in its wake. But war will always be with us as long as the red-faced war-god Ares stamps about in our psyches, soothed only by his lover, Beauty herself – sexy, promiscuous, adulterous, maddening, worshipped Aphrodite, goddess of Love, who is married to the lame cuckold Hephaestus. As armourer to the gods, working with his Cyclopes in the great forges beneath Mount Etna, he is the god behind our technology, perhaps, which, having divine sanction, is therefore not necessarily inimical to soul and only grows lethal when Love is taken away from it by War.

There are deities behind social movements. Hera's little *hausfrau* daughter, Hebe, is behind the ideal of the wifely and motherly domestic goddess who was worshipped in the 1950s. Then the great wheel of the world-soul turns, Hebe retreats into the wings and Aphrodite takes centre stage to inaugurate the sexy, promiscuous '60s. But we must not forget the great goddesses who will have nothing to do with sex and marriage. The virgin Athena sprang fully armed from her father's head, as if she were the strong right arm of his very thoughts. An intellectual blue-stocking – with teeth – Athena is the goddess of feminism, of social justice and civic virtue, her Parthenon ('virgin') presiding over the city of Athens. The other virgin goddess is Artemis, goddess of hunting and the wilderness, and also, strangely, of childbirth. Might it be children other than the literal kind – ideas and inspirations – which her remote beauty helps bring to birth? We recognize these goddesses in modern women, though we do not have to take their attributes of warrior-dress and hunting, midwifery and even virginity literally. But a man who marries a woman under the aegis of Athena or Artemis would be well advised not to tangle with her when she's on the warpath or pursuing one of her crusades; nor to try and prevent her from taking off, free-spirited, into the wild.

We are all very naive about our own unfathomed unconscious lives and the gods, both savage and wise, who dwell therein and shape our attitudes to the world.

Dame Kind

For example, our attitude to Nature, or Dame Kind as she was known in medieval times, depends on the deity whose point of view we unwittingly take. Through the eyes of Demeter, so to speak, we see Nature as the abode of green growth and fertility. Gaia, or Ge, governs the realm just below the earth's surface. From her outlook we see the deeper meaning of places, as not simply subject to brute biology, but as sacred – places where we perform rituals and to which we make pilgrimages, whether for picnics at standing stones or prayers at holy wells. She is not the goddess of fertility, but of the rites which guarantee fertility.[8]

If Gaia is the goddess of the ecological movement, Artemis is the goddess of conservation, the Virgin whose inviolacy we must preserve at all costs. She presides over wild Nature where we do not grow things or perform rituals. If anything, we hunt – a perilous business because we might lose ourselves in the wilderness while chasing a magical white hart or, worse, become the hunted ourselves. The story of Actaeon is a cautionary tale. He saw what no one is permitted to see: the goddess, bathing naked. We are allowed to hunt the animals who are in Artemis' care or which are, like white harts, manifestations or masks of Artemis herself (providing always we show the proper reverence); but we are not allowed to see Artemis herself, as if in her nakedness. In striving to see too much, and lusting after the goddess, Actaeon is like the natural scientist who knows no bounds to his enquiry and seeks to penetrate Nature to her core. Myth tells us that this is indecent. Artemis punishes Actaeon by turning him into a stag. The hunter becomes the hunted. He is torn to pieces – not by the goddess, but by his own hounds, emblems of his own lust. Here we see that the vision of Nature as 'red in tooth and claw', which the old survival-of-the-fittest scientists held up as the true version of Nature, is actually a reflection of their own lustful and aggressive stance towards her. By imagining that she is soulless machinery they can despoil at will, they open themselves to destruction by their own impious desires.

Like an embodiment of the world-soul, Nature reflects back at us the face we show her. She is not the fixed entity we fondly think she is, but a sea of metaphors, constantly shape-shifting – the inviolate nymph we must preserve; the dangerous animal who destroys; the temptress we must penetrate or rape; the pregnant mother who gives birth to abundance; and so on. She can even be Dionysian when the Maenads go out to her rocky places at dead of winter to 'commune' with the god. At her most tranquil, dozing in the heat of the noon-day, there comes the terrible shout of Pan, which sends us running for our lives.

Ideology
Religion is successful when it acknowledges soul and does not exclude other gods too fervently in favour of one. Even

Christian monotheism was subverted by soul. Its one God became a Trinity. The Virgin Mary was elevated by popular demand to the status of a goddess behind whom stand all the great goddesses, from Astarte to Artemis, Isis to Sophia. The daimons crept back in as mediating saints. Christ Himself was multifarious in the early days of Christianity, being freely identified with pagan gods and heroes from Osiris, Apollo and Dionysus, to Eros, Orpheus, Prometheus, Adonis and, especially, Heracles.[9]

As I have mentioned, the more we insist on monotheism and shut out other gods, the more they clamour at the back door – and the more rigid and puritanical we must become in order to keep them at bay. Our religion narrows to ideology. We cling to a single, literal creed and condemn any imaginative variant as deviant or heretical. We become fundamentalists, whether Christians or Muslims, Marxists or fascists, rationalists or materialists.

All ideologues are monotheists without knowing it. They have been ambushed by one or other of the gods. They use the perspective of a single god to suppress all the others. But the gods do not want to be treated monotheistically. They are all married or related to each other, as mythology makes clear. If we isolate them, their virtues turn against us. In seeking to reconnect with their fellow deities they become ruthless and possessive, and this is reflected in our fanaticisms.

For example, we all need a portion of Dionysian ecstasy from time to time to 'take us out of ourselves'. But to be only Dionysian is to suffer that degradation of ecstasy familiar to the addict and alcoholic. If we isolate Gaia, we no longer revere the Soul of the World and promote the sanctity of certain sites. She becomes the goddess of an ecological ideology which has replaced religious instruction in many schools. Mostly this does no harm; but we should be aware that it can turn a beautiful sacred world into a profane 'environment' whose spoliation we

combat with the same literal and scientistic attitude that caused
the damage in the first place. Analogously, to pursue Artemis
alone is to make a religion of 'conservation' and to foster puritanical 'green' movements which would not just reject
consumerism but spread abstinence everywhere, curbing all
our pleasures along with our carbon footprints. But ideologies
can only ever hope to change our lifestyles; it takes soul to
change our lives. Clever Athena[10] who inspires our desire for
justice and equality in the community becomes a harridan
when she is isolated. She turns us into oxymoronic fanatical
liberals who detect political incorrectness everywhere, like the
old Puritans who, condemning all sensuality, saw wantonness in
every innocent gesture.

Many ardent atheists think that by rejecting the Judaeo-
Christian God they have vanquished religion. They do not
notice that they are in thrall to gods of their own, such as
Apollo. For when he is alone and untempered by his brother
Hermes or his counterpart Dionysus, he ceases to be sweet
and enlightening reason and becomes rigidly over-rational,
violently opposed to anything that smacks of soul, of the
daimonic, of the divine. The materialists, on the other hand, are
unconsciously possessed by the Mother – probably Hera, who
reduces all points of view to her own, just as the materialists
reduce everything to matter; and, like many materialists, she is
notoriously vindictive towards her husband's lovers; that is,
towards any other perspective with which he might ally himself.

Unfortunately ideologues can never be talked into adopting
any other perspective. They have to be, as Christians would say,
converted; or, as we might say, initiated – that is, transformed.
But how might an Apollonic rationalist, for instance, be
persuaded to release his iron grip on the world?

One way might be to introduce him to Dionysus, whom
Nietzsche famously paired with, and opposed to, Apollo. We
can see how, to Dionysus, god of collective abandonment,

Apollo must seem dangerously cold, tight-arsed, individualistic, aloof and intellectual. From Apollo's point of view, Dionysus can only appear dangerously irrational, undifferentiated, out of control, prone to contagious hysteria. It is obvious that we need something of both their outlooks if we are not to become either intolerable prigs or dissipated ne'er-do-wells. Although Apollo and Dionysus share a father – Zeus – their perspectives are poles apart. So how are they to be brought together?

Like the rationalist, Apollo on his own over-values consciousness; he needs to be acquainted with the 'irrational' unconscious. Fortunately, the god whom Jung called the 'god of the unconscious' is not far away – is, in fact, his younger brother, Hermes.

The Hermetic way

One of Hermes' first actions after his birth is to steal Apollo's cattle. He twists their hooves around, and makes himself a pair of sandals which he wears back to front, so that his pursuers will be misled into thinking that he has gone in the opposite direction. From Apollo's standpoint he is at best a trickster, at worst a thief and a liar – when he is accused of thieving, he flatly denies it. Duplicity is the air he breathes, and very different from Apollo's unity.

When he is not in relation to Apollo, however, Hermes appears quite otherwise. He is not only the god of thievery but also the god of communication. He presides over trade and commerce, crossroads and boundaries, magic and oracles. He is marginal, shady, even occult – the most daimonic of the gods – but also known for his wisdom and the depth of his hermeneutics. As messenger to the gods, he is the only one who can travel freely between their skyworld, the human world and the Underworld. He mediates between different planes of existence and separate levels of the psyche. He specializes not only in leading astray, but also in guiding – notably guiding the souls of the dead down into Hades.

Hermes is highly ambiguous, transcending all boundaries because he is himself the god of boundaries; difficult to pin down because he has no home except the road he travels, constantly enabling exchange to take place between this world and the Otherworld, the above and the below, consciousness and the unconscious – as I have already mentioned when identifying him with alchemy's Mercurius. His thieving from Apollo is only the thievery which the unconscious is always practising on consciousness, snatching away words, ideas, memories and dreams just when we most need them. If we want to retrieve them or interpret their depths, we cannot follow their literal tracks on the straight sunny path of Apollo. We have to be devious, following the twisted path that Hermes has ordained, even going in the direction opposite to the one the tracks are pointing to.

If we take the winding, backward, downward path of Hermes, we not only connect with the soul's deepest perspective – that of Hades, Death – but also, and paradoxically, with the gods of the high Olympian world. Hermes connects consciousness to the unconscious, and psyche to the world. He may be a thorn in the side of righteous, moralizing, pompous Apollo, but he does initiate the reconciliation between them: he offers his brother the lyre he has made out of a tortoise's shell. Apollo is so delighted with the instrument that he gives his cattle to Hermes, and appoints him Lord of the Herds. Hermes understands that barter and reciprocal exchange are as important in the life of the soul as they are in trade. He enables different worlds to be bridged, different perspectives to be mediated. He invents fire-sticks and lights the primordial fire long before Prometheus steals fire from the gods. He cooks a couple of cattle and sacrifices the meat to all the gods, including himself, dividing it up into twelve portions. Thus he gives all the gods, every perspective on the world, their due. He not only reconnects himself to Apollo, he is also the first to carry the infant Dionysus – standing in for the Dionysian stance while it matures, perhaps – and so maintains the connection between the god of ecstatic disorder and orderly Apollo.

Eleusis

We are all to some extent innocent Kores, children of Nature, picking posies in the tranquil fields and blissfully unaware of the imminent eruption of Death's chariot, which will carry us off to the Underworld to be violated. Such a rape is indispensable to real life because it drags us out of our merely natural, merely human life and initiates us into the life of the soul. We are all Kores who have to become Persephones. The myth of Demeter and the Kore was central to the Mysteries of Eleusis, which, the myth tells us, Demeter founded in the course of her search for her daughter. We do not know much more about these Mysteries, except that they were considered indispensable to the citizens of ancient Athens. But we can be sure that they entailed death, that is, the 'dying to ourselves' without which we remain childish – psychic 'maidens' who lack the reflection and double vision of those who have been woken into soul life. It is unfortunate that initiation seems to have to be so sudden and brutal; but then again, there is no gentle way to encounter death. Like the Kore we can learn to love Hades. Her abduction and rape is a narrative that is eternally present in our own souls. It tells us we must be penetrated by death. From our normal sunny conscious outlook in the green, growing, fertile, physical fields, Hades' cold Underworld makes us shudder and fills us with dread. We think it is a drear and chilly place, perhaps even unreal, like the shades who are said to populate it. But Hades is also known as Plouton, 'the Rich One'. And his riches are not of silver and gold, but the limitless riches of Imagination, beside which it is our fields – even ourselves – that seem mere shadows.

Eros and Psyche

The myth of Demeter and the Kore is about soul, and it underlies the rituals of the Eleusinian Mysteries. There is another myth which is clearly related to it, like a variant of it, which is even more fundamentally about soul, and which underlies the Mysteries of Isis: the story of Psyche and Eros, Soul and Love. It is like the story of Cinderella, for which it is doubtless the blueprint, except that it is inverted: it is the rich prince Eros who flees from Psyche rather than the other way round.

Psyche has married Eros, who has been sent by his mother, Aphrodite, to inflict the pangs of love on the girl because she is jealous of Psyche's beauty. But Eros, who inspires love in everyone but is never in love himself, falls for Psyche. His palace is alive with disembodied voices and everything is invisibly laid on – now the story is like Beauty and the Beast – but Psyche is forbidden to see her husband. Her two older, jealous (no doubt ugly) sisters persuade her that he is a monster, an enormous snake who will devour her, and her child – for she is now pregnant. So, when she is lying with Eros one night after he has fallen asleep, she quietly lights an oil lamp – only to behold the beautiful and winged young god. Here, the story is like the reverse of Sleeping Beauty, only she does not wake him with a kiss but by mistake – a drop of hot oil from the lamp falls onto his shoulder. He wakes; and, without a word, flies off – back to his jealous mother, Aphrodite.

Being connected to the Mysteries of Isis, the story is a myth of initiation. It is much older than the version from Apuleius' *The Golden Ass* which I am paraphrasing here. Initiation is about the transformation of the soul through death and rebirth; and, here, the transformation takes place through love, and especially through the archetypal pattern of union, separation, suffering and reunion, as the gradually awakening Psyche is connected to the creative power of Eros. This is the basic pattern of romantic fiction, the myth of soul, of which we – and especially women – never tire, just as we – and especially men – never tire of adventure stories, the myth of the hero.

Psyche has been loving blindly, and so her first awakening occurs when she shines the light on Love itself. She wishes to love in the light, truly, but her first attempt drives love away. She is then condemned to embark on a long search for her lost love. It is a gruelling tale of suffering, which tells us that in order for soul to awake and fulfil its potential, pain is necessary. Her journey involves different kinds of death.

For example, she originally goes to her wedding as if to a funeral because the Oracle predicted that her husband, for whom she was to wait on the precipitous Oracle rock, would be immortal, viperous and feared even by great Zeus. She is wafted off the high rock by the west wind and brought to Eros' palace, just as if Love itself had wafted her into another world of unimaginable opulence. However, when her sisters, mad with jealousy – and believing that they can win Eros for themselves after his flight – ascend the Oracle rock, they do not notice that the west wind is not blowing. They jump off and are dashed to pieces. Absence of love, or delusions of love, will transform what should be the beginning of initiatory death into actual death.

Meanwhile the distraught Psyche has tried to commit suicide, as if to forestall the pain of her initiatory death by seeking oblivion. She throws herself in a river, but is gently washed back to shore. She will try to destroy herself again, later on, after she has implored both Demeter and Hera for help and been refused. At last, in despair, summoning all her courage, she is forced to surrender to Aphrodite.

Aphrodite is like the wicked stepmother. She is violently opposed to the love of Psyche and Eros for each other because her love is the opposite of soul love. It is a sexy and possessive kind of love – she wishes to keep Eros for herself and apart from soul. She fears transformation at the hands of Eros through his connection with soul, who will give love depth and the perspective of death. She wishes also to keep soul as a slave and to block her transformation via the engendering power of Eros, who has impregnated her and allowed her to give birth to her own potential. Love can be both freedom to fulfil oneself and also enslavement to Aphrodite's needs.

Thus Aphrodite now gives Psyche over to her two servants, Anxiety and Grief, to flog and torture her. In addition, she sets Psyche some impossible tasks, just like the folk heroines who must spin gold out of straw or guess secret names; and, like them, Psyche is helped by unlikely assistants, such as an ant, a reed and an eagle.

The last task is to take a box down to Hades and bring back a day's worth of Persephone's beauty. Psyche realizes that she is, literally, being sent to her death. She climbs a high tower in order to throw herself off. Unlike the first suicide attempt, born of panic and despair, this second attempt appears nonsensical: how can you put off death by death? The answer is that Psyche fears entrance to Hades because it signifies the last stage of her initiatory death – that 'dying to oneself' which can be worse than literal physical death. To confront Persephone, 'Bringer of Destruction', is to be destroyed in a more radical way than simple physical death. It is the relinquishing of all that the ego clings to, all the things by which we define ourselves, a fate worse than death.

Fortunately, the tower stops her from jumping off by telling her of a secret route into the Underworld. In fact he gives her long and detailed instructions on how to proceed. She has to carry two bits of bread soaked in honey water to pacify Cerberus, the three-headed dog who guards the Underworld, on the way there and back. She has to carry two coins in her mouth to pay Charon the ferryman, also there and back. The tower describes three ways that Aphrodite will try and make her drop the sops and coins. He also tells her to refuse Persephone's offer of a cushioned chair and magnificent meal and, instead, to sit on the ground and ask only for a piece of bread. Above all, she must not open or even look at the box she is carrying back. All these details must have been elements of a death and rebirth ritual undertaken by initiation candidates during the Isis Mysteries. At any rate, Psyche does as she is told – and makes it back.

But, of course, her curiosity is too great not to open the box and borrow a bit of Persephone's beauty for herself. When she opens it, however, no beauty emerges – only a death-like sleep which wraps her in a dark cloud. She falls like a corpse and lies there, the open box beside her.

This is Psyche's last kind of death, the opposite of her first. For now she possesses the beauty of the knowledge of death which, just as she could not at first survive in the Underworld, cannot survive in the 'upper' world of consciousness. Only Love can revive her, by putting that portion of beauty which belongs to the Underworld back where it belongs.

Beauty is at the heart of this myth. Eros is sent to exact his mother's revenge on Psyche for being too beautiful – he is supposed to make her fall in love, only to be overpowered by her beauty himself. Beauty, as Plotinus remarked, is the first attribute of the soul.[11] Where beauty is, or is perceived, there soul is also. Aphrodite is the most beautiful of the goddesses. Yet she is jealous of Psyche for being universally acknowledged as more beautiful than she. Aphrodite also lacks and craves Persephone's beauty, which is of a different kind. It is an Underworld beauty: an inner beauty, invisible, as Hades is, to outward eyes and only perceptible to those who have undergone death. Aphrodite can only acquire this beauty through Psyche because soul alone mediates between the beauty of the invisible inner world and the visible outer.

This is why the box of beauty appears to be empty. The beauty therein cannot be seen in the upper world, with ordinary perception. To put it on is to be returned to the Underworld – that is, to die; or to have one's literal perception, one's everyday senses, plunged into Stygian unconsciousness. Only love can see through this darkness and banish the sleep. Now it is Psyche who is Sleeping Beauty, and she is woken by Eros who flies down, brushes away the cloud of sleep and shuts it up in its box again. Psyche wakes, and takes the box to Aphrodite.

Zeus reprimands Aphrodite and decrees that Eros shall settle down and marry Psyche. He gives her a cup of nectar so that she may become immortal (nectar is food exclusive to gods). All the gods attend the wedding on Mount Olympus; and, in due course, Psyche gives birth to her child, a daughter whose name is Pleasure.

The tale of Psyche tells us that soul has two constants: she is beautiful and she comes into her own through love. It tells us that we become immortal and unite with the gods on high, not through mystic flights of the transcending spirit, but by the downward path of suffering towards the goddess of destruction and the god of death: we have to embrace the bitterness of a soul made flesh – of the soul's mortality – before we are received among the gods and attain immortality.

It is a shock, too, to the Western mind, stamped with its Puritan ethic of 'ascent' through will and work, self-control and self-denial, to find that one way of uniting soul and love is . . . Pleasure.

Dreams

If myths are like collective dreams, dreams are like personal myths. One thing we learn from Freud and Jung is that dreams are the best model of the psyche. To begin with, they teach us that although the soul is not located anywhere, being non-spatial, it always represents itself spatially – as an Otherworld. We dream that we are in a secluded valley, a foreign city, a desert, a dense wood, an old family home, another planet, a supermarket, an airport, a riotous party, a lunatic asylum . . . . All such places are specifically chosen by soul to represent its own condition at any one time. The people, animals and even the objects in this psychic space are daimons. They embody the state of our souls while, at the same time, point back to the archetypes.

Dreams can refer to our personal history, as Freud said. But they do not end there. As manifestations of soul they lead down to the bottomless Underworld. Concealed behind or within each image taken from our personal life there are impersonal resonances. Sometimes the transition between the two is marked by a dramatic device. How often do we find ourselves saying, when describing a dream, 'I was sorting through my laundry, when, *suddenly* .' or 'I was driving down a dark road, when, *suddenly* . . . '?

'When, *suddenly* . . . ' is often the moment when we pass from an ordinary dream to what some tribal cultures call a 'big dream'. They understand that some dreams are personal to us, while others are bigger, concerning the whole tribe. These are manifestations of the collective unconscious; and I guess that we have all had at least two or three 'big dreams' which have seemed more real than everyday life, and which stay with us for years as a source of wonder. However, there is no dream so archetypal that it does not contain some residue of the dreamer's personal imagery, just as there is no dream so personal that it does not contain a whiff of the archetypal. The visionary dream of the Great Goddess might retain traces of a great-aunt or a childhood sweetheart; the businesswoman glimpsed on the underground train can lead us in dreams down to Hecate, goddess of the Underworld, if we but read the dream aright.

The trouble is, dreams are notoriously difficult to read aright. We try to 'interpret' them, but this is a dubious way to proceed. It implies that dreams are allegories whose single 'real' meaning has to be revealed, or that their symbols can be translated from a handbook. It is better to treat dreams like poems or plays, able to be read at several different levels at once, especially when there may be more than one deity inside them. By using imagination and insight, by being sensitive to its resonances and references, we can learn to appreciate a dream's style as well as content – it may be lyric, epic, tragic, comic, melodramatic, farcical . . . .

We complain that dreams are vague. But this very vagueness may be the meaning. They may not be visually clear, but they may nevertheless carry a strong charge, like a scent, of nostalgia, joy or menace. We complain that dreams are fleeting, always disappearing over the horizon of consciousness just as we wake. We strain to catch them, but perhaps their evanescence *is* their meaning, like the nymphs whom we glimpse disappearing into the wood; or sprinting Atalanta who can outrun any man. Such dreams lead us to dream on or dream again, leading us farther in and out of our depth.

Dreams may also be vague and fleeting because of the strength of our daylight outlook. Our waking consciousness, so contained within our heads, so ego-centred, so floodlit, makes the dream seem dim and ill-defined. It naturally flees from the light and from a consciousness which would grab it, badger it for subliminal messages, interpret it, handcuff it and interrogate it for its secret. If, however, we were to cultivate a more daimonic consciousness, we could slide more easily into dreams, adapt to them, changing shape if necessary, and so return to wakefulness with full memory of our Otherworldly sojourn. We might even learn to let the dream surface while we are awake, for dreaming goes on all the time – it is nothing other than soul's imagining. We only associate it with night and sleep because that is when our guard is down and we let the dreams in, or let ourselves be taken down into the dream. If we allowed the dream back in daylight hours the hardness of our literal reality would be emulsified. Daimons would be released from their prison of literalism, emerging from rock and forest to repopulate the landscape and re-ensoul the world.

Incubation

Like modern depth psychologists, the ancient Greeks took dreams seriously and believed that they could help cure sickness. At temples of Asclepius, son of Apollo and god of medicine, people underwent a procedure called incubation.[12] They lay down to sleep in a sacred precinct and dreamt the solution to their disease. In old accounts of incubation we find descriptions of the amazement people felt when the state they entered was not like ordinary sleep but more like an Otherworldly vision, often continuing regardless of whether they were asleep or awake, whether they opened their eyes or shut them. 'Often you find mention', writes the classicist Peter Kingsley, 'of a state that's like being awake, but different from being awake, that's like sleep but not sleep . . . . It's not the waking state, it's not an ordinary dream and it's not dreamless sleep. It's something else, something in between'[13] – a good description of daimonic consciousness.

Some dreams can undeniably be taken literally, as precognitive or prophetic, for instance – their personages are spirits who give us a winning horse or tell us not to board an aeroplane. But the overwhelming majority are not spirits but daimons. They may appear as people we know, such as a neighbour, an old school friend or a sibling, but they are both themselves and not themselves – they invite us to see through their apparent selves to the archetypal beings beyond. They are metaphorical people, like characters in a play, to whom we have to bring our imagination.

Studies have shown that most dreams are nightmares.[14] We sit our school exams over and over again; we lose our teeth or trousers in the restaurant or in front of Buckingham Palace. These repetitions are, as we have seen, part of soul-making, like the circular distillations of the alchemists. We find ourselves on stage, but naked; or unable to remember our lines, because to the soul it is our lives which are like a play. The role we call real life does not work in the theatre of the soul. We are stripped to our naked selves, lost for words – only, if we allow it, to learn new modes of speech and to acquire new clothes, new shapes, along with the many parts we are composed of.

Because we have so sternly set consciousness and the unconscious in opposition to each other, our dreams are often compensatory, seeking to redress the imbalance in the psyche as a whole. They show us what we are neglecting. If we do not attend to them, their daimons show up as demons, breaking into our dream houses like burglars or wild animals.

When we dream about the cripple or the boy with the suppurating wound; the awful murder scene full of body parts or the menacing robot; the sly thief or preening film star – we ask not only what they mean to our lives but also what their mythic context is. Is the cripple really lame Oedipus or Hephaestus? Is the wounded boy Philoctetes whose wound would never heal, telling us that we cannot always cure what ails us? The murder scene, the ritually dismembered body of Dionysus or Orpheus? The robot, Talos the bronze man whom Daedalus made to guard Crete? The sly thief, Hermes himself, filching things from our everyday life to weave dreams out of? The film star, Narcissus who gazes endlessly at his own reflection?

Since myths have their share of sickness and madness, horror and perversion, these things are properties of soul. Thus the most disturbing dreams can be the best. They show us that we are in touch with soul. We must try therefore not to turn shuddering away from nightmares, nor to demonize them, but rather to discern the daimons in them.

The same is true of our psychopathology – our psychological ailments. They are not like organic diseases. They are the torments and distortions which signal the twisting of the fettered psyche. It was just such twistings – the obsessive, compulsive, neurotic and 'hysterical' symptoms – that led Freud and Jung to discover the unconscious, and hence to rediscover soul. But, as James Hillman has pointed out, the result of these discoveries has too often been to confuse three different things: the unconscious, pathologizing and soul.[15] That is, we confuse the rediscovery of soul with the place where it happened: the psychoanalyst's consulting room. Consequently we begin to believe that our souls can only be found through therapy and analysis. But, really, it was the crazy symptoms, like nightmares, which first flagged the soul's awakening from its Enlightenment sleep, and not the treatment of these symptoms. They were only the muffled cries of the outcast daimons returning from exile.

In fact, symptoms notoriously resist treatment: do away with one and it comes back as another. The wise therapist follows where the symptoms lead, using them as the threads which will lead him or her through the labyrinth to whatever daimon is at work in the patient's psyche. The god who is behind the symptoms also therefore cures them. We cannot deny those who suffer mental affliction the short-term benefits of drugs, behavioural techniques and aversion therapies; but in the long run these tend to repress the cure, and what they repress comes back in another guise. We must always try and trace the symptoms back to their source, and this means connecting them to a bigger picture, an archetypal context, a mythic narrative. In this way they will become less literal, compulsive and all-consuming. They will begin to move more freely, acquire meaning and so unblock our choked psyches, letting them breathe again.

Our neurotic fears, our anxieties and Achilles' heels do not necessarily signify weakness or failure. Each is a complex which contains an archetype, which in turn opens onto a deity who introduces us to a whole new cosmos, a new world-view. What seem to be our weakest spots can really be portals to another world; or fault lines through which the gods boil up into consciousness.

Dreams remind us that there is an Otherworld. Do not let anybody tell you otherwise. Do not let the world-weary literalist or stentorian scientist disenchant you. What you knew in your bones during childhood is true: the Otherworld of magic and enchantment is real, sometimes terribly real — and certainly more real than the factual reality which our culture has built up, brick by brick, to shut out colour and light and prevent us from flying.

SEVEN

Soul and daimon

There is an aspect to the question of what the soul is which is startling and strange, but so widespread that it cannot be avoided. It is connected to the popular idea that we all have a guardian angel. According to a US poll in the 1990s, sixty-nine per cent of Americans believe in angels. Forty-six per cent have their own guardian angels and thirty-two per cent have felt an angelic presence.[1] For example, in her book *When Angels Appear*, Hope Macdonald describes an incident in which a young mother sees that her three-year-old daughter, Lisa, has escaped from the garden and is sitting on the railway line beyond. At that moment a train comes around the bend, its whistle blowing. 'As she raced from the house screaming her daughter's name, she suddenly saw a striking figure, clothed in pure white, lifting Lisa off the track with an arm around the child . . . . When the mother reached the daughter's side, Lisa was standing alone.'[2]

Not many tales of guardian angels are as dramatic as this one; but a surprising number of people attest to some experience that they ascribe to the action of a guardian angel, even if it is only a single word of warning or, as is commonly reported, a simple touch on the shoulder or tug on the sleeve.

While Lisa's angel conforms to popular expectations of an angel – a white, possibly winged, powerful and protective being – they may not always be thus. The folklorist Katharine Briggs reported how a friend of hers, a clergyman's widow who suffered from an injured foot, was sitting one day on a seat in London's Regent's Park, wondering how on earth she would find the strength to limp home. Suddenly she saw a tiny man in green who looked at her very kindly and said: 'Go home. We promise that your foot shan't pain you tonight.' Then he disappeared. But the intense pain in her foot had gone. She walked home easily and slept painlessly all night.[3]

And what are we to make of the 'angels' – as terse as any doctor – in this next account, related in the *British Medical Journal* for December 1998? A woman referred to only as AB heard a voice while sitting at home reading. It told her not to be afraid and said that it was here with a friend to help her. Although AB had no history of psychological problems, she went straight to a psychiatrist who 'treated' her with counselling and medication, and pronounced her cured. But while she was on holiday soon afterwards, AB heard the voice again – or, rather, two voices. They told her to return immediately to England because something was wrong with her. She did as they said. Back in London the voices gave her an address to go to. It turned out to be the brain-scan department of a hospital. As she arrived, the voices told her to ask for a brain scan for two reasons: she had a tumour on her brain and the brain stem was inflamed. Her original psychiatrist, wishing to reassure her, arranged for the scan, even though there was no indication of any tumour. He was criticized by his colleagues for pandering to AB's hypochondriacal delusions. However, the results showed that she did indeed have a tumour, which was removed. After the operation, the voices came again. They said: 'We are pleased to have helped you. Goodbye.' AB has since made a full recovery.

Already we see that the idea of guardian angels is both puzzling and varied; and so it might be useful briefly to review their origins in Western culture. These are bound up with the origins of angels in general.

A little history of angels

Angels enter our culture via the Old Testament, but they do not feature strongly there. They only become dominant figures in the Jewish apocalyptic writings which date from about the third century BC onwards. It is likely that this is because such writings were influenced by the Zoroastrian religion of Persia, where the Jews had been held captive. The Zoroastrians had complex ideas about angels, including a well-developed doctrine of guardian angels – celestial beings of light who act a bit like the prototype of us humans. But the later Jewish angels tended to be impersonal rather than personal; and, as Harold Bloom reminds us in *Omens of Millennium*, not at all composed of sweetness and light. Like the archangel Metatron, angels were highly ambiguous, awesome, even terrifying.[4] We might remember how Muhammad the Prophet asked to look upon the angel Gabriel, who had dictated the Koran to him. As the agent of the Prophet's revelation, Gabriel could well be called his guardian angel. However, when the Prophet was granted his wish, he fainted dead away at the shock of seeing such a vast being, filling the horizon and stretching upwards out of view.[5] In the Book of Enoch (Enoch was held by some to have been transformed into Metatron when 'he walked with God, and was not, because God took him') angels lust after Earth women,[6] like the mysterious angelic Nephilim, who suddenly came down from above in the book of Genesis and 'mated with the daughters of men'. No wonder St Paul warned women in Corinthians 'to have a veil on their heads, because of the angels . . . .'[7] In Colossians he warns against worship of angels, implying that there is no difference between angels and demons.

However, angels found their way into European culture less through the Jewish tradition than through the Greek, notably through Dionysius the Areopagite. He was originally believed to have been an Athenian disciple of St Paul's, but is now reckoned to be a Syrian monk of the late fifth century. His book *The Celestial Hierarchy* is the most influential text in the history of angelology. It was Dionysius who tried to settle the question – raised by the likes of St Augustine – of whether or not angels had a material body. He came down decisively on the side of immateriality. Angels were pure spiritual beings, he said – and this idea was taken up enthusiastically by St Thomas Aquinas, and hence by the Roman Catholic Church. It was Dionysius who arranged the angels into the nine orders adopted by Catholic orthodoxy, from Cherubim, Seraphim and Thrones, through Dominions, Virtues and Powers, down to Principalities, Archangels and Angels – each order a link in the Great Chain of Being which stretched from God down to mankind, the animals, plants and stones.

The idea that angels mediated between God and mankind was actually a much older idea which Dionysius derived from the Neoplatonists. His whole system of theology, in fact, was cribbed wholesale from Plotinus, Iamblichus and Proclus and then Christianized. But in the original, Neoplatonic 'theology' the mediating beings were not angels but daimons. The idea of guardian angels comes from the Greek notion of the personal daimon.

Personal daimons

In the *Symposium*, Socrates tells us that 'only through the daimonic is there intercourse and conversation between men and gods, whether in the waking state or during sleep. And the man who is an expert in such intercourse is a daimonic man . . . .'[8] Socrates could speak with authority because his personal daimon was the most famous in antiquity. Apuleius, of *Eros and Psyche* fame, wrote a book about it, explaining that Socrates' daimon was responsible for mediating between him and the gods. Daimons, claimed Apuleius, inhabit the air and have bodies of so transparent a kind that we cannot see them, only hear them. This was the case with Socrates, whose daimon was famous for simply saying 'No' whenever he was about to encounter danger or do something displeasing to the gods. It was not just Apuleius, but all the Neoplatonists, incidentally, who believed that daimons are as much material as spiritual, despite what later Catholic apologists such as Aquinas claimed. To say they inhabit the air is a metaphor for the middle realm they inhabit between the material and spiritual realms, as it were participating in both. It is the realm which the great scholar of Sufism, Henri Corbin, calls 'the imaginal world' in which a different, daimonic reality prevails. It is the middle realm described by C. G. Jung, who called it 'psychic reality'. Above all, of course, it is the Soul of the World.

We all have a personal daimon, whose duty is not only to protect us but also to summon us to our vocation. But perhaps it is only in those with an exceptionally powerful summons, a striking vocation, that their daimons become unusually apparent. These are the shamans, poets, medicine men, mediums and witch-doctors whom Socrates called 'experts in daimonic intercourse'.⁹ Jung was just such a medicine man, as his journey into the Underworld of the unconscious makes plain. His first overt encounter with his daimon came in a dream of a winged being, sailing across the sky. He saw that it was an old man with the horns of a bull. He held a bunch of four keys, one of which he clutched as if he were about to open a lock. The lock he was about to open, of course, was the locked unconscious psyche of Jung. This mysterious figure introduced himself as Philemon; and he visited Jung often after that, not only in dreams but while he was awake as well. 'At times he seemed to me quite real,' wrote Jung in *Memories, Dreams, Reflections*, 'as if he were a living personality. I went walking up and down the garden with him, and to me he was what the Indians call a guru . . . . Philemon brought home to me the crucial insight that there are things in the psyche which I do not produce, but which have their own life . . . I held

conversations with him and he said things which I had not consciously thought . . . He said I treated thoughts as if I generate
them myself but in his view thoughts were like animals in the
forest, or people in a room . . . It was he who taught me
psychic objectivity, the reality of the psyche.'[10]

If this is an unconventional picture of a 'guardian angel', it is
conservative compared to Napoleon's 'familiar spirit', as
described by Aniela Jaffé in *Apparitions*: 'it protected him . . .
guided him, as a daemon, and . . . at particular moments took
on the shape of a shining sphere, which he called his star, or
which visited him in the figure of a dwarf clothed in red that
warned him.'[11] On the other hand, it was not so eccentric
when we consider that, according to Iamblichus, daimons
favour luminous appearances or 'phasmata' second only to manifesting in personified form. The phasmata of daimons are
'various and dreadful'. They appear 'at different times : . . in a
different form, and appear at one time great, but at another
small, yet are still recognized to be the phasmata of daemons.'[12]
Thus it is not so surprising if a personal daimon shape-shifts,
showing itself now as a Gabriel-sized angel, now as a red dwarf.

The Ka

The idea that we each have a personal daimon is surprisingly
widespread. The Romans, of course, called it the *genius* – to
which they made sacrifices on their birthdays.[13] It is the *nagual*
of Central America and the *nyarong* of the Malays.[14] It is the
'guardian spirit' or 'personal god' of many North American
tribes, whether the 'agate man' of the Navaho, the *sicom* of the
Dakota or the 'owl' of the Kwakiutl – all of which accompany,
guide, protect and warn. It would be tedious to trawl through
every culture that subscribes to it; but it is worth mentioning
two or three to show how subtle the differences can be in its
conception, within a broad general agreement about its
function as guardian and guide.

Among the Australian Aboriginals, for example, C. Strehlow has described how the Aranda recognize an Iningukua, who accompanies us through life, warns us of dangers and helps us escape from them. We are both at one with this guardian and separate from it – it lived before us and will not die with us.[15] The anthropologist Lucien Lévy-Bruhl succinctly sums up the puzzling ambiguity of a person's daimon, 'who is undoubtedly in him, is himself, makes him what he is, but at the same time surpasses him, differs from him, and keeps him in a state of dependency.'[16]

Many West African peoples believe that before you enter the world you draw up a contract with a heavenly double who prescribes what you will do with your life – how long you will live, whom you will marry, how many children you will have and so on. 'Then, just before you are born, you are led to the Tree of Forgetfulness, which you embrace, and from that moment you lose all conscious recollection of your contract.' However, if you do not live up to your contractual obligations 'you will become ill, and you will need the help of a diviner, who will use all his skill to make contact with your heavenly double and discover what articles of the contract you are failing to fulfil.'[17] I cannot help feeling that our psychotherapeutic techniques could learn something from this procedure . . . .

More specifically in West Africa, Major A. B. Ellis reported that the Ewe-speaking peoples believe they have a second individuality living inside them called a *kra*. As usual, it is a guardian spirit which goes on existing after our death, either entering a newly born human or an animal; or wandering about the world. Like the Roman *genius*, it receives homage from its host, especially on his birthday, when an animal sacrifice is made to the kra.

At the same time, the kra can behave like the 'shadow' or soul I described in Chapter One. For instance, it can leave the body at will and wander in the Otherworld. Dreams are the adventures of the kra in the Otherworld, and we feel the effects of its actions when, for instance, we wake up with aching limbs after the kra has been working or struggling in the dream-world. The kra looks like us because when it meets others in dreams it is really meeting the kras of others, yet it can recognize the people to whom they belong because of the physical resemblance. Like the soul, then, it can leave the body – and we become cold and pulseless until it returns (if it does not, we die). Yet, say the Ewe-speaking peoples, the kra is not the soul, which goes on living after death independently of the kra.[18]

The neighbouring Ga-speaking peoples call the kra the *okra*. They sometimes identify it with the soul, or *susuma*. But, then again, it is not really the soul because it is more often spoken of as a guardian who has stood by them in times of danger or, in times of misfortune, turned away from them.[19]

According to Vilhjalmur Stefansson, when an Inuit child is born it comes into the world with a soul, or *nappan*, of its own. But this soul is so foolish, inexperienced and feeble, just as a baby is, that it needs a wiser and more experienced soul than its own to look after it. Accordingly, the soul of a dead ancestor is summoned to become the child's guardian soul, or *atka*.

The atka enters the child and teaches it to talk. But when the child talks it is really the atka who speaks, with all the acquired wisdom of the ancestor. Therefore, whatever the child says, it is really the wisest person in the family, regardless of how foolish its words or actions may seem. If the child cries for a knife, for example, its mother should give it a knife at once because it is the ancestor who wants it, and it would be presumptuous of the young mother to think that she knows what is better for the child than its atka. More importantly, if she refused the knife, she would offend the ancestor, who in his anger might abandon the child, causing it to fall ill or even die. So the child must be indulged at all times in order to propitiate its atka, the ancestor.

As the child grows up, its own soul or nappan gets stronger and develops in wisdom so that after ten or twelve years it is competent to look after the child. At that point it becomes less vital to please the atka and so it becomes customary to start punishing and disciplining children at that age.[20]

Similarly, the Bantus of Southern Africa assert that a man has a daimon, with the same name as himself, who is the spirit of an ancestor or godfather reincarnated within him. This daimon is 'the sovereign part of his soul, within him and yet without him, surrounding him, guiding him from birth to death.'[21] Once again, the daimon is seen to be intensely personal – it 'belongs' exclusively to oneself – yet strangely impersonal, existing outside oneself. Among the Ashanti of West Africa, the *ntoro* is a spirit which protects and guides.[22] However, it is transmitted from father to son via sexual union with the mother ('ntoro' is sometimes the word for semen).

In ancient Egypt the *ka* – as opposed to the ba I have already described – was a person's vital force, but experienced as something bestowed from outside rather than as emanating from themselves. It was represented in wall paintings by two upraised arms, either on their own or else attached to the head of the person's 'double'. However the ka was only a personal, protective daimon in the true sense for the king, and perhaps some of the elite nobles, who had been initiated like shamans into the world of the dead where the ka resides. For the ka 'energy', so to speak, was pooled among the ancestors – the dead – who directed it towards the physical realm, infusing humans, and also animals and crops, with the ka's vital force. When a person died, they were said to 'go to their ka' – that is, the ancestral ka group or clan. Tombs were important because they were 'the places of ka', like exchanges where the dead and living could communicate.[23]

Ordinary people would only experience the ka after death, and probably not as an individual entity but as the ancestral group which absorbed them. For the king, though, the ka was a kind of protective daimon, often depicted as walking behind him like a servant, and whom he could experience as a separate 'person'. As the Old Kingdom King Pepi says:

'It goes well with me and my name;
I live with my ka.
It expels the evil that is before me,
It removes the evil that is behind me.'[24]

Doubtless ordinary folk, the uninitiated, experienced the ka at times as a heightened sense of individual power, as we do; but to experience it as part of the psyche's infrastructure was the prerogative of the king alone. The average ancient Egyptian certainly never felt the sense of personal identification with the ka they felt with the ba.[25]

The raising of Plotinus' daimon

The paradox of the personal daimon is that it can also be impersonal. Katharine Briggs' friend with the injured foot encountered a being that was clearly and intimately to do with her – yet also almost part of the landscape, like a fairy. I suggest that while the personal daimon is exactly that – personal – it is also always grounded in the impersonal and unknowable depths of the psyche. It is also, in other words, a manifestation of the Anima Mundi, or Soul of the World – as the case of Plotinus makes clear.

While he was living in Rome, he was approached by an Egyptian priest who, wishing to show off his theurgical powers, asked if he might be allowed to invoke a visible manifestation of Plotinus' daimon. The sage agreed. The rite took place in the Temple of Isis, the only pure place in Rome according to the priest. But to everyone's surprise, the daimon turned out to be a god – the priest was so shocked that the god disappeared before it could be questioned.[26]

Plotinus himself was eloquent on the subject of the personal daimon. He held that every human psyche is a spectrum of possible levels, on any one of which we may choose to live (each of us is an 'intellectual cosmos'); and, whatever level one chooses, the next one above that serves as one's daimon. If one lives well, one may live at a higher level in the next life, and then the level of one's daimon will accordingly rise, until for the perfect sage the daimon is the One itself, the transcendent source and goal of everything that is. In other words, the daimon was not, for Plotinus, an anthropomorphic being but an inner psychological principle – notably the spiritual level above that on which we conduct our lives.[27] It is therefore both within us and, at the same time, transcendent; and this suggests that it is simultaneously as personal as a 'familiar' and as impersonal as a god. Iamblichus went further, to assert that personal daimons are not fixed but can develop or perhaps unfold in relation to our own spiritual development, rather as Jung might say that in the course of individuation we move beyond the personal unconscious to the impersonal, collective unconscious – through the daimonic to the divine. We are *assigned* a daimon at birth, said Iamblichus, to govern and direct our lives; but our task is to *obtain* a god in its place.[28]

This doctrine comes from a story or myth told by Plato in *The Republic* concerning a man called Er, who had what we now call a Near-Death Experience.[29] He brought back news not just of what happens after death, but what happens before birth. We choose the lives we are about to lead, he said, but we are allotted a daimon to act as guardian and to help us fulfil our choice. Then we pass under the throne of Necessity, the pattern of our lives having been fixed, to be born. Our daimons carry the imaginative blueprints of our lives. They lay down the personal myth, as it were, which we are bound to enact in the course of our lives. It is the voice that calls us to our true purpose, our vocation. The reality of the personal daimon is affirmed by the fact that it persists in the human mind, so that no matter how we wish to grow out of Plato's old tale, it crops up in different guises again and again.

The psychologist Julian Jaynes was guided by his daimon while he was writing a book about the problem of what knowledge is and how we can know anything at all. He had become hopelessly bogged down and lost. One afternoon he lay down, as he tells us, 'in intellectual despair' on a couch. 'Suddenly, out of an absolute quiet, there came a firm, distinct loud voice from my upper right, which said: "Include the knower and the known!" It lugged me to my feet absurdly exclaiming "Hello?", looking for whoever was in the room.'[30]

But Jaynes was a scientist of the mind, and so he naturally thought that the voice had been an 'auditory hallucination'. To his credit he thought that it was probably quite a common occurrence, especially in the past before our brains had split into right and left hemispheres. Formerly, he thought, the right-brain 'person' would talk directly to the left-brain 'person' – the 'I'. Now this communication had been disrupted and we no longer, or only intermittently, heard instructions from the 'gods'. He described his conclusions in an influential book, *The Origin of Consciousness and the Breakdown of the Bicameral Mind*. But we are in a position to see that he only did what scientism so often does: it takes up an old myth and reinvents it, but in a literalistic way.

Another example of this literalizing is the Just So story[31] of the 'selfish gene'. In the early pages of his book of that name, Richard Dawkins finds it impossible to avoid talking about our 'selfish genes' as if they are personal daimons. They 'create form', he says, and 'mould matter' and 'choose'. They are 'the immortals'. They 'possess us'. We are merely 'lumbering robots' whose genes 'created us body and mind'.[32] This anthropomorphic language, I suggest, is hardly the language of science, but let it pass. For Dawkins is unconsciously literalizing a myth and part of him knows that it is natural to personify. When he asks us to believe that our most treasured attributes are mere biology, pressed into the service of our genes, he is unwittingly inverting and literalizing the traditional – and, I would assert, the true – order which sees our bodily life, on the contrary, as the mere vehicle of our daimon, soul or 'higher self'.

According to Dawkins, and indeed to most scientists, the 'selfish gene' is allotted to us by Chance and thereafter subjects us to its inexorable Necessity – the pattern we are forced by the genes to live out. Chance and Necessity, the twin goddesses of science, are supposed to rule our lives. But Plato's daimon tells another tale, one which science has, once again, not so much replaced as inverted and made literal. The daimon is allotted to us in accordance with the life we have already chosen. We are not merely the random result of the chance meeting of our parents for we have chosen them just as they have, willy-nilly, chosen each other. We really do come into the world as Wordsworth says, 'trailing clouds of glory'. Thereafter we are subject, certainly, to Necessity; but it manifests as a fate or destiny we are also free to deny. Of course, it is not advisable: to cut oneself off from our daimon is to lose its protection and guidance, to court accidents and to lose our way. Besides, to deny the daimon turns out to be only the illusion of freedom. Real freedom, it turns out – paradoxically – is freely to choose to subordinate our egotistical desires and wishes to the imperatives of the personal daimon, whose service is perfect freedom.

Acorn and oak

In *The Soul's Code*, James Hillman – the best of the post-Jungian analytical psychologists – develops a whole child psychology based on the idea of the personal daimon. He calls it the acorn theory, according to which 'each life is formed by its unique image, an image that is the essence of that life and calls it to a destiny. As the force of fate, this image acts as a personal

daimon, an accompanying guide who remembers your calling
. . . . The daimon motivates. It protects. It invents and persists
with stubborn fidelity. It resists compromising reasonableness
and often forces deviance and oddity upon its keeper and
especially when it is neglected or opposed.'[33] Indeed, the
daimon can manifest itself in both psychic and physical
symptoms and disorders, as a kind of preventive medicine,
holding us back from taking a false path.

Since it represents the fate of the individual – since our
adult 'oak' life is latent in our acorn state – the personal daimon
is prescient. It knows the future – not in detail, perhaps, because
it cannot manipulate events, but as regards the general pattern.
It is that within us which is forever restless and unsatisfied,
yearning and homesick, even when we are at home. The existential philosopher Martin Heidegger is referring to exactly
this when he speaks of 'that weird and yet friendly feeling that
we have always been who we are, that we are nothing but the
unveiling of things decided upon long ago.'[34]

But we should note that the daimon is not our conscience,
which was unknown in the ancient daimon-ridden world.
Conscience is a product of Judaeo-Christian culture. It belongs
to the idea of morality and, later, to the Freudian superego: the
voice of parents, Church, state, whatever social institution prescribes what is right and wrong for us. But the daimon is not a
moralist. In fact, it may oppose conscience, as when we think we
must 'do the right thing' – marry the girl, take the safe job –
while the daimon whispers: 'No, don't. They will lead you
away from your true self, and you will be left empty and bewildered.' Disconcertingly, it is even possible to ask our daimon to
fulfil our own desires, even evil or selfish ones – we can appropriate the daimon's power for our own egotistical ends.

In short, our behaviour is not just formed by the past, as psychology tends to suppose; it can be formed retroactively by the
future – by the intuition of where our calling will take us and

what we are destined to become. Hillman cites many examples from famous people's biographies. Sometimes the child knows what he might become, like Yehudi Menuhin insisting as a tiny child on having a violin, yet smashing the toy violin he was given: his daimon was already grown up and disdained to play a child's toy. Sometimes he fears to know what he must become – Manolete, bravest and best of bullfighters, clung to his mother's apron strings as if he already knew the dangers he would have to encounter as an adult.[35] Winston Churchill was a poor scholar, consigned to what we would now call a remedial-reading class, as if putting off the moment when he would have to labour for his Nobel Prize for Literature. Thus, when we see bright children going off the rails, we should hesitate to blame their parents and their past. Their daimons are, after all, parent-less and have plans for them other than the plans of parents or the conformist demands of school. It is notable that our passion for attributing aberrant behaviour in children to inadequate parenting is highly eccentric: in traditional societies, whatever is wrong always comes from elsewhere. It is attributed to witch-craft, taboo-breaking, neglected rituals, contact with unfavourable places, a remote enemy, an angry god, a hungry ghost, an offended ancestor and so on – but never to what your mum and dad did to you, or didn't do, years ago. Just as we often find in the biographies of exceptional people clashes with authority and unruliness at school – all the symptoms of 'attention-deficit disorder', hyperactivity and truancy – might it not be that such behaviour can in some cases herald an individual whose intuition has told them that mere tuition is an irrelevance to, or distrac-tion from, their high daimonic purpose? It is a constant task for us to look for the angel in our children's errancy, and not be too quick to medicate, subdue or hammer them into line.

Those exceptional souls who become aware of their daimons, as Jung did, have the satisfaction of fulfilling its purpose and hence of fulfilling their true selves. But this does not make them immune to suffering; for who knows what Bad Lands the daimon would have us cross before we reach the Isles of the Blessed? Who knows what wrestling, what injury, we are – like Jacob – in for at the hands of our angel? What our daimon teaches us, therefore, is not to be always seeking a *cure* for our suffering but rather to seek a supernatural *use* for it.[36] 'I have had much trouble in living with my ideas', wrote Jung at the end of his long and fruitful life. 'There was a daimon in me . . . . It overpowered me, and if I was at times ruthless it was because I was in the grip of a daimon . . . . A creative person has little power over his own life. He is not free. He is captive and driven by his daimon . . . . The daimon of creativity has ruthlessly had its way with me.'[37]

While the daimon may be harder to spot in someone who is apparently unexceptional, it is still present. It may not be a call to worldly success or glamour, or to greatness and even holiness, but it is nevertheless a call to *character*.[38] We all know people who lead outwardly humdrum lives; who have not been called to exceptional tasks, whether as poet, shaman or world-conqueror. But they seem grounded, fulfilled, relaxed, interested, humorous, *good*. Moreover they seem happy. The Greek for happiness was *eudaimonia*, having a good or well-pleased daimon. It is not what they do – they may be shoe-salesmen or shepherds – but *how* they do it, with what style, integrity, wholeheartedness. Their calling is not in their work but in their life: in the pub, in the family, in their hobbies. In their unspoken imaginative lives. The unregarded but selfless mother of five is as likely – perhaps more likely – to achieve sanctity as any grand artist. For their call might be to efface themselves, to be as conventional as possible, not in a stultifying way but in a celebratory way – celebrating attention to the small details, from washing up to driving a car; spreading harmony, cooper-ation and well-being. They are attractively unheroic in an age where suspicion attends the heroic approach: the empire-building, the money-making, the artistic prima-donna-ing, the over-achieving . . . . No life is mediocre when it is seen from the inside, from the daimon's point of view.

This leads us to one of the thorniest problems surrounding the personal daimon: why does it only protect us sometimes? For every person who obeys the daimon's whisper and refuses to board the faulty plane there are a hundred who perish. There is no decisive answer to this. We might say that either the daimon's promptings were not heard or heeded – and this is common enough; or that it was the destiny of the hundreds to die exactly when and where and how they did. What we can say, though, is that what looks like chance or misfortune from the outside can look like destiny from the inside, through the daimon's eyes. Destiny is the inner meaning of chance. Besides, we might note that the Greek idea of fate had none of the inevitability of fatalism.[39] It referred to a class of events which, however much we rationalize them in retrospect, remain untoward. Fate was responsible for essentially uncaused events, the ones that do not fit in. In other words, not everything is rigidly laid out in an infallible divine plan, but is subject to daimonic intervention of the sort that simply jogs your elbow or tips you the wink. *Moira*, fate, means a share or portion. Fate, like the daimon, has only a portion in what happens. So when the daimon thwarts or obstructs or alters our intention with its interventions – perhaps with something as small as a hesitation or uncanny feeling – we later say: 'It was fate.'

Hillman adds an important rider to his acorn theory. The very phrase suggests growth and development, and this is congenial to us because we take it for granted that progress is a good thing and that our lives are all about personal 'growth'.[40] However, as I have already suggested, we forget that these ideas are not absolutes but comparatively recent inventions. They are the product of the eighteenth-century Enlightenment, which promoted the sovereignty of Reason and the myth of advancement and development. We forget that these words are only metaphors we ought to be chary of taking literally, as if they were facts. We should remember that before the Enlightenment – at the Renaissance, for instance – we thought that human nature was unchanging and that a return to a more ideal past was the way forward.

Thus, although we are certainly in the business of 'making our souls', the metaphor of rational 'progress' can be misleading. Nor can we model the daimon on metaphors of organic growth or maturation, as so much psychology does in relation to the psyche. For what Plato calls our paradigm (*paradeigma*), our life image, is carried by the daimon from birth. We are complete at the start. 'I don't develop;' said Picasso; 'I am.'[41] We are more like a many-faceted whole, and it is our task in the course of a lifetime to realize each facet of our selves, as if the daimon were introducing us to different deities in turn – a journey that is more likely to be downward, circular and labyrinthine than upward, onward and straight.

The daimon overturns the conventional view held by psychotherapy: that what happens early in life determines what happens later. Our lives are not a chain of cause and effect, according to the daimon. We are not the products of our history. Rather, we are ahistorical creatures for whom historical events in our childhood and later development are mirrors in which we catch glimpses of our primordial image.

Lastly, to remind us that we are all in cahoots with a divine being, no matter how worthless we appear to others or to ourselves, we can turn to one of the archetypal depictions of the relationship between human and daimon. I am thinking here less of Faust and Mephistopheles than of P. G. Wodehouse's Wooster and Jeeves. How does such a bumbling, footling, useless sort of chap as Bertie Wooster manage to hold on to such a manservant as the godlike Jeeves? The answer, I suppose, is: humility.

'I say, Jeeves, a man I met at the club last night
    told me to put my shirt on Privateer for the two
    o'clock race this afternoon. How about it?'

'I should not advocate it, sir. The stable is not
    sanguine.'

'Talking of shirts, have those mauve ones
    I ordered arrived yet?'

'Yes, sir. I sent them back.'

'Sent them back?'

'Yes, sir. They would not have become you . . . '

'All the other great men of the age are simply
    in the crowd, watching you go by.

'Thank you very much, sir. I endeavour to give
    satisfaction.'[42]

Daimon and muse

For the poet, the daimon is not his Muse exactly but it can sometimes look like her. She is often a mixed blessing if Keats's portraits of her in *Lamia* and *La Belle Dame sans Merci* are to be credited: white-skinned, cold, irresistibly alluring figures who seduce the poet, drain him like a vampire for their own purposes and leave him 'alone and palely loitering'. For once she is awakened, the Muse will drive relentlessly to become the centre of the personality, casting aside whatever we think of as ourselves. The rewards in terms of achievement can be enormous, but they are also dangerous; and everyday life, with its little comforts and satisfactions, can be a casualty.

The late Poet Laureate Ted Hughes called his Muse the 'poetic self'. It is identical to the daimon. As he writes feelingly in *Winter Pollen*, it is 'that other voice which from earliest times came to the poet as a god, took possession of him, delivered the poem, then left him.'[43] It was axiomatic, he says, that it lived its own life separate from the poet's everyday personality; that it was entirely outside his control; and that it was, above all, supernatural. Moreover, he goes on, its first principle is 'the ancient and formerly divine law of psychodynamics, which states: any communion with that other personality especially when it does incorporate some form of the true self, is healing, and redeems the suffering of life, and releases joy.'[44]

Hughes consciously related the vocation of poet to that of shamans who, in Siberia at least, often owed their power to female daimons to whom they were symbolically married or else whose female attributes they incorporated in their dress, sometimes even performing women's work and speaking women's language. One rule was paramount for those who were called by the daimon: you must shamanize – or die. That is, you must learn to make the dangerous journey into the Otherworld, retrieving souls who are lost there and bringing back the songs and myths on which social order depends. If you do not, you may not literally die, but you will lose any life worth living. For you will lose your way, lose your meaning and purpose, lose your own soul. Nor can you easily shake off the faithful daimon which, if it is neglected, will plague you with dreams and images, compulsions and obsessions, driving you mad.

W. B. Yeats was one whom Hughes identified as having the shaman's vocation; and, like Jung, he often experienced the daimon as antagonistic. It comes, said Yeats, 'not as like to like but seeking its own opposite. Man and daimon feed the hunger in each other's hearts.'[45] Here is an image of a dynamic, even erotic relationship between us and our daimons. Indeed, Yeats thought of it as feminine, and equated her with the Anima Mundi. She is the sleeping as opposed to the waking mind. That is, Yeats seems to identify his daimon with the unconscious and, more particularly, as a personification of the collective unconscious or world-soul. His relations with her were inverse and reciprocal, 'each dying each other's life, living each other's death',[46] as he says, adapting a fragment of Heraclitus' and harking back to the Neoplatonic view that the soul grows more beautiful and vigorous as the body diminishes in strength. And so we see that the daimon not only comes to us as a mentor, guru or guide, but can come, as it did for Hughes and Yeats, as strife and opposition – feeding their hunger and their art, yes, but at what cost to their lives?

Ted Hughes' vocation as a poet came in a strange dream, his shape-changing daimon taking an unexpectedly shamanic turn. In his second year at Cambridge University, he tells us, where he was reading English in the hope that it would help him with his writing, he began to feel an inexplicable resistance towards producing essays every week, even though he liked his supervisor and had a strong interest in the subject. This resistance grew and grew. 'It had a distressful quality, like a fiercely fought defence.' In the end, 'it brought me to a halt.'

On the last memorable day, he was completely bogged down in an essay, toiling for hours every day and covering many pages – which he promptly tore up. It was two in the morning again, and he was 'exhausted, sitting in my college room at my table, bent over a page of foolscap that had about four lines written across the top of it . . . . At last I had to give up and go to bed . . . .

'I began to dream. I dreamed I had never left my table and was still sitting there, bent over the piece of foolscap, staring at the same few lines across the top. Suddenly my attention was drawn to the door. I thought I had heard something there. As I waited, listening, I saw the door was opening slowly. Then a head came round the edge of the door. It was about the height of a man's head but clearly the head of a fox though the light over there was dim.

'The door opened wide and down the short stair and across the room towards me came a figure that was at the same time a skinny man and a fox walking erect on its hind legs. It was a fox but the size of a wolf. As it approached and came into the light I saw that its body and limbs had just now stepped out of a furnace. Every inch was roasted, smouldering, black-charred, split and bleeding. Its eyes, which were level with mine where I sat, dazzled with the intensity of the pain. It came up until it stood beside me. Then it spread its hand – a human hand as I now saw, but burned and bleeding like the rest of him – flat palm down on the blank space of my page. At the same time it said; "Stop this – you are destroying us." Then as it lifted its hand away I saw the blood-print, like a palmist's specimen, with all the lines and creases, in wet glistening blood on the page.

'I immediately woke up. The impression of reality was so total, I got out of bed to look at the papers on my table, quite certain that I would see the blood-print there on the page.'[47]

The daimon takes striking, even desperate measures to announce itself to those who are denying it. It took animal shape to summon Hughes away from that academic approach to literature which would stifle his poetic creativity and the instinctual life it depended on. He gave up studying English and completed his degree in the school of Archaeology and Anthropology.

Every shaman would recognize his dream as a qualification for the magic drum which they ride like a horse into the Otherworld. We also see how ambiguous the daimon can be in the forms it takes. It can even trick you into truth. Jack Preger, who had been a farmer for twelve years, was ploughing a field one day on his tractor when he clearly heard a voice telling him that he should be a doctor. He was suspicious. He asked the voice who the hell it was. The voice said: 'I am the Paraclete.' The word meant nothing to Jack, so he looked it up in the dictionary. It turned out to mean 'the Holy Spirit'. He was impressed that the voice had as it were proved its objective validity by announcing itself as someone he, as a subject, could not have known. He concluded that the voice was not a delusion but a vocation. He became a doctor and spent many years helping and treating the poorest, most disenfranchised people on the streets of Calcutta.[48]

It is not unusual of course to encounter the daimon as a religious figure, as Jesus or Buddha or the Blessed Virgin Mary. Nor can we categorically assert that people are not encountering the holy personage they claim that they are. We can only remember that the daimon is universal and non-denominational; that it can appear in any guise that most suits the recipient; and that it is the intermediary between us and whatever deity we hold dear. There is no objection to calling it, for instance, God's will.

Soul, self and daimon

To try and summarize: the personal daimon has been called, with good reason, the soul. Or the 'higher soul'. Or one of several souls. But really it is the guide and guardian of the soul whose potentiality, like a paradigm, it bears. The harder we look for it, the more it evades our grasp; for, like all daimons, it is elusive and shape-changing. We cannot even assign it a gender since it may appear as angel or animal, masculine or feminine – or neither. Socrates always referred to his daimon in the neuter gender: *daimonion*.

The daimon can be understood, like the ka, as a personification of the ancestors – an apt metaphor because, like the daimon, the ancestors are both intimately related to us yet, like the dead, separate and remote. It can be thought of as a specific ancestor, as the Inuit believe, standing in for our fledgling soul until its wings are formed and it can fly for itself. It is like the voice of the unconscious, or of our 'higher selves'. It is the 'still small voice' we must listen for in the midst of the turbulence and earthquake of existence. If it is not itself a god, as it may very well be, it is the intermediary through whom we communicate with the gods and they with us. It can be a Doppelgänger whose estrangement means illness, madness or even death. It is most alive when we are dying, most conscious when we sleep. It directs the unfolding of our souls, but it does not itself develop. It is a paradox.

If we are in harmony with our daimons they will draw near, filling us with a sense of unique purpose. Our egocentric life dissolves and we see beyond ourselves, wondering at how far we have come, at how we have accomplished far more than we thought ourselves capable of. We are amazed at how much we have changed – and at how little, being at the same time the same person we were in earliest childhood. We have all looked momentarily through the daimon's eyes and glimpsed the vista of our lives stretching forwards, foreshadowing what we have yet to perfect; or, rather, since it is the viewpoint of completion, the life we must live as if backwards. We have all, I dare say, been vouchsafed a visionary inkling of the pains we will have to endure, perhaps; but this is palliated by the sense of destiny, of rightness and of a life filled with meaning.

The last word on personal daimons goes to Yeats, who wrote in his book *Mythologies*: 'I think it was Heraclitus who said: the Daimon is our destiny. When I think of life as a struggle with the Daimon who would ever set us to the hardest work among those not impossible, I understand why there is a deep enmity between a man and his destiny, and why a man loves nothing but his destiny . . . . I am persuaded that the Daimon delivers and deceives us, and that he wove the netting from the stars and threw the net from his shoulder . . . .'[49] Here is a portrait of the personal daimon which is both daunting and beautiful and, like Jung's, tinged with a poignant melancholy. For the daimon is our hard taskmaster, driving us to perform the most difficult work possible for us, no matter what the human cost. No wonder our feelings for it are as ambiguous as it shows itself to be. Anyone who invokes their guardian angel, therefore, should beware. It may not be as friendly and sweet as the many little New Age books on angels would have you believe. It will protect you, yes – but only the 'you' who serves its plan for your self. It will guide you, certainly – but who knows what sojourn in the wilderness this might entail? And, because the personal daimon is, finally, grounded in the impersonal Ground of Being itself, you will inevitably be led way, way out of your depth.

EIGHT

Soul and spirit

In 1600, Jacob Boehme was sitting in his room one day when 'his eye fell upon a burnished pewter dish which reflected the sunshine with such marvellous splendour that he fell into an inward ecstasy, and it seemed to him as if he could now look into the principles and deepest foundations of things. He believed that it was only a fancy, and in order to banish it from his mind he went out into the green fields. But here he noticed that he could gaze into the very heart of things, the very herbs and grass, and that actual nature harmonized with what he had inwardly seen.'[1]

There are two kinds of mystical experience: the vision of the Creator and the vision of the created. The latter can be further subdivided into two sorts: the vision of the Beloved and the vision of Nature. Boehme was one of the great Protestant mystics, a key figure in the link between Renaissance Neoplatonic thought and the Romantics. His experience is the first I am aware of which constitutes what I am calling the vision of Nature. It is still quite common these days. For example, in 1969, Derek Gibson was travelling to work by motorcycle when he noticed that the sound of his engine had faded to a murmur. 'Then everything suddenly changed. I could clearly see everything as before with form and substance, but instead of looking *at* it all I was looking *into* everything. I saw beneath the bark of the trees and *through* the underlying trunks. I was looking *into* the grass too, and all was magnified beyond measure. To the extent that I could see moving micro-scopic organisms! Then, not only was I seeing all this, but I was literally *inside* it all. *At the same time* as I was looking into this mass of greenery I was aware of every single blade of grass and fold of the trees as if each had been placed before me one at a time and entered into.'[2]

In the vision of Nature, every object is imbued with signif-icance and importance. Everything is a presence. Everything is ensouled. In religious language, everything is holy – sometimes filled with as much holy dread as holy joy – but always awe-inspiring. The ego is abolished, one is neither self-conscious nor detached, but conscious of one's self in intimate participation with every other self. There is no desire, except to continue in that state of what the art connoisseur Bernard Berenson called Itness:

'It was a morning in early summer. A silver haze shimmered and trembled over the lime trees. The air was laden with their fragrance. The temperature was like a caress. I remember – I need not recall – that I climbed up a tree stump and felt suddenly immersed in Itness. I did not call it by that name. I had no need for words. It and I were one.'[3]

The Jesuit priest and poet Gerard Manley Hopkins called 'It' the inscape of things:

> Each mortal thing does one thing and the same:
> Deals out that being indoors each one dwells;
> Selves – goes itself; *myself* it speaks and spells
> Crying *what I do is me: for that I came.*[4]

The Vision of Nature does not seem to have been recorded much before the beginning of the seventeenth century. This time was a historical watershed, when the old medieval world-view began to be turned upside-down by our modern scientific world-view. We suddenly found ourselves standing apart from

Nature and observing it objectively rather than, as before, participating in it. So we might say that the vision of Nature is only a return to the norm before we divided consciousness from the 'outside' world. Do we now call mystical what is commonplace for traditional cultures and once was for us?

If so, this is perhaps why the vision of Nature in our culture most often occurs in childhood or adolescence, before we have become 'educated'; or in those people, such as Wordsworth, who – according to his friend Coleridge – never lost that child-like perception of Nature by which

> . . . with an eye made quiet by the power
> Of harmony, and the deep power of joy,
> We see into the life of things.[5]

Such visions are the impetus not only behind works of art but also behind scientific investigation because, as Plato remarked, the beginning of every kind of philosophy is Wonder.

Mystical experience is also an extreme example of a kind of knowledge we all have, even those scientists who deny that it is knowledge at all. It is not objective cognition, but subjective recognition – in Plato's sense, of knowledge as a recollection of the reality we knew before birth. It is immediate and intuitive, what used to be called gnosis: we know a thing by imaginatively participating in its unique quality rather than by objectively measuring its quantity. The sudden illumination at dead of night, the flash of lightning in the darkness, the 'Newton's apple' moment – these provide the germ of a theory or of a whole vision of the world which is then painstakingly confirmed by empirical methods. A single mystical experience, maybe lasting only a minute – whether of Nature, of another person or of God – will be one of the defining moments of our life, a touchstone of knowledge against which we measure all other kinds of knowledge for their portion of truth. It is a rare experience, but not as rare as we think. Sir Alistair Hardy's research project at Oxford in the 1970s found that thirty-six per cent of British people have had mystical experiences.[6]

Wendy Rose-Neill's encounter with Dame Kind took place while she was gardening. She suddenly became intensely aware of her surroundings: the scent of grass, the sound of birds and of rustling leaves. 'I had a sudden impulse to lie face down in the grass,' she said, 'and as I did so, an energy seemed to flow through me as if I had become part of the earth underneath me. The boundary between my physical self and my surroundings seemed to dissolve and my feeling of separation vanished. In a strange way I felt blended into a total unity with the earth, as if I were made of it and it of me ... I felt as if I had suddenly come alive for the first time – as if I were awakening from a long deep sleep into the real world ... I realized that I was surrounded by an incredible loving energy, and that everything, both living and non-living, is bound inextricably within a kind of consciousness which I cannot describe in words.'[7]

Everyone who has a mystical experience agrees on three things. First, it is difficult to talk about, not just because it is intensely personal but also because the experience itself transcends language. Second, it is always *given* – that is, it cannot be induced by an effort of will, although a degree of preparation or training can help. What Christians call grace, the free gift of God, seems to be operative. Third, all mystical experiences are not only more important to the beneficiaries than their normal state, but infinitely more meaningful. They are revelations of reality. No one says after the experience, 'I see now that it was all a dream or a hallucination or a delusion, but now I've come to my senses.' They say the opposite: 'Ordinary life seemed like a dream in comparison to the reality I saw.' At the same time, ordinary things are not distorted as they can be in dreams. Everything is the same as usual, but more vivid, colourful and above all charged with significance.

It is impossible to say for certain whether different accounts of mystical experience among, say, Christians and Hindus are accounts of different experiences or of the same experiences filtered through different languages, cultures and beliefs. All we can say is that the experience is never completely separate from the subject's culture.

The Vision of the Beloved

Whereas the Vision of Nature seems to be available to everyone in all cultures, there is another kind of mystical experience which seems to be peculiar to Western culture. It might be called the Vision of the Beloved. The English language is hand-icapped here because our word 'love' has to stand for at least four distinct kinds of love for which the Greek words are *epithymia*, which is, roughly speaking, synonymous with lust; *philia*, which is the mutual love of friends or family; *eros*, which is sexual love; and *agape*, which in Greece signified a 'love-feast' or community of love, but which Christians adopted to indicate love between members of the Church and, notably, pure love of God. So the Vision of the Beloved might more accurately be called the Vision of Eros.[8]

If the Vision of Nature is the mystical experience of the multiple, non-human, impersonal Soul of the World, the Vision of Eros is the mystical experience of a single, human person, like the very image of one's individual soul. It can happen on the instant — love at first sight — and its characteristic features are an experience of awe: the Beloved you revere is above you, and you are beneath their notice. There is sexual desire, but not lust in which, by definition, the Beloved is made an object and is therefore inferior.

This vision of love seems to have arisen among the medieval troubadours, who sang of a 'courtly love' in which knights chastely adored and obeyed their ladies, who were placed on pedestals and worshipped from afar. Indeed the beloved lady might not even know that she had a knightly lover, secretly performing noble deeds he dedicated to her. This kind of love became the template for our modern idea of 'romantic' love, which we believe transforms the lover's character for the better. We also believe that it is available to everyone, almost that we all have a right to fall deeply in love, even though it is in fact a comparatively rare experience. Nevertheless its after-image, so to speak, persists today for everyone who is tortured by unrequitable love for some remote Beauty, from an unattainable film star or pop icon to a senior boy or girl at school. Like courtly love there is no question of *philia* – that love which is based on friendship, companionship, shared interests etc. – which, mixed with *eros*, seems to give the best chance of a happy marriage.

In addition, our modern emphasis on falling in love is an experience unknown to tribal people and to Western culture before the medieval period. In other words, it is culturally determined, more the effect of the cult of courtly love than its cause. The most famous example is that of Dante. He sees Beatrice on the streets of Florence and is instantly smitten. A voice says, 'Now you have seen your beatitude.'[9] Her beauty is not like Plato's idea of it, as if there were some objective and impersonal standard of beauty. On the contrary, Beatrice may or may not have been more or less beautiful than other girls. The point is that, to Dante, she is absolutely beautiful because she is Beatrice. There is also a strong sense that love of her is analogous to love of God; that to love her is a short step to loving God, and the more so because her beauty is a sign of her grace – when she dies she will go to Heaven. Famously, she does die; and Dante's *The Divine Comedy* is the account of his journey through the Otherworld – Hell, Purgatory, Paradise – in order to find her again. For Beatrice is the very image of his soul; his journey, like all our journeys, a search for his own soul.

A further development of the Vision of the Beloved was the

various stories which together comprise the myth of Tristan and Isolde. It provides the root-metaphor for our modern belief – I should say, hope – that romantic love need not be the unrequited yearning for a superior beloved, but a relationship in which love is mutual. Tristan and Isolde are both heroic figures in the epic style: they are both aristocratic – he, the most handsome, brave etc.; she, the most beautiful, virtuous etc. They fall in love. But they cannot marry because Isolde is already married to King Mark, to whom Tristan owes absolute loyalty. Their relationship is a torment, not because they cannot have sex – they do have sex, albeit very infrequently – but because their sexual desire is actually 'the symbolic expression of their real passion which is the yearning of two souls to merge and become one, a consummation which is impossible so long as they have bodies, so that their ultimate goal is to die in each other's arms.'[10] Which is what happens, because the merging of two souls can only happen after death.

Their love is essentially religious because each is an absolute, and the ultimate good, for the other. All relations to other people or to the world pale into insignificance beside it. In his book *Passion and Society*, Denis de Rougemont argues – convincingly, I think – that such tales of the troubadours were in fact propagating a heretical, Catharist form of Christianity, and that their courtly love of a knight for his unattainable lady was code for the soul's yearning for a remote God. At any rate, both Plato and Dante agree that love of a beautiful human is meant to direct the lover beyond the human to the 'uncreated source of all beauty'.[11] The difference is that, with Plato, the ascent is impersonal and transcends the body; in Dante's Christian vision, it is personal and includes the body. When he at last meets Beatrice again in the Earthly paradise he re-experiences his original love, but more intensely. And Beatrice now stays with him as he makes his last ascent towards God.

This suggests that love does not have to be either unrequited yearning or the desire to become one person. It can be mutual, providing that each person also loves something greater than the other, as if love must circulate through the other to the Source of love and back again in a dynamic reciprocal process. We retain an inkling of this idea when we insist on getting married in church, 'in the eyes of God', as so many people do who otherwise never set foot there. An essential part of this dynamic is the imaginative ability to put yourself in the other's shoes. It is the prerequisite of compassion, of course, but it is also the beginning of love. This love becomes mutual when the Beloved reciprocates by putting himself or herself in your shoes. In his book *The Descent of the Dove*, Charles Williams called this reciprocity the doctrine of substitution ('I am in you') and exchange ('as you are in me').[12] He thought that it only occurs in a Christian culture because it is founded on the idea, unknown to the Greeks for instance, that we can be 'in Christ' as Christ can be 'in us'. 'I have been crucified with Christ,' as St Paul said, 'and I no longer live, but Christ lives in me.'[13] For Williams, substitution and exchange is the model for all relationships, especially that of lover and beloved. It is what marriage is about. Even the impersonal Vision of Nature is about experiencing yourself as 'in' everything, as everything is in you.

Substitution depends on the imaginative act of placing oneself in the Other; exchange depends on faith – that the Other will reciprocate. The Greeks could make the first movement, but they lacked the idea of the second. They had the concept of an individual soul but they lacked the concept of the personal. Other people were not immortal souls analogous to oneself in whom one could find mutual love, like Dante and Beatrice. Their beauty was an impersonal attribute by which one climbed the ladder of contemplation to a knowledge of the Form of Beauty itself. So, too, the Greeks lacked the idea of a God who could love one personally – an idea also absent in the

Old Testament but introduced by Christ. We are so imbued by Christianity, whether we know it or not, that we have forgotten that mystical experience – indeed, love – can be impersonal, as it was for the Greeks. It is quite possible that many people who call themselves atheists simply have a much stronger sense of the impersonal order of the world than of a personal God. They love the Soul of the World in its impersonal aspect, so to speak, rather than in its manifestation as a personal deity.

The consummation of desire is what we spend most of our lives seeking. If we find it, it is fleeting and we long to recapture it. If we do not find it, we still try to recapture it because we have all seen the divine Forms, including the Form of Beauty, before birth. And so desire is nothing other than the unconscious longing for a return to that unutterable fulfilment. Desire itself is an expression of our mortality, our separation from the Ground of all Being to which we ache to return.

Our separation brings suffering. We cannot stand the pain of unconsummated desire. It creates in us an emptiness, a void. We are tempted to fill it illegitimately. (The modern mystic Simone Weil puts it starkly: 'All sins are attempts to fill voids.')[14] Desire, which is good, becomes degraded. In seeking to assuage our pain we distort infinite desire into that limitless craving which used to be called concupiscence. Its essence is to want pleasure and satisfaction through another – but not to want the other. The soul's yearning for the unattainable Beloved becomes the promiscuous person's attempt to leave soul out of sex altogether, and to substitute numerical quantity for the quality of intimacy and depth. As for Don Giovanni, we recall from Mozart's opera, what is important to him is not love, or even sex – but the list of his conquests. Women become an interchangeable set of parts, like the hard-core pornography which butchers the beauty of women down to anatomical detail. Porn is not about evoking Eros but about disenchanting beauty of its power to evoke the pains of love.

Analogously, the shadow of mutual love is the sickness of sexual infatuation so well described by Marcel Proust. Here, even the act of sex brings no satisfaction because what is desired is the total absorption of the other, body and soul, into oneself. A hopeless desire, in other words, which Tristan and Isolde could only resolve by death; which brings us jealous possessive rage, anguish, despair and an exponential increase in craving, like an addict's, as each act of sex fails to assuage a desire grown limitless. The Greeks may not have had a concept of the transforming power of mutual love made possible by the Christian concept of a personal soul, but they knew all about violent sexual passion. They regarded it as a kind of madness – possession by Eros – which deprived you of all dignity and made you betray your friends.

Nowadays we are particularly prone to such madness because we have lost the religious depth which would contain and define the soul's desire for something beyond the human. This loss forces us to invest far more in other individuals – family, children and friends as well as lovers – than they can bear. This leads to inevitable disappointment when our Beloveds turn out not to be the idealized divine figures we adore. The paradox is that we can only truly love each other when we also love something beyond each other.

The Vision of God

If, on the other hand, we do not try to satisfy our desire; if we simply hold fast to our hunger, then we are transformed by our longing, as if desire were cutting into itself. We are emptied of everything until we are an aching void which, like a vacuum, draws in the mighty rush of Love itself. This can result in a vision of God. It takes place, as one anonymous medieval mystic put it, in 'a cloud of unknowing' where you must 'reconcile yourself to wait in this darkness as long as is necessary, but still go on longing after him whom you love . . . . You must enter a state of nothingness . . . a state of "nowhereness", where you are not outside or above yourself, nor behind or beside yourself either.'[15]

Unlike the Vision of Nature or of the Beloved, this experience does not usually happen spontaneously, to anybody at any time – it needs a degree of preparation, such as prayer, fasting, meditation and self-denial. Some may attain it sooner than others if they have a talent – that is, a vocation – for it; others may never attain it at all. It is the kind of experience that Plotinus had those four times: a union with the One, with God, with the Ground of all Being; but it is most associated with Christians in medieval times, from Walter Hilton and Richard Rolle in England, to Johann Tauler and John Ruysbroeck in Germany, to the great Spanish mystics of the sixteenth century, St Teresa of Avila and St John of the Cross.

Of course mystical experience had been acceptable in the Christian world ever since St Paul's second letter to the Corinthians. 'I know a man', he writes, referring to himself, 'who fourteen years ago was caught up to the third Heaven. Whether it was in the body or out of the body or apart from the body I do not know – God knows. And I know that this man – whether in the body or apart from the body I do not know, but God knows – was caught up to Paradise. He heard inexpressible things, things that man is not permitted to tell.'[16]

But the man who was most responsible for the medieval outpouring of mystical experience was Dionysius the Areopagite, whom we met earlier. As well as his thoroughgoing angelology, Dionysius outlined two ways of salvation, two paths to God. The first was the Affirmative Way, whereby the soul reaches God through intermediaries, from the hierarchy of the Church in the Earthly sphere to the hierarchy of angelic powers in the heavenly. His system of divine intermediaries was lifted straight out of Neoplatonism, whose daimons he Christianized into angels. This Way asserts that all things are good, and from

God; and He can be reached through the things of this world, whether through Nature or through other people, just as the two visions of Nature and of the Beloved suggest.

The second path to God is the Negative Way, whereby all sensory experience, all desire, all thought – even all understanding – have to be renounced in order to reach God. Even the idea of God Himself has to be given up. The soul enters a profound darkness from which only the grace of God can deliver it.[17] There, in the darkness that is not even darkness but beyond darkness and light, the spirit merges ecstatically with the Uncreated Light, yet its identity is not submerged; for all things in the 'Super-Essence' are 'fused yet distinct'.[18] Sometimes the darkness is no darkness at all but the illusion of darkness created by the light of God which blinds the soul with its brilliance. No genuine mystic, incidentally, has ever claimed that such an experience is either necessary for salvation or a proof of sanctity. As St John of the Cross reminds us: 'All visions, revelations, heavenly feelings, and whatever is greater than these, are not worth the least act of humility . . . .'[19]

Because there are no words to describe the encounter with God, the mystic can only say what it is not; or else use metaphors drawn from human love (just as the Vision of Eros uses metaphors drawn from divine love). In his most famous poem, St John describes the rapture of his soul's union with God in terms of a lover slipping away at dead of night, climbing the secret stair of the hushed house, with no other guide than his own burning heart, to where his Beloved is waiting.[20] The night is his 'Dark Night of the Soul', in which he is purged of all natural sense, all human longing and knowledge, in order to achieve divine vision. The myth of Psyche and Eros also seems to tell in terms of human love a tale of the soul's initiation into divine love.

Another popular metaphor for the love of God is light and, in particular, fire, like the 'flame-coloured cloud' which suddenly enwrapped Richard Maurice Bucke while he was driving home in a hansom cab. 'For an instant I thought of fire, an immense conflagration somewhere close by . . . the next, I knew that the fire was within myself. Directly afterwards, there came upon me a sense of exultation, of immense joyousness . . . an intellectual illumination impossible to describe . . . .'[21]

Bucke called this experience 'cosmic consciousness'; and it seems to have been the same kind of experience that the religious mathematician Blaise Pascal underwent on 23 November 1654, when 'From about half past ten in the evening until half past midnight,' he wrote on a piece of parchment found sewn into his clothing at his death in 1662,

FIRE

'God of Abraham, God of Isaac, God of Jacob', not
   of philosophers and scholars.

Certainty, certainty, heartfelt joy, peace.

God of Jesus Christ . . .

Joy, joy, joy, tears of joy.[22]

Plotinus describes the path to mystical union with the One in three ways or, rather, a single way expressed in three spatial metaphors:[23] a journey *upwards* towards a spiritual summit; a journey *within*, where the summit is found within one's own depths, from which all external images – sensory perceptions, intellectual ideas or spatial concepts – have been removed; and a journey *back*, an *epistrophé* or 'turning back' to the origin and source of everything, including oneself.[24] Self-knowledge is knowledge of that from which we came. All these can be summed up in his last words (according to Porphyry's arrangement) of his writings: 'The flight of the alone to the Alone.'

For Plotinus, uniting with the One was also a uniting with oneself, and so the soul does not lose its identity in the One. Nor is the soul's path linear but, rather, a circular turning about its source and centre, just as Jung describes, in order to weave itself into a unity where the two become one. Plotinus preferred the first way, the journey 'upwards', which he based on the ascent to absolute beauty as described by Plato in *The Symposium* – which can therefore be understood as an initiatory text as much as a dialogue about human love. Plotinus describes his own mystical experiences enigmatically as being awakened out of his body into himself, becoming external to all things and contained within himself. He sees a marvellous beauty and is sure that he is communing with the highest order of things, becoming one with the divine.[25]

His ascent, unlike that of Christian mystics – which it closely resembles – is intellectual, non-reciprocal (the soul desires the One, which cannot itself desire) and less the result of supernatural grace than of a natural predilection of the soul. Since it is naturally rooted in the divine ground, the soul can return there in accordance with the psychic law that all things tend to revert to their source.[26] Plotinus' union with the One therefore sounds a bit cool to our sensibility, a bit impersonal compared to the Christian encounter with a personal God whose sudden flaming out of the darkness burns you away in ecstasy.

Our double nature

The Negative Way and the Affirmative Way are extreme examples of two basic human constituents or tendencies. There have been many ways of characterizing them: male and female, intellectual and emotional, consciousness and unconscious, yang and yin, left brain and right brain, sun and moon, unity and multiplicity, Classical and Romantic, Apollonic and Dionysian, light and dark and so on. Each pair is a metaphor for the two-fold tension in our lives or selves. The terms I have chosen to express this tension are 'spirit' and 'soul' because they are large resonant terms with religious connotations. They are not to be understood as substances or even as theological concepts, but rather as symbols.[27] As such they cannot be exactly defined. They can only be grasped elliptically, by the associations they evoke.

The Vision of Nature and the Vision of Eros belong to the Affirmative Way. They are visions of what is created. They are so to speak *soul* visions.

The Vision of God belongs to the Negative Way. It is a vision of the Creator, or of the Source. It is a *spirit* vision, which always desires unity and rejects soul's vision of multiplicity.

Spirit is expressed in metaphors of ascent, height and light. He flies and soars like Peter Pan or Icarus. He longs for transcendence, to rise above the world. Quickly, arrow-straight, he climbs the holy mountain of self-denial and prayer towards Illumination; or the ladders of Reason towards Enlightenment. Pure reason, pure philosophy, pure mathematics, pure light, pure love . . . . Spirit is a Puritan, his goal the pure life of the ascetic monk in his cell or the pure scientist in his hygienic laboratory. He turns his back on what he sees as soul's contamination and muddle.

Soul is expressed in metaphors of descent, depth and darkness. She favours the Underworld and the circuitous route. She is not transcendent but immanent, lying hidden within the world. Slowly, meanderingly, she follows the downward spiral of imagination towards its dark wisdom. She prefers the twilight to the light, where things mingle and worlds intersect. She is suspicious of 'purity', knowing that reality is complex and muddy.

Spirit resents the way that soul is always trying to hold him down or entangle him just as he has leapt out of bed to make a fresh start, wipe the slate clean, embark on a big new adventure. Soul brings him down with the residue of an anxiety dream or clips his wings with a sudden fit of peevishness or mood of pointlessness. Her images and urges, memories and fears, farts and fits of giggles are always breaking in on his high-minded, solemn meditations. His important work is interrupted, as mine is now, by stomach-rumblings and daydreams. He strives to bring soul to heel, control her desires, empty out her imagination, make her forget her dreams; but the more puritanically he denies these daimons the more strongly they return, ever more distorted, like the sexy demons who tempted poor St Anthony in his desert cave.

Spirit wishes to die literally to the world, shedding all its images and its attachments in the pure, clean, empty air of the desert and mountain-top; soul dies to the literal world, finding truth and meaning in the depths of all images and attachments.

Spirit is humourless. If he makes a joke, it is of the 'cosmic' variety – that is, not funny. Soul adores every kind of joke, from the finest wit to the most grotesque buffoonery.

Soul says that the basis of all reality is image, myth, story, fiction – in short, imagination. Spirit says that all this is unreal, illusory, against reason. He prefers 'facts', preferably 'hard' facts. If a thing is not literal, it is not real. Soul replies that it is literalism that is not real but only a product of spirit's literalistic perspective, like the ascents he turns into literal mountain-climbing or the Otherworld journeys he turns into literal pilgrimages, while she stays put in Imagination's gleaming caverns. Facts, she says, are only spirit's fictions.

Sharp-edged spirit always wants things cut and dried, black and white, either-or; soul says that things are not like that: they are always ambiguous, paradoxical, both-and. Spirit has big ideas which he insists are brand new. Soul says that there are no new ideas, only old myths recast in modern garb, which we need new insight to see through.

Spirit resists disease and flees death; soul sees disease as one of her treasured manifestations, and death as her own proper realm. She savours death, whose bitterness is an initiation; spirit leaps over death and its darkness to emphasize the light of rebirth.

Soul is poetry; spirit, prose. Books with 'soul' in the title are usually about, and by, spirit – and full of abstractions and generalities about the delights of Light, Love, Oneness, God, Energy, Consciousness. Our difficulty in staying awake when reading such books is owing to soul's desire that we should return to her realm of dreams and images, or pick up a book with a good story in it. She closes our eyes against the mystic dazzle; she closes our ears against the banality of transcendence, against large pronouncements, against the preachy platitudes of would-be gurus or of 'channelled' spirits, angels and space brothers. 'Glory be to God,' says soul (through G. M. Hopkins) 'for dappled things', whatever is 'counter, original, spare, strange; Whatever is fickle, freckled (who knows how?)'.[28] She regards spirit much as Virginia Woolf regarded Lowes Dickinson: 'Always live in the Whole, Life in the One; always Shelley and Goethe, and then he loses his hot-water bottle; and never notices a face or a cat or a dog or a flower, except in the flow of the universal.' For the trouble is, said Woolf, 'One can't write directly about the soul. Looked at, it vanishes; but look at the ceiling, at Grizzle, at the cheaper beasts in the zoo which are exposed to walkers in Regent's Park, and the soul slips in.'[29]

Spirit wants to commandeer soul for his own purposes – progress, growth, improvement. He turns soul's playful self-sufficiency into practical self-help. Indeed, our passion for self-help is underpinned by that muscular Protestant work ethic, replete with guilt, which was so admirable in the Pilgrim Fathers and still sees America as its spiritual home. Soul sees spirit's rigorous regimes of meditation as a form of repression, denying her infinite variety of images.

Spirit loves humanity but, unlike soul, is less interested in people. He is high-minded and serious, looking down on soul's love of gossip, rumour and myth-making. He is suspicious of appearances, disapproves of make-up and fancy hair-dos and smart shoes. He does not see that soul's gossip and chat is a concern with relationship and personal connections; her liking of personal adornment, an expression of her concern with Beauty, which spirit always tries to 'get behind', get to Truth.

It is spirit which always postulates something 'higher' 'behind' the image, such as a noumenon behind a phenomenon, a god behind a daimon, or one God behind the gods. But soul says that this is not literally so. The sense of 'behindness' is built into soul's vision, supplying her sense of dimension, mystery and depth. So, too, the structures and hierarchies we are so attached to are spirit's impositions on soul's flow. We are allowed hierarchies, as Plotinus is allowed his system of emanations and the evolutionists are allowed their vision of a great chain of being, providing only that we use them as tools, as ways of seeing, rather than asserting that they are the case.

It was this perceived rigidity that caused W. B. Yeats temporarily to 'mock Plotinus' thought and cry in Plato's teeth', as he writes in his poem 'The Tower'; but, later, he recanted. 'I forgot that it is something in our eyes that makes us see them as all transcendence. Has not Plotinus written: "Let every soul recall, then, at the outset the truth that soul is the author of all living things, that it had breathed the life into them all, whatever is nourished by earth and sea, all the creatures of the air, the divine stars in the sky; it is the maker of the sun; itself formed and ordered this vast heaven and conducts all that rhythmic motion – and it is a principle distinct from all these to which it gives law and movement and life . . . ." '[30]

To spiritual, hierarchical thinking, the daimons are at best the missing links between this world and the world 'above'. But to soul they are the very fabric of a single world which shifts shape – shows us many different aspects, including the spiritual and the material, according to whatever perspective, whatever god, we are looking through.

Spirit is a Utopian, always flying off to forge a new future, always plotting a social programme to usher in the New

Jerusalem. He cannot wait to forget the past, leave home, shake off family ties and old traditions. Soul is an Arcadian, always wishing to return to the Golden Age, always waiting to reinstate the conditions of Eden.[31] She loves memory, the past, the ancestors and old customs. She likes the unchanging cycles of seasons, festivals and sagas.

Whereas spirit sees the past as a static, backward, primitive, superstitious and unhygienic Dark Age, soul sees it as a nourishing wellspring of sacred culture, social harmony and right relations with Nature. In our secular culture soul returns – if the British TV ratings are anything to go by – as an interest in gardens, old buildings, antiques, archaeology, genealogy and Nature programmes.

When the poet Kathleen Raine heard two young girls singing as they brought in the washing on the Scottish island of Eigg, with no accompaniment other than birdsong, the sound of sheep and of the sea – no modern sound – she remarked: 'it was not so much the past that we seemed then to enter, but the permanent, the enduring norm, the familiar.'[32] And this, too, is part of the joy of the vision of Nature, that it seems the way things should be – and are, if we but open our eyes and hearts to what is not beyond this beautiful world but enfolded within it.

One and Many

If I am giving the impression that spirit and soul are opposed to each other, it is not necessarily so. It is the result of the preponderantly 'spirit' perspective of our culture, founded on a monotheism which tends to polarize – whether spirit and soul, Affirmative and Negative, this world and the next, angels and demons or spirit and matter. Such oppositions have been carried over into modern society where subject is at odds with object, mind with matter, fact with fiction and so forth.

A wholesome life, it seems, is made out of holding spirit and soul together, in tandem and in tension. Religiously speaking, this means balancing the One and the Many – one God with many gods. All the great Renaissance magi, from Ficino and Pico to John Dee, were Christian polytheists. Ficino, for example, 'worshipped God simultaneously both beyond and within Creation.' For him, 'the world was "full" of a god who transcends it: *Iovis omnia plena* [all things are full of Jupiter].'[33] Their faith was biblical and monotheistic, but their theology, as it were, came from Plato and Plotinus. The Romantic poets too were usually Christian; but they also were drawn to pagan Neoplatonism. William Blake's work is the paradigm for Christian polytheism. They all managed to resist monotheism's tendency towards superiority and its perennial wish to break free from soul's manyness. Even Iris Murdoch, who as a novelist as well as a philosopher should have known better, asserts that 'theological mythology, stories about the gods, creation myths and so on, belong to the realm of image-making and are at a lower level than reality and ultimate religious truth, a view continuously held in the east, and also in western mysticism: beyond the last image we fall into the abyss of God.'[34]

Soul might well expostulate: 'But, but . . . "abyss" and "God" are also only images in my vast treasure-house of images. Indeed, I am myself the abyss – for I am, as Heraclitus says, fathomless – in which the image of God is contained.' Recognizing this truth, perhaps, the Protestant theologian Paul Tillich was forced to postulate, in the fashion of pure spirit, a 'God above God';[35] a God, that is, who is unknown and unknowable, beyond any image of God we can conceive of. But is this not also an image . . . ? Must there not then be a God above God above God . . . ?

In other words, there is no monotheism which is not besieged by soul's fragmenting daimons; and there is no polytheism which does not acknowledge, however dimly, some overriding deity,[36] whether it is Zeus among the Greek gods,

Ra among the Egyptians, Wakan-Tanka among the Native Americans of the Plains, the 'Spirit of the Forest' among the Pygmies or the shadowy creator god of the Eveny reindeer-herders, Hövki. Even Plato's Form of the Good can be seen as the assertion of an impersonal unity over against the many personified gods of Homeric polytheism, rather like the way the Buddha emptied out the Hindu deities into the 'void' of nirvana. However, neither of these banished the gods altogether as jealous Jehovah did.

In his desire to break free of soul, spirit turns his back on her and flees as if from his own shadow. But if he faces his own shadow he finds his own reflection. For when soul is working together with spirit, she contains and defines him, slows him down and fleshes him out, gives him bulk and substance, roots his airy ideas in concrete images, brings imagination to his single-mindedness, encourages him to turn things over in his mind, to brood and gestate before bringing forth. Above all, soul reflects; and spirit can only know his own truth through her.

Reciprocally, spirit invigorates soul, who is tempted to remain in the valley of dreams, to hide in fetid mists, to stagnate in the past[37] – her love of beauty degenerating into an empty aestheticism, her polytheism surrendering to fatalism. She needs spirit's fire and wind to burn away her haze and give her lift-off. She needs his lightning-strike to germinate her imaginative fertility, his inspiration to breathe zest into her. In spirit soul sees her own beauty.

Thus soul and spirit can only be grasped in relation to each other. I have been opposing them in order to bring out their differences; but opposition is only one way in which they relate, albeit the way favoured by modernity. Really, they are forever intertwined, mutually mirroring. Whatever is said about the one is necessarily from the standpoint of the other, like Jung's anima and animus. Jung called this pairing a syzygy. It is a term taken from the conjunction of planets in astronomy. Our imagination is bounded by syzygies. We can only imagine in pairs, like the tandems of our mythic tales: twins, brothers and sisters, heroes and damsels, heroes and dragons, fathers and daughters, mothers and sons, and so on. The union of consciousness and the unconscious in the Self is symbolized in alchemy by a hermaphrodite. The usual symbol of the union of soul and spirit is, of course, simply marriage – for every Dante a Beatrice, for every Psyche an Eros. All the Elizabeth Bennets get their Mr Darcys. Every soul is secretly a Princess with her own Prince Charming.

This implies that this book should be as much a study of spirit as it is of soul. I expect you have noticed that it already is, because all descriptions or 'definitions' of soul are reflections of one or another perspective of spirit; or, to put it slightly differently, soul's own reflections in spirit's mirror.

Nowadays the outlook of spirit is most often carried by what we call the ego. And it is this archetypal 'spirit' perspective which I want to look at in the next chapter. But before I do this I would like to append a cautionary tale about the fate of daimons who fall into the hands of unbridled spirit.

The flaying of Marsyas

Marsyas was a daimon – a satyr, in fact – who stumbled one day across a flute that, unknown to him, had been cursed by Athena. He went about Phrygia in the train of Cybele, one of the great Middle Eastern goddesses, delighting the peasantry with his playing. It was soon rumoured that even Apollo himself could not make such marvellous music. This made Apollo angry. He invited Marsyas to meet him in a musical contest, the winner of which could choose whatever punishment he wished for the loser. Marsyas foolishly agreed. The Muses, who were elected to judge the contest, were equally delighted by both contestants. So Apollo challenged Marsyas to do as he did, which was to turn his instrument upside-down, and play and sing at the same time. This was quite easy for Apollo to do with his stringed lyre, but impossible for Marsyas to do with his flute. The Muses had no choice but, in spite of the cheat, to declare Apollo the winner. Whereupon the god took a cruel revenge on the satyr: he flayed Marsyas alive and nailed his skin to a tree.

Now, this may be a reference to the ritual removal of an animal skin from a satyr or silenos, a man who danced in a Dionysian rite while wearing a goat-skin and horse's tail. But it also tells us a lot about unbridled Apollo. Although there are many kinds of spirit, 'more and more the notion of "spirit" has come to be carried' (James Hillman tells us) 'by the Apollonian archetype, the sublimations of higher and abstract disciplines, the intellectual mind, refinements and purifications.'[38] A-pollo means 'not many', and so 'far-seeing' Apollo is the god of unity. As we have seen, he is also the god of science who, unrestrained by the influence of Hermes or Dionysus, may lapse into monomaniacal scientism, which feels it is above soul – but not above tampering with the facts in order to defeat its competitors. Scientism hates and, I dare say, fears soul's irrational eruptions of goaty daimons, playing their maddening Dionysian flutes – and wishes to flay them alive.

NINE

Soul and ego

T he main bearer of spirit in our times is what we call the ego. Plotinus was the first person to recognize the ego psychologically – that is, says Professor Dodds, 'the first to make the vital distinction between the total personality (*psyche*) and the ego-consciousness (*emeis*).'[1] But it was known mythologically much earlier: as the hero. The hero is the archetypal image of the ego, and in myths he usually has one divine parent. The mother of Achilles, for instance, was the goddess Thetis, and the father of Heracles was Zeus. This parentage makes the hero especially useful for understanding the relationship between spirit in its guise of hero or ego, and soul. For the myths about the heroes represent a pattern of estrangement and reconciliation between the two. I shall be relating several examples shortly, but the formula is universal.

The action begins when the hero feels the imperative to separate himself from his mother, cutting the ties to her apron strings and making his own way in the world. Typically he encounters obstacles and suffers ordeals. These he must overcome or endure, by guile or strength, in order to win the beautiful woman (usually a princess) with whom he has fallen in love.

Jung described this motif in psychological terms. It is essential, he said, that the ego differentiates itself from the unconscious as the archetypal 'Mother', in order to be reunited with it as 'anima' at a higher level. In other words, just as in myth the hero is that offshoot of the gods who wants to break free of the gods, so the ego breaks free of the soul, its matrix, in order to reflect soul, to make its potential actual, and eventually to be reunited with the realized soul to form the totality of the self.

This pattern is not confined to Greek myths, of course – it is re-enacted every day in popular fiction and cinema. Nor is it confined to Western culture. Tribal peoples enact the same pattern in their rites of passage, especially those designed for boys and girls at puberty. The rites involve exile, isolation and physical suffering – but also revelations of the tribe's myths. When the young people return to their tribe they are no longer children but individuals in their own right. They can then go on to the next rite of passage, which is marriage and child-bearing.

Like the hero, the ego is the indomitable 'spirit perspective' without whom we would remain in thrall to the perspective of the archetypal Mother. The heroic ego supplies our drive to activity and exploration; he gives us our feeling of strength, independence, willpower and our need to overcome challenges.

The problems begin when these virtues become overween-ing, too 'masculine' and single-minded. The heroic ego begins to believe that he is not that child of soul launched outwards to experience the world and return, but wholly free of the soul as if he has escaped soul's gravity. He starts to believe that he is – the sin of hubris – not derived from the gods but self-derived. This type of ego-consciousness, arriving in Western culture at the beginning of the seventeenth century, has come to dominate our world-view. It has been called the heroic ego, the rational ego and, by James Hillman, the Heraclean ego.[2] This is because the most admired hero of the Greeks, Heracles (in Latin, Hercules), has a darker side to him which we, glorying in his strength and triumphs, have chosen to ignore.

Heracles in Hades

Heracles is most famous for his 'twelve labours' – mighty tasks he has to perform in order to expiate a crime. They mostly involve capturing or slaughtering exotic creatures, such as a legendary lion, a miraculous deer, the many-headed Hydra, a giant boar. Since they symbolize the Otherworldly powers of the Imagination, it is doubtful whether the tasks should have been approached in this way, or even undertaken at all. For example, in his fifth labour he undertook to clean out what should clearly be left alone – the vast and filthy Augean stables, whose dung and putrefaction signal them as a place for allowing images to brew and simmer in an alchemical fashion.

The most telling labour from our point of view is his last: the capture of Cerberos, the three-headed hound who guards the way to Hades. Heracles behaves in an extraordinary and disgraceful way. Brandishing his club, he bludgeons his way into the Underworld. First, in order to cross the river Styx, he simply intimidates Charon the ferryman into carrying him. Once on the other side, he aims an arrow at the shade of the hero Meleager, and has to be told by Hermes (who has of course accompanied him down, as he accompanies everyone down to Hades) that Meleager is not the 'real' Meleager, but only a shade. Hermes is similarly embarrassed when Heracles draws his sword on the shade of Medusa the Gorgon. She, too (explains Hermes), is only a shade. But Heracles is incapable of learning that shades, *eidola*, are real – as images; but are unreal as soon as we take them literally. He treats everything as literal. The shades of the dead flee from him in terror, just as the daimons run from our strong-arm rationalism.

And so he goes muscling his way through the Underworld, wrestling Hades' herdsmen and slaughtering their cattle in order to feed the shades of men with blood – a technique for bringing them back to life. Finally he chokes Cerberos, chains him and drags him like a reluctant dream up into the daylight world of the living.

The natural way to enter Hades is to die. But you do not necessarily have to die literally. You may, like Orpheus – like all shamans – die metaphorically. This means the death of the ego and its literalistic perspective in order that the daimonic, imaginative self can come into being. This death is the kind experienced during the rites of passage I mentioned earlier in this chapter. It is called initiation. In fact, before his last labour Heracles specifically asked to experience this kind of death by being initiated into the Eleusinian Mysteries. He knew that only by becoming assimilated to death, as it were, could he pass freely into the Underworld. However, he was refused permission. So, denied a metaphorical death, Heracles inverts the situation – and kills literally.

The daimons or images which would have initiated him if he had met them with humility madden him instead. He cannot grasp any reality he cannot grapple with, or club. He fears and shuns imagination, image, daimon – just as our modern rational world-view does. Instead of embracing the god Hades in his realm, as the welcome death of his literalistic stance, Heracles attacks him, wounding him in the shoulder and driving him from his throne.

The story of Heracles shows something extraordinary: that there is a perspective within myth that denies myth, together with its gods and daimons.

Like Heracles, the rational ego does not recognize images, daimons or even death. It regards all viewpoints other than its own as delusional, and does not notice that the literal world it inhabits is the product of its own perspective. If we want to know what will happen to us if we cling to the life of the rational ego alone, if we deny soul and the initiatory death that its recognition implies, we have only to consider the final fate of Heracles.

His wife, Deianeira, is unhappy at Heracles' neglect of her.

When he asks her to weave him a special shirt to be worn at a sacrifice, she sees her chance to rekindle his interest. She has procured a love-potion from a centaur called Nessus and made out of his blood. She dips the shirt in the blood and sends it off to her husband.

Deianeira represents Heracles' soul, as the wives and girl-friends of heroes usually do. Like all our souls she is constant and patient and goes on loving us no matter how much we forget or neglect her. But if we are determined to deny her, her love can only reach us in a distorted form. It may even appear destructive because it is love directed at our true selves, not at our egos – the very means by which we shut soul out. The soul's love, in other words, can look like forcible initiation as it assaults the stone walls of the ego.

Consequently, the blood that the shirt is dipped in is, unknown to Deianeira, not a love-potion but a poison. For Nessus the centaur is a vengeful daimon whose comrades Heracles has previously killed. One version of the myth tells us that Nessus' blood is only poisonous in the first place because he had been wounded by Heracles' poisoned arrow. This dramatic irony points to a poetic justice because it is really Heracles who has poisoned love. The myth tells us that poison is sometimes the only way love can reach us. It is a metaphor for the corrosive force that love is perceived to be by the impregnable Heraclean ego which, if it will not die to itself, must finally consume itself. So Heracles puts on the shirt, whose poison eats into his flesh. Mad with pain he tries to tear it off, but it cannot be removed, and he succeeds only in tearing himself to pieces.

Siegfried's loss of soul

In my book *Daimonic Reality: A Field Guide to the Otherworld*, I suggest that there is a heroic pattern that mirrors even more faithfully our modern rational ego. It is the Germanic myth of

Siegfried, 'the great hero of the German people'.[3] Even more than the Heraclean, he provides the archetypal background for that singular perspective of spirit we might call the northern Protestant ego, originating in Germany, from which the rational ego derives.

It may seem eccentric to cite a pagan myth as underlying a Christian development; but we will remember how thinly Christianity sometimes veils paganism, especially when we consider the dramatic resurgence of Germanic myth (notably Siegfried's) under Hitler's regime. At any rate, Siegfried and the northern Protestant ego share an important feature: they both suffer from loss of soul. The best-known version of the Siegfried myth is Wagner's operatic treatment of it in the *Ring* cycle. However, the version to which I will refer is the earlier Norse one, where Siegfried is known as Sigurd, and Brunhilde as Brynhild.[4] The parts of the plot which concern us are briefly as follows.

Sigurd's first major heroic task is to kill the dragon Fafnir, as a result of which he is bathed in the dragon's blood, which renders him invulnerable, except for a small spot on his back where a linden leaf has fallen. He also cooks and eats the dragon's heart, which enables him to understand the language of the birds – who at once tell him to seek out Brynhild.

To be invulnerable is a dubious distinction; it implies that one is armoured, intransigent, unwilling to let anything through. Here, we sense the beginning of a spirit perspective rigidifying into a single-minded rational ego. Its soul counterpart in this case is personified by Brynhild. But she is not the usual princess; she is a Valkyr, one of Odin's warrior-maidens, cast out of the Otherworld for disobedience. There is no one like her in Greek mythology, except perhaps great Artemis, the cold huntress and moon-goddess. As a pair, Sigurd and Brynhild, ego and soul, both determine and reflect each other; and, splendid as they are, they are also hard and ruthless and martial.

Sigurd finds Brynhild on a mountain peak, in a tower surrounded by a wall of flame which only he can breach on his magical horse, Grani (reminiscent of the shaman's 'spirit horse'). Even though he represents the ego, Sigurd is still flexible and, so to speak, daimonic – able to adapt to Otherworldly conditions; and so he is in harmony with soul. Accordingly, he and Brynhild spend three days together and fall in love, avowing that they are each other's very souls. He then leaves her in order to perform more deeds of derring-do, so that he can be worthy of her exalted hand in marriage on his return. Actually, he at once falls in with a king called Gunnar, and his two brothers, Hogni and Gotthorm. He gets on so well with Gunnar that he becomes his blood-brother, incidentally confiding to him the secret of his weak spot.

In this twinning of Sigurd and Gunnar we are invited to see them as two aspects of the same person. The flexible, spirited Sigurd who was Brynhild's lover is now under the influence of Gunnar and his worldly household, where he meets Gunnar's mother, and his sister Gudrun. As the story unfolds we become aware that Gunnar now represents the rational ego which splits off from spirit, and denies its connection with soul. That the connection is lost is represented by the fact that Sigurd forgets all about Brynhild. He has fallen prey to an enchantment concocted by Gunnar's mother to make him fall in love with Gudrun instead. The enchantment is like that waking daylight consciousness which banishes the dream images and returns us to this mundane world. Thus Sigurd forgets his true soul, Brynhild, in her Otherworldly tower and marries Gudrun, the charming but shallow *hausfrau*.

Meanwhile, Gunnar has heard of the beautiful warrior-maiden Brynhild and determines to win her. Sigurd, oblivious of his connection to Brynhild in another life, offers to help. But, arriving at the flame-encircled tower, Gunnar cannot traverse the fire, even when Sigurd lends him Grani. However, remembering another of his mother's spells, Gunnar decides to change shape with Sigurd in order that Sigurd can win Brynhild on his behalf. This can be seen as the rational ego imposing its perspective on spirit. Thus, in the guise of Gunnar, Sigurd breaches the wall of fire for the second time and wins Brynhild, who reckons herself (correctly) forgotten by Sigurd and reasons that this 'Gunnar' must be worthy since he was able to penetrate the ring of fire. She does not see Sigurd resuming his own appearance and galloping off home in advance to warn the household of the real Gunnar's return with his duped bride. When Brynhild arrives she recognizes him and realizes that he has apparently betrayed her and married another. At this, her demeanour grows increasingly icy and remote – incomprehensible to Gunnar and Gudrun.

As soon as he sees Brynhild at her wedding feast, Sigurd remembers everything – but can say nothing of his past connection with her out of loyalty to Gunnar, his blood-brother, and Gudrun, his wife. A year passes before Gudrun reveals to Brynhild during a quarrel that it was in fact not Gunnar who won her, but Sigurd in disguise. Brynhild confronts Sigurd, and he stumblingly explains what happened: that he had been put under an enchantment and had no memory of her. Brynhild begs him to leave with her at once so that they may live together as originally planned. But Sigurd will still not betray Gunnar and Gudrun.

Here, Sigurd gives up his second chance to become reconnected to the Otherworld of the Valkyr, as if he had become too contaminated with this world. What he had lost the first time through forgetfulness, he now wilfully denies.

I would just like to summarize the important movement in the relationship between Sigurd and Gunnar. At first, they were like twin brothers, two aspects of the same person, spirit and ego. However, Sigurd's entry into the worldly, richly familial atmosphere of Gunnar's domain changes him: he forgets he was once conjoined to another world, as spirit is rightly conjoined to soul. He now identifies wholly with Gunnar, the rational ego. This situation might still have been reversible – he recognizes Brynhild, she invites him to flee with her – but is in fact made permanent by his refusal to join her. It is precisely this wilful denial of soul which is most relevant to us because it is the hallmark of the rational ego, the dominant perspective of our own culture. Even its close kin, the iconoclastic northern Protestant ego, is prefigured in Sigurd's choice of the ethical perspective (his duty to Gunnar and Gudrun) over the erotic (his desire for Brynhild).

The spurned Brynhild vengefully tells Gunnar that Sigurd really loves her and wishes him, Gunnar, dead (which is, from soul's point of view, no more than the truth). Gunnar then plans a pre-emptive strike. However, we notice that Brynhild has also engineered Sigurd's death, which is what she now wants; for if soul cannot be united with spirit in this life, she must snatch him into her own realm where, as for Tristan and Isolde, there are no obstacles to union.

Neither Gunnar nor Hogni can kill Sigurd because of the blood oath that binds them; so they persuade their younger brother, Gotthorm, to do the deed during a hunting expedition. When they stop to drink from a stream, Sigurd kneels to scoop up the water. The noise of the stream drowns the sound of the birds who are warning him of his danger – and Gotthorm plunges his sword into the vulnerable spot on Sigurd's back. With his last ounce of strength, Sigurd kills Gotthorm – and dies.

Gudrun weeps bitterly at the news of Sigurd's death; but Brynhild says not a word. She simply arrays herself as if for a marriage feast. Then, lying on her bed, she stabs herself in the breast. As she bleeds to death, she calls for Gunnar and tells him how Sigurd loved her before *he* ever did and how Sigurd was a good friend to him, refusing to betray him. Finally she asks that she may be placed on the funeral pyre next to her beloved.

Gunnar, as rational ego, is left in charge of a world devoid of both soul and of any alternative heroic perspective.

The violation of Nature

In the stories of Heracles and Sigurd we see the consequences of severing spirit from soul, and beyond that, the rational ego from its blood-brother spirit. Their myths are especially pertinent to us because something similar has been happening in Western culture over the last four hundred years. As we have seen, one of the rational ego's postures is to depict itself as detached and objective; a perspective which, emerging in the seventeenth century, made scientific enquiry possible. As Francis Bacon's new empiricism and René Descartes's dualism gave rise to rationalism, contemporary scientists, such as the founders of the Royal Society, claimed exactly this detachment from Nature – a severance which, they believed, would allow them to examine her dispassionately and so discover her secrets.

The reality was – and perhaps is – somewhat different. The philosopher Mary Midgley in her research into scientific papers of the seventeenth century found that, far from being neutral and objective about Nature, the fledgling scientists unfailingly depict her as a wild and dangerous harlot who must be *fought, tormented, uprooted, interrogated, held down and penetrated, pierced and vanquished*. The language of rape and torture is not exceptional, she remarks; it is 'the common and constant idiom of the age.'[5] Yet, amazingly, the scientists went on believing in their own rational detachment. Even today, scientists like to dramatize the universe they see as inanimate by calling it 'hostile'; yet hostile is exactly what an inanimate universe cannot be. Thus in metaphors do the daimons creep back in, subverting scientists' claims of objectivity by colouring their unconscious use of language.

There is, however, more to the scientistic fantasy of complete detachment from Nature. It can be read as a literalized version of the disembodied ascent of the mystic or the Otherworld journey of the shaman. It substitutes objective, cerebral cognition for true knowledge, gnosis, in which the knower is profoundly implicated, even transformed. Just as the mystic on the Negative Way is prey to a return of the repressed daimons in diabolic form, so the materialist is haunted by the Nature he has objectified and unsouled. No wonder she comes back as a harlot, vengeful goddess or Valkyr, all the more violent for being unrecognized.

Nature was only the first casualty of the rational ego. It was followed by all the other manifestations of soul: imagination was downgraded to fantasy, the province of women and children, whose status was equally reduced; and the past was no longer a perfect state we had descended from, but a dark superstitious place we must transcend. Eventually soul itself was looked upon as a fantasy or illusion. If spirit is always striving to break free of soul, the rational modern ego is precisely the delusion that it has succeeded.

The chameleon ego

Just as soul banished from the world returns as a threatening goddess, so soul banished from the mind returns as a hostile unconscious, nagging us with neurotic symptoms or ravaging us with madness. And the more the ego insists that consciousness only resides with him, that only he lives in the light, the more distorted and threatening the unconscious seems.

From soul's point of view, she has been banished from Nature, which is now soulless machinery. She has no choice but to take refuge within the human psyche. But she also fails in this because she is excluded by the narrow, brilliant spotlight of consciousness which casts everything else into shadow. She is compelled to hide behind consciousness – in the unconscious. Except that she does not so much fill the unconscious as *form* it. The unconscious is the product of the rational ego which cast the soul into darkness. It remained in abeyance for some three hundred years until its daimons began to cry out for recognition once more from the couches of the psychoanalysts. But we were never meant, surely, to be divided from Nature and from our own souls by the heroic ego's rational scalpel.

I have been describing the way the rational ego separates itself from the 'outside' world (of Nature, for instance) and from its own 'unconscious mind' as two different movements. But really they are one. Each is the consequence of the other because soul is located both in the world outside and in the world inside. However, soul does not recognize the distinction outside/inside – it is a distinction made by the rational ego, and not operative in the medieval world-view or in traditional cultures.

Among tribal peoples, for instance, personal identity is not confined within the body or head or brain, as we assume it to be. On the contrary, it can take on different social roles, or overflow a person's body, extending to their personal possessions and even to the remains of their meal or their footprints[6] – it depends on the amount of mana they possess. We look askance at this notion that objects in the world can be regarded as an extension of a person's individuality; but perhaps we should, on the contrary, regard our own idea of individuality as having been cramped and reduced. For the tribal person, psychic life is fluid, his ego's borders less well defined. He is able to merge with the life of things outside his body. But this is simply common sense if you live in a culture which experiences everything as ensouled as you are, with a world-soul underlying and connecting every individual manifestation of itself.

Western culture used to judge tribal thought as childish and primitive, but we can now see that it is more like imagining. Anyone who has engaged in intense imaginative activity understands what it is to be 'primitive' – knows the feeling of entering another world, of abolishing distinctions of subject and object, of experiencing Nature as animate, of sensing the presence of daimons moving like greater powers within and around them. In bowing our heads humbly before the Muse, and losing ourselves in her imagery, we paradoxically gain greater freedom and meaning, and come to know what it is to be our true selves. This happens spontaneously, for instance in the Vision of Nature I described in the last chapter; but it can be induced by an act of imagination such as we make in the creation of art. In both cases, the ego is absent or, to put it another way, is absorbed in the object of contemplation. Keats describes this when he speaks of the 'Camelion Poet' as 'the most unpoetical of any thing in existence; because he has no Identity.' That is, he is always identifying with something else, 'filling some other body', says Keats, such as the sun, the moon, the sea – just as we are able to do in dreams. Indeed, Keats' description of the 'poetical character' may be read as a description of soul itself: it 'is not itself – it has no self – it is everything and nothing – has no character – it enjoys light and shade; it lives in gusto, be it foul or fair . . . . What shocks the virtuous philosopher delights the Camelion Poet . . . .'[7]

The alienated ego

If I wanted to be charitable towards the rational ego I might say that it enables us to imagine deeply into separateness and singleness and loneliness. It shows us what it is to be vulnerable because the more it boasts of its strength, the more we perceive an underlying weakness. The more self-centred it is, the less real connection it has with others. In short, the more and the bigger ego we have, the less self.

The reason for this is given in myth, as usual. As I have said, a hero always has one divine parent. The ego is partly born of the gods who constitute soul. If that parentage is spurned, then the divine ground of the ego has to be wholly assumed by the human part. The result is what psychologists call 'inflation': the ego is puffed up with a sense of his own divinity and godlike self-sufficiency, denying any gods outside himself. He seals himself off in his sense of superiority – with the unhappy consequences we know only too well. 'The achievement of human autonomy has been paid for by the experience of alienation'.[8]

The isolation experienced by an ego conscious only of itself can be devastating, especially when it first emerges in our teenage years. The tension between spirit and soul, potentially so fruitful, can seem intolerable. We feel cut off from ourselves and from the world, like outsiders. Our awareness of ourselves as unique beings just feels like the impossibility of ever being known or understood. We want to regress – to childhood, to our mother's breast, to the state of Eden where we are at one with ourselves and the world, before we became this tormented, two-fold, self-transcending chimera, both embedded by our bodies in Nature, yet exiled by consciousness from it.

No wonder we hide in our rooms and refuse to leave home; no wonder we throw ourselves at the opposite sex, hoping that love – or sex – will, Tristan and Isolde-like, annihilate alienation; no wonder we cling to others in gangs or groups, hoping to dissolve our identity and cease to stick out like sore thumbs. We take drugs or drink to try and dull the razor of consciousness or break through to some 'higher' consciousness where the stress-fracture of consciousness will be mended.

When the rational ego opposes soul, it polarizes body and spirit, denying them their own harmonizing links to soul and to each other. The practical effects are everywhere recognizable: if we deny body, we end up as arid intellectuals or as rigid Puritans; if we deny spirit, we fall into self-indulgent hedonism, or hopelessly cultivate what we imagine to be the instinctual life of animals. If we try to express spirit directly through the body we fall prey to ideologies of Nature worship or free love; if we try to express body solely through spirit, we counterfeit true asceticism with strict dietary programmes and keep-fit regimes.

Such attempts to extinguish one side or the other of our contradictory nature, whether through adolescent binges or adult abstentions, are – paradoxically – a blind groping towards initiation of the very kind which Heracles and Sigurd refused.

It is an initiation which seeks the death of the partial self and thus the birth of the realized soul in all its wholeness, wherein our two-fold nature and all the contradictions of existence can be accommodated in a dynamic equilibrium. I shall be tackling initiation in the next chapter. But to end this one, I want to mention that, of course, not all egos are of the soul-destroying rational kind. Not all heroes are Heracles. Myth provides us with many models of how a heroic ego happily relates to soul.

Odysseus and Perseus

Red-haired Odysseus, for instance, has relationships with many soul figures. His wife Penelope waits patiently for him to return home to Ithaca from the Trojan War; but he is waylaid for twenty years. He is enchanted en route by the demi-goddess Calypso, side-tracked by the witch Circe and delayed by the innocent Nausicaa. He is always called wily, crafty and devious. He is *polytropos*, an epithet which means 'turning many ways'. He is flexible and multifaceted. His is the perspective which finds many and different reflections of himself in the mirror of soul, just as soul appears to him in many different female guises, like the shape-shifting anima. More of a trickster than a conventional 'hero', he may not be as strong as his comrades Diomedes and Aias; he may not have armies like Agamemnon and Achilles (he only contributes one ship to the war effort); but only he is able to think up the Trojan Horse trick that will win the city.

When he encounters the Underworld, he does not pillage like Heracles. He just wants information about his future from it, and meets it calmly as if he were already acclimatized. In fact, he does not go there – he summons the Underworld to him by filling a trench with cattle blood and inviting the dead to drink.

The blood confers temporary substance on the shades of the dead, notably allowing them to speak, and therefore to prophesy or give advice.

Perseus also travels into a kind of Underworld where he has been commanded to confront and slay the ultimate horror: Medusa the Gorgon, whose look turns us to stone, as if she represented some deep shadow part of the psyche where we are frozen, stuck, petrified. To cope with Medusa, Perseus needs the help of more than one god, more than one perspective. From Athena he acquires a polished shield. She shows him how he must not look directly at the Gorgon but walk backwards towards her, using her reflection in the shield to guide him. Reflection, then – the backward-looking contemplation and absorption of images from the unconscious – is a key to approaching the deep psyche.

From Hermes, Perseus acquires an adamantine sickle. This is a lethal weapon for decapitating Medusa; but, unlike the Heraclean bludgeon, it is sharp, incisive and less connected with warfare than with harvesting. (Indeed, the death of Medusa brings forth an unexpected harvest: her corpse gives birth to Pegasus, the winged horse, and Chrysaor, the 'golden' warrior, both of whom had been begotten on her by the sea god Poseidon.)

The shield and sickle will enable him to kill Medusa. But if he is to escape the wrath of Medusa's deadly sisters and get out alive, he needs three more things: a pair of winged sandals for speed of flight; a wallet to contain the dangerous, still-active head of the Gorgon; and the dark helmet of invisibility which belongs to Hades. In order to get these things he has to make a preliminary trip into the Underworld, to the Stygian nymphs (they inhabit the underworld river Styx) who have charge of them. It is wise, it seems, to reconnoitre the unconscious, acclimatize and acquire its gifts before we broach the deepest Gorgon-levels . . . .

Once he has found Medusa, Perseus approaches her by walking backwards and holding up the polished shield to catch her image so that he can avoid looking directly at her. Thus he is able to behead her over his shoulder with the sickle. We notice that his approach is the opposite of Orpheus'. In looking back at his wife Eurydice as he is leading her out of the Underworld, Orpheus prematurely 'reflects' – that is, he adopts an ego perspective which belongs to the upper world of consciousness and is inappropriate to the realm of soul. He thus separates himself from soul, driving it back and losing it, as in fact he loses Eurydice.

Perseus, on the other hand, does not look at the underworld image head-on. He knows that the direct and literal approach of Heracles is useless in a realm of images. Instead, he adopts a hermetic procedure: he advances backwards and reflects forwards. Psychologically, he is the ego which lets itself be guided forward by the image of soul on which it is reflecting. He knows that the Gorgon is an image which is dangerous if taken literally, 'head-on', but which is neutralized when treated as the image of an image. His method is like a double negative: reflection renders Medusa positive in the sense that it recognizes her as real, but not literal. Taken literally, the image is lethal; but, taken seriously as an image, the Gorgon becomes vulnerable and able to be slain.

Now, Perseus flies off on his winged sandals, invisible under his helmet. These pieces of shamanic kit are really powers he has gained. Hades' helmet signifies the perspective of death, which, once acquired, assimilates you to the Underworld and makes you 'invisible' within it. The sandals signify the perspective of Hermes which enables us to travel freely, as he did, between this world and the Otherworld both above and below. It is Hermes, too, who arrives in time to help Perseus carry the magical wallet containing the Gorgon's head. In fact it is too heavy to be carried without him. The wallet signifies the way we have to create a sort of Stygian space in our consciousness so that when unconscious contents surge up – they may be petrifying – we are able to contain them and not be overwhelmed. With the help of Hermes' perspective, too, we can secure them and prevent them from falling back into the Underworld of the unconscious. We are then able to assimilate them so that they are no longer antagonistic but helpful, as the Gorgon's head helped Perseus to defeat his enemies. It will be obvious how much more subtle Perseus' approach to the Otherworld is than that of Heracles; how much less rigid than that of Sigurd; and how much wiser than both he is to enlist a variety of deities, a range of perspectives, with which to broach the terrible Unknown.

Soul and initiation

I t is an axiom for all religions that to understand reality, arrive at Heaven or achieve bliss we must die and be reborn. That is, we must 'die to ourselves' and be reborn as new selves. This metaphorical death takes precedence over literal death. It is the death of the ego in order that the self may come into being. Every society has developed so-called rites of passage to promote this metaphorical death and rebirth at biologically significant times: birth, puberty, sex/marriage and death. Western culture has all but done away with formal rites so that all-important initiations have to be reinvented and undergone informally.

Unlike monotheistic cultures such as ours which have polarized and opposed body and soul, life and death, traditional cultures see death as the corollary of birth – while life is continuous. Like the Greeks they distinguish, as it were, between *bios*, which is life in the biological sense, and *zoe*, which can be applied to the life of the individual soul as well, going on beyond the death of the body. Initiation is the continuous adjustment of ego to soul through a series of discontinuities – a series of deaths and rebirths, from ancestor to child, child to adult, adult to parent, parent to elder and elder to ancestor. Actual rites of passage tend to be seen as culminations of much longer processes. For example, when children are initiated into adulthood, they are often still regarded as incomplete until they are married – and even until they have children themselves, as if the whole of life were an initiation.

The most striking rites of passage are usually male puberty rites. Young boys are typically abducted at dead of night by frightening daimons, who snatch them away from the safety of their families into the wilderness or bush where they are starved, deprived of sleep, buried in shallow graves, incised with scars and, above all, circumcised.[1] The daimons are played by elders, disguised as sacred animals perhaps, or ghostly ancestors, or uncanny Otherworldly beings. The important thing is that the candidate should 'die' and become assimilated to the dead. Sometimes, among Australian Aboriginal tribes for example, they are not allowed to use their hands, to speak or even to look, except at the ground; and they have to be fed by their sponsors. This is a symbolic death but also a rebirth because the rite is seen as a return to babyhood where the initiate has to be taught how to eat and talk all over again.[2] Puberty rites are not perhaps so much an initiation into manhood as into 'personhood': beforehand the candidate is a non-person, rather as the Maoris say that a child is 'dumb' before he is tattooed on the face and thereby enabled 'to speak'. Girls are typically secluded with the women of the tribe at the time of their first menstruation, and initiated into the mysteries of womanhood, together with its sacred lore, stories and songs. If for some reason initiation is delayed, a boy or girl can enter their twenties without becoming a proper person. Physiological change is subordinate to psychical transformation. Initiation is like the inner meaning of biology.

After the very real pain and fear of the symbolic death, the initiates are taught a new secret language or allowed into a secret society; or simply granted admission to the 'men's house'. They learn how the world and its inhabitants were made – the Creation Myths – and how the arts of fire-making, cooking, hunting, planting, weaving, pottery-making and so on were introduced by daimonic or ancestral 'culture-heroes'. Beneath the surface of ordinary life there is another more potent life which suffuses every area of existence with a divine order. Initiation is the acquisition of the double vision which enables us to see through this world to that Otherworld; or to see this temporal world through the eternal viewpoint of that other.

Sex, drugs and rock 'n' roll

Rites of passage are what Western culture conspicuously lacks. Even the Churches' acknowledgement of their necessity – baptism, confirmation or first communion, marriage rites and funeral obsequies – have fallen into desuetude. It is unsurprising, therefore, if teenagers are troublesome. Either they stay at home, or as if at home – tied to their family in a childish state – and growing ever more sulky, self-centred and self-pitying candidates for 'Brat Camps'; or else they are driven unconsciously to try to initiate themselves through danger and pain. Young men spontaneously cluster into tribal initiation groups who get drunk and take drugs; get scars, piercings and tattoos; get into fights. In his book *One Blood* John Heale makes it clear that the younger members of gangs in London and Manchester regard a prison sentence or even getting shot as a rite of passage.[3] Desperate to prove their manhood, they welcome rather than fear these calamities because they are more afraid that, without them, they will never gain 'respect' – the recognition owing to persons as such. They would rather die, literally, than live without having undergone the metaphorical death of initiation. They might try sex, too, in the hope that this will somehow induce manhood. But it only induces, for all their swagger, despair because manhood must precede sex and cannot be attained through it. Many marriages are essentially the union of children, who want more from marriage – a sense of self – than marriage can supply.

For a while the gang, with its private language, rules, taboos and fierce comradeship, can provide a dawning sense of manhood; but it is, of its nature, a transitional state and cannot be prolonged indefinitely. Each member must be initiated into the tribe at large if the rites are not to become meaningless ends in themselves – and end in tears. But the tribe at large is a fragmented secular society with no formal connection to the imaginative life of the soul, no sacred consensus of myths. Worse still, it is organized horizontally rather than vertically. That is, there are no elders who, wiser by virtue of their greater age, can initiate the young because the young inhabit a different culture from the elders, to whom it is unintelligible, and vice versa. The only formal societies in which the elders can successfully break down the initiation candidate, instruct him in 'sacred' lore and reconstruct him as a full member are hierarchical organizations such as the armed forces, sports clubs, organized crime rings – and even the pecking orders of office life.

It is no wonder, then, that attempts to 'educate' youth into 'responsible behaviour' or to lecture it on 'Health and Safety' fall on deaf ears. A youth craves danger and pain to find out whether he can stand it, whether he is a man or not.

Wish and desire

So, what looks like self-destructive behaviour in young people is the result of confusion: they do not want to die in actual fact, they want initiatory death – and rebirth into a greater reality, a larger imaginative world, that will release them from the tormented consciousness confined within their heads. Many suicides are a failure of imagination. We are trapped inside ourselves, in an ever-narrowing cell, and cannot imagine a way out. In despair, that is, we know the situation must change, but we do not realize that it is ourselves which have to change in the first instance. We cannot make this imaginative leap, so we make the literal one – the only change left to us. If we had been able to manage some small measure of initiation we might have glimpsed the eternal world of imagination itself, in whose light temporal problems and prisons are put in perspective and seem more like opportunities for further transformation than dead-ends.

Unlike the tribal child who experiences that imaginative fullness at first hand, we have come to believe that there is no Otherworld. The old Greeks knew about it: Athenian citizens were initiated into the Mysteries of Eleusis. So secret was the rite that no one ever did more than hint at its content; but we know that a great revelation was vouchsafed to the participants, whose lives were not the same again. Imagination thrives on mystery. But mystery has come to be rather frowned on, as insufficiently 'accessible', like the Latin Mass; or else treated as a 'problem' to be solved.

Children retain a proper desire for the mysterious Otherworld. They like fantasy literature, comic-book superheroes, horror films; they like daimons, from elves and orcs to vampires and werewolves. Unfortunately, they are given fake daimons in *ersatz* Otherworlds provided by the prancing 'little people' on a television screen or by computer role-playing games – virtual realities of which they remain essentially passive observers.

The idea of imagination implies deep participation and the harnessing of real desires in order to effect self-transformation. Passive fantasy is ruled, not by desire, but by wish. The fantasy world of wish is the powerless world of the child, who can make any wish it wants because all are equally impossible. We may wish for many things – money, power, happiness, glamour, fame – but all wishes boil down to the same wish: to be magically and effortlessly changed into someone else. Of course, we might desire wealth and celebrity, for example, and we might acquire them if we have talent, an ability to work hard and a bit of luck. Whether or not our desire is *gratified* is another question because the desire for wealth is at root a desire for freedom, notably freedom from anxiety; while the desire for celebrity is at root the desire for the glory of soul. In the world of wish, however, no talent or effort is required: riches or celebrity are got by winning the lottery or appearing on television. Untalented children – girls even more than boys, it seems – on the TV show *Pop Idol* tend not to say, 'I want to be a good singer'; they say, 'I want to be famous. I want everyone to know who I am.' Behind this sad wish is the fear of the uninitiated: that they are not proper humans; that they are invisible. They long to be seen – seen as proper and whole individuals.

If we lose the transforming power of initiation, we go on living in the childish wish-world where self-transformation is feebly counterfeited by literal attempts at change, whether through travel, hoping to return as new people, or buying new things we don't need, or 'making-over' our homes or ourselves – if clothes and make-up fail, we try surgical alteration. Such measures can be manifestations of soul's beautifying impulse; but more often they are ways of disengaging with soul. It depends on whether there is a face behind the make-up or an empty mask.

Soul in general may desire many things, and our souls in particular may all need different things. But what all souls want is attention. Like the daimonic elves and fairies we used to leave food out for, or the dead we used to propitiate on Hallowe'en, or the sacrifices we burned for the gods, the soul needs feeding – where 'feeding' signifies heeding. Soul will not abide neglect. If we want to avoid the poison shirt, we must attend closely to all the images in which she appears to us, no matter how apparently inferior or insignificant, repellent or frightening. Only by talking to soul, and listening, can we know ourselves. If our puffed-up egos ignore her, we will lose her – not really, for soul cannot finally be lost. She is the Ground of all Being. But we can temporarily drive her away and stalk the Earth as disconnected empty shells, like zombies.

Taken

Just such a 'loss of soul' is a condition recognized by all traditional societies, for whom it is the principal cause of illness. Since it cannot be lost forever, it is simply lost in the Otherworld; and since this is also the world of the dead, we are in danger of having to follow it there, i.e. dying. In the folklore of Ireland, it was common to find humans who had been abducted by the fairies and compelled to live in their realm for seven, fourteen or even twenty-one years, when they were allowed to return to their Earthly village, old spent men and women – mere husks of humanity – to die.[4] For the people of fairy, the Tuatha dé Danann, were pleased to take young men for their strength, to help them in their wars and games; young women to marry; young mothers to suckle their young. For all their dazzle and glamour, riding in laughing cavalcades, their silver eyes flashing, as witnesses tell us, the Tuatha dé Danann seem to long for the robustness and substance of humans, just as we long for their beauty and wisdom.[5]

Those who are 'taken', as the Irish say, are said to be 'away'. What remains – what the fairies leave behind in the beds of the taken – is a 'log', or else 'a body in its likeness or the likeness of a body'.[6] This occurrence was presumably pan-European in the old days, for the elves, hulder-folk, trolls, vilas etc. of mainland Europe were no less rapacious than the Irish 'Good People'. It is the equivalent of what modern tribal cultures call loss of soul. It is so serious a condition that the afflicted person wastes away to an empty husk and, unless the soul is retrieved, dies. This is why the chief function of shamans is to retrieve souls which may have wandered off during sleep or illness; which may have been lured away or even violently abducted by daimons, sorcerers or the dead.

In Ireland people were especially vulnerable to abduction before the Church had performed its rites of passage for them. Babies before baptism, young women on the eve of marriage, young mothers who had not yet been 'churched' after giving birth – all these could be the more easily snatched because they were in an in-between state.[7] Soul loss is explained by modernity as a primitive diagnosis for babies who do not thrive, for young girls who are anorexic, for mothers who lie like logs in bed with post-natal depression. But since these sorts of disorder are more psychological than organic, the 'primitive' explanation may be just as near the truth – certainly the afflicted could well benefit from a shamanic cure, if we still had such a thing.

Sometimes a shaman cannot retrieve a soul. As the northern Australian shaman Willidjungo remarked, 'I can look right through a man and see that he is rotten inside . . . sometimes when people steal a man's soul in the bush he comes here to my camp. I go look; he is empty inside. I say, "I can't fix you up. Everything is gone. Your heart is still there, but it's empty. I can't fix you up." Then I tell everybody he is going to die.'[8] We have all met someone like that, I guess. Willidjungo is vividly describing a common malaise among Westerners: that sense of emptiness which comes from having lost any connection with a deeper self. We go to psychotherapists much as Willidjungo's clients go to him. They do not retrieve our souls as shamans do; but, if they are any good, they help us to travel into the Otherworld of the unconscious and locate our own souls, often lost at some decisive moment in the past.

If we do not lie down and die like Willidjungo's extreme cases or like the hexed African, it is probably owing to the strength of our egos, which go on driving us through our increasingly meaningless lives. We are not as vulnerable as members of traditional cultures whose egos are so intimately connected to the soul that they can easily wither away once the soul is lost, like the man who dies when his animal counterpart – his 'bush-soul' – is killed. But at the same time, the tribesperson is less vulnerable to the emptiness which so often besets us, who have severed the multiple tremulous threads which connect us to other souls, not only the collective soul of the tribe, but also to the souls of Earth and sky, animals and rocks and streams. We can even suffer from a condition unknown to the African or Australian Aboriginal – what psychologists call 'depersonalization'.

It is not like depression, although sufferers are depressed. They feel strange and changed, 'unlike themselves'. They no longer recognize themselves. Their actions seem to be automatic, as if they are robots. This lack of connection with themselves – their souls – is also, of course, an alienation from the world, which sometimes looks, literally, two-dimensional. It seems, as it seemed to Hamlet, 'weary, stale, flat and unprofitable'. Everything is monotonous, dry, empty and dead.[9] Enough to wither away any member of a traditional culture. But our indomitable egos go on driving us through our routines as if we were the machines we feel ourselves to be.

Indeed, we may begin to suspect that the materialistic view of humans as nothing more than computer-driven machines is the result of the collective depersonalization to which our culture has in large measure succumbed. Estranged from soul we have cut ourselves off from that imaginative life which naturally shows itself to us in brilliant personifications. So our psyches now present themselves as dark, empty voids. Worse still, because loss of soul is also loss of world-soul, our cosmos reflects our individual psyches. It becomes the black, empty, 'hostile' abyss of outer space. Such a view of the universe simply did not exist before the seventeenth century. The mathematician Blaise Pascal was perhaps the first scientist to take on board the modern vision of space, and to shudder at 'the infinite immensity of space of which I am ignorant and which knows me not . . . . The eternal silence of those infinite spaces frightens me.'[10]

It is disconcerting to suspect that 'depersonalization' is not just a psychopathological condition but to some extent our common state of mind; sad to think that we have swapped a vibrant, animate cosmos for a mechanical soulless universe, like the perpetual winter presided over by the wounded Fisher-King in the Arthurian legend. Only the Holy Grail can heal his wound and restore fruitfulness to the Waste Land. And what is the Holy Grail? Nothing less than the Soul of the World. Only a conscious effort of imagination to summon her daimons back can save us, together with an act of psychological faith that they will come.

Lost souls

In 1938, the psychoanalyst Bruno Bettelheim was snatched from his comfortable home and sent to Dachau and then Buchenwald. He was amazed at how fragile his world was, how easily it could be smashed. In less than a day he lost his belief in the strength of order and civilization. It was not so much the brutal beating he took on the train en route, but its senseless and arbitrary nature. On his arrival he found that these conditions continued: the smallest infringement of arbitrary rules was savagely punished. In fact you did not even have to break a rule – 'punishment' was random and indiscriminate. He came to believe that the purpose of the camps was not to punish, nor to create workers, nor even to exterminate – it was to destroy the prisoners' belief in their self-determination and their belief that they were persons as such. It was, we might say, to destroy their souls. According to the chemist and novelist Primo Levi, who spent time in the death camps, forcing the prisoners to operate the crematoria themselves 'had a meaning, contained a message: "We, the master race, are your destroyers, but you are no better than we are; if we so wish and we do so wish, we can destroy not only your bodies but also your souls, just as we have destroyed ours".'[11]

What was important to the Nazis was that every prisoner should live in fear of death at every moment. And it was this fear that corroded the soul, causing prisoners to turn on each other, even to police each other, so that there was little need for external force. It was the unspoken aim of the Nazis to prove a point: that the Jews, for instance, really were *Untermenschen*, sub-human, without souls. When the point was proved, as it were, they could be burnt as so much rubbish. If the Nazis' aim had been merely to kill, they would not have punished so brutally those who tried, and failed, to commit suicide.[12]

Those who did not kill themselves tried to hang on to their humanity. There were a few who were able to use the privation and violence as a means of initiation, but only those already advanced in sanctity could do so, given the extreme nature of the 'initiation'. For the remainder there was the constant fear of being reduced to the condition of *Müsselmanner*, or 'Muslims' – so-called because they had succumbed to a kind of fatalism, as Muslims were erroneously supposed to have. These unfortunates, reduced by the unremitting fear of death to naked egos, single points of craving, clinging to life and burning with desire, mostly for food, soon burnt out, and were left dragging themselves around like automatons. They even ceased to feed themselves. But the other prisoners were reluctant to help feed them because their condition was highly contagious. So the 'Muslims' were shunned, and soon died.[13] They formed 'the backbone of the camp,' writes Primo Levi, 'an anonymous mass, continually renewed and always identical, of non-men who march and labour in silence, the divine spark dead within them, already too empty to really suffer. One hesitates to call them living: one hesitates to call their death death, in the face of which they have no fear, as they are too tired to understand.'[14] The soul, it seems, can be all but extinguished before bodily life has ended. It cannot be destroyed, but it can be irretrievable – in this life at least. Nothing is clearer proof of the vulnerability of the soul than the fate of the 'Muslims'; yet, paradoxically, nothing is clearer proof of the soul's existence than to look into the vacant eyes and naked craving of one whose soul is lost.

Bettelheim was interested in what he called the psychology of extreme situations, such as he encountered in the concentration camp. But we are all liable to suffer soul-mutilation in far less extreme circumstances, whenever we are faced with tyranny, whether from a parent or a peer, a boss or a spouse. All they have to do is have power over us and to abuse that power, especially by imposing arbitrary rewards and punishments. As we have seen, arbitrariness is the key to successful brainwashing. It is in our nature to seek order and meaning so that we try to satisfy the powerful ones by predicting what they want and carrying it out. But we can never satisfy them, or detect their plan. Just when we think we are doing the 'right thing', we are reprimanded; but we might find ourselves being praised for something we simply guessed at. We endlessly debate with ourselves as to whether or not we are doing the 'right thing', or doing the thing right or not – and we end up policing ourselves. The powerful one becomes internalized, replacing our own selves.

Looking back, I was perhaps not as unfortunate as I thought at the time when, at puberty, I was isolated in the bush with my peer-group, deprived of food and sleep by elders, subjected to arbitrary and complicated rules, tortured and made to learn large amounts of sacred lore before I was deemed worthy of entry into the tribe. This was called a British public-school education, where the 'bush' was a rural spot and the 'elders' were those seniors who took it upon themselves by tradition to initiate new boys with ordeals and to make them learn all the school slang, like a sacred language, along with all the arcane customs, rites and meanings of ties, badges, colours and so on. Everyone colluded in the view that the school was providing education, but in fact the education was poor and secondary.

It was unwittingly providing initiation, to 'make a man of you'.

It is important that the fear and pain inflicted on initiation candidates is not personal. The smallest pinch delivered with malice hurts more than the hardest knock incurred by accident. In tribal life, it may be your father or uncle who is circumcising or starving you; but, painted or masked, he has become an impersonal daimon who is conducting you by force into the Otherworld. It is equally important that fear and pain are the prelude to an unmasking and a revelation of the beauty and mystery of tribal myth and religion. For if the torment is personal and prolonged beyond a certain point it does not bring the soul forth, but brutalizes it. Certain boys at school were not admitted to the 'tribe' but went on being tortured in a personal way – that is, they were victimized and bullied. For some, the consequent loss of soul led to nervous breakdowns, or even suicide.

The shaman's dismembering

All rites of passage are 'little deaths' in preparation for the last rite of physical death – and rebirth into the ancestral afterlife. However, all cultures recognize a special class of person who undertakes this final death and rebirth as it were prematurely. These people are the medicine-men, witch-doctors or shamans who are in charge of the tribe's sacred life as opposed to the secular life managed by the chief or elders. Their highly specialized initiation provides the blueprint for other, more usual initiations, rather in the way that mythic heroes pattern our own styles of ego and their stances.

The life of the shaman can be a lonely one. He is singled out and set apart from the tribe. He often does not marry, unless he marries a female daimon, rather as a poet 'marries' his Muse. Thus it is not uncommon for a shaman to try to ignore his vocation, which typically comes in the form of a sudden illness or apparent madness, a violent revelation or a 'big dream'. The sickness is essential because all shamans are 'wounded healers' who cannot heal until they have healed themselves. To this end, they leave their bodies and fly into the Otherworld.

The topography of the Otherworld shows a surprising uniformity across the world: an upper and lower region such as a sky world and an underworld; a world-tree which links them; dangerous means of access, such as narrow bridges or gaps, gates and rocks which slam and clash.[15] After the perilous journey, uncanny daimons – often the souls of former shamans – kill, flay or dismember the shamans. Then they are re-made, raised up and taught the sacred songs they will need to summon their daimonic helpers or familiars, and master the demons of disease. For their principal task is to tend the souls of the tribe when they are sick and retrieve them when they are lost. They combine the roles of doctor, priest and poet, which we have, whether wisely or not, divided and deprived of proper religious initiation – especially our priests who, instead of being chewed up like Inuit shamans by huge spirit bears, spat out and reassembled, simply sit theological examinations and dine with a toothless bishop.

The shamanic calling – perhaps I should say, the heroic vocation – is universal, but only occurs to the few. Since our culture has no official place for shamans, I dread to think how many go unrecognized or do not understand their calling. How many are madmen in an asylum, or suicidal poets, or anorexic girls fasting like saints? For it seems to be the rule that once a shaman is called he or she must shamanize, or die.

But, in a way, this is the rocky boat we all find ourselves in because we are all called by a daimon. If our fate is less dramatic than that of shamans who refuse or fail to understand their vocations, still we are liable to wither away or lead only half a life if we ignore the daimon's call.

We may further wonder whether the rise of the modern rational ego with its Heraclean strength, its sense of being the heroic exception and its corresponding obduracy, does not mean that we all require something more stringent than the usual rites of passage (which in any case we are largely denied). Perhaps because we all, to a greater or lesser extent, participate in a world-view which is radically estranged from the reality of soul, we all need the equivalent of the shaman's initiation if we are to open friendly relations with the Otherworld; or, to put it psychologically, to maintain equilibrium between our consciousness and the unconscious. If this is so, we should face up to what exactly is required by the shamanic vocation. And, if the shaman's initiation seems at first sight shockingly violent, it is not more so, I suggest, than the psychological wrenching we suffer in psychotherapy – or simply in the course of lives beset by the agonies of love affairs and bereavements, and illnesses which have strong elements of psychopathology.

First of all, we have to travel into the Otherworld. Of course, we all can – and sometimes do – travel involuntarily or spontaneously into the Otherworld; but only the shaman can travel there and back at will. He can do this because he has himself become a denizen of the Otherworld – become, that is, daimonized. This is why he is such an ambiguous figure, both central to the tribe and also marginalized; both welcomed and feared. He is uncanny, and a shape-shifter who may take animal forms. He is certainly not the serene, spiritual guru-like figure which some New Age devotees would have him be – he is more likely to be turbulent and trickster-like, colluding with the psychopathology soul is so fond of, rather than promoting the calm transcendence of spiritual disciplines.

Central to the shamanistic cultures of the Arctic and sub-Arctic regions, from North America to Siberia, and then down through Asia to Indonesia, is the necessity of dismemberment.[16] This occurs, too, among the shamans of South America, who use one or more of over a hundred hallucinogenic plants to effect initiation. The Siberian shaman Dyukhade was dismembered by an Otherworldly blacksmith, who seized him with tongs the size of a tent, cut off his head, sliced his body into pieces and boiled the whole lot for three years. Then he put the head on his anvil and hammered it, dipping it in cold water to temper it. He separated the muscles from the bones, and then put them together again. He covered the skull with flesh and re-joined it to the torso. He pulled out the eyes and replaced them with new ones. Lastly, he pierced Dyukhade's ears with his iron finger and said that, now, he would be able to hear 'the speech of plants'. After this, Dyukhade found himself on a mountain. Soon after, he woke in his own tent.[17]

A Yakut shaman described how his disembodied head watched the preparation of its body. In a procedure analogous to the butchering of reindeer, 'they hook an iron hook into the body and distribute all the joints; they clean the bones, by scratching off the flesh and removing all the fluid. They take the two eyes out of the sockets and put them on one side.' The bits of flesh are then scattered on all the pathways of the Underworld, or else they are eaten by the nine (or three times nine) spirits that cause sickness, whose ways the shaman will thereby know in the future.[18] While the shaman is being system-atically dismantled and reassembled, blood oozes from his inert body as it lies in his tent surrounded by anxious relatives.[19]

If dismemberment is not universal, something very like it is so widespread that it might be called archetypal. In the early stages of initiation into Tibetan Buddhism, for example, the neophyte must meditate in a graveyard and be dismembered by the spirits of the dead. Throughout Asia and the Americas, it is common for initiation candidates to see themselves as skeletons[20] – that is, stripped down to the bone before they are reconstituted. Amongst the Aranda of Australia, the initiate is lanced through the neck by a 'spirit' while sleeping at the entrance to the initiatory cave. The spirit then carries him inside the cave, tears out his internal organs and replaces them with new ones. Instead of the 'iron bones' of the Siberian shaman, the Aranda initiate has quartz crystals inserted into his body. These are supposed to be of celestial origin and only quasi-material as if they were 'solidified light'. They confer powers, such as the ability to fly.[21]

Meanwhile, shamans among the Angmagsalik of Greenland are initiated by a shamanic bear, which is larger than an ordinary bear but so thin that its ribs are visible. Sanimuinak was eaten by such a bear. It came out of the sea, circled him for a while and then bit him in the loins and ate him. It was painful at first; but then all sensation left him. However, he remained conscious until his heart was eaten. At that point he lost consciousness, and was dead. He woke some time later, at the same spot. He walked by the sea. He heard something running after him. It was his breeches and boots and frock, which fell down so that he could put them on.[22]

Initiations are not always so violent. The farther south in North America you travel, the more the motif of dismemberment is replaced by the more familiar fasting and praying of, say, the Plains peoples. A characteristic Native American initiation has been described by the Sioux medicine-man Leonard Crow Dog, who was only a boy at the time. The ritual process may not involve dismemberment but it is not without its trials, tribulations and horrors. The whole experience is one of radical transformation, beginning with Leonard's symbolical 'cooking' and purifying in the sweat lodge. He is then taken to his 'Vision Pit', dug like a grave on a nearby hill. He stays there for two days and three nights without food or water, praying for a vision until the tears run down his face. At last an inhuman voice speaks to him out of the darkness, saying, 'This night we will teach you.' He finds himself out of the pit and in another world – a prairie covered in wild flowers and with herds of buffalo and elk. He meets supernatural beings: an ancestral wise man, an eagle who confers power on him, a pale hairy formless creature whom he has to wrestle. Then someone is shaking his shoulder. It is his father. The Vision Quest is over, and Leonard returns, reborn, to the village where he begins life as a medicine-man.[23]

Raising the dead

Shamanic dismembering may seem alien to us until we remember that something like it lies at the roots of Western culture and is therefore an active component of our psychology. The core myth of dynastic Egypt, for example, was the death and resurrection of the god and culture-hero Osiris. His brother Set trapped him in a sarcophagus which was flung into the river Nile and floated out to sea. His sister Isis roamed the world looking for him, like Demeter searching for the Kore. She finally rescued Osiris, only to see him torn by Set into fourteen pieces. She reassembled and revived him, and he became the ruler of the Underworld.

In Greek mythology, 'twice-born' Dionysus was torn to pieces as a child by Titans, and then boiled in a cauldron. He was rescued and resuscitated by his grandmother Rhea. His dismemberment was repeated ritually by his Maenads during his Mysteries, with a goat playing the part of the god. Orpheus, the archetype of the shaman in our culture, was also of course dismembered by Maenads after he had returned from the Halls of Hades, having failed to retrieve Eurydice, his very soul. It was said that his head floated all the way to Lesbos, where it was enshrined and able to utter prophecies.

In Norse myth the all-father Odin, chief among the gods, but also a culture-hero, is hung for nine days on the wind-swept world-tree without food or drink and pierced with a spear, in order that he might receive the runes – the precious art of writing. He even plucks out one of his eyes in exchange for knowledge.

Christian mystics can sometimes be recognized as shamanic

types. We think of St Francis of Assisi fasting in the wilderness, where a fierce angel pierces him with fiery darts, giving him the first stigmata – the five wounds of Christ; or of St Teresa of Avila whose exquisite agonies were inflicted by heavenly arrows; or St Mary Alocoque, whose heart was ripped out in an ecstatic trance by Christ Himself. He put it in His heart – the Sacred Heart of subsequent veneration – where it was inflamed before being replaced in her body.[24]

The pain of initiation is like an operation by soul on the body to free itself from an identification with the body. Like all ascetic practices, it opens us into a more imaginative state of mind, transcending biology. Our culture tends to treat us humans as only biology, as sorts of organic machinery. If we get ill our medicine is geared up for mechanical solutions. It is particularly admirable in its assiduous efforts to keep us alive. Death is medicine's enemy. The reason for this is that the archetype behind medicine is personified by Apollo's son, Asclepius. He was so good at medicine that he started raising people from the dead. Naturally Hades complained to Zeus that he was being deprived of his rightful subjects – whereupon Zeus put a stop to Asclepius' activities by striking him with a thunderbolt.

Soul lives in the realm of the dead and so will always under-mine Asclepian projects, such as our own medical ideal, to promote physical life at all costs; will always undermine the ego's project of building bodily strength, health, fitness and fantasies of immortality. As an expression of soul, though, the body is a rich mine of images. Its ailments are metaphorical as well as physical, its symptoms are questions. What burden am I carrying, asks Backache; what do I not want to hear, asks Ear Infection; what am I loath to swallow, asks Eating Disorder; what is wrong with my emotional life, asks Heart Disease; what is constricting me, asks Lung Problem . . . . Even crass physical ailments such as a broken leg may be soul's way of compelling the head-strong ego to stop dead and reflect on her. Every pain is a potential portal onto the Underworld where the Rich One waits with death, yes, but also with his unimaginable treasure.

One of Christianity's strengths lies in its treatment of suffering. Its God was the first not only to incarnate himself as an ordinary man, but to experience through crucifixion maximum suffering. Thus Christians can detach themselves from personal suffering by the double movement of substitution and exchange, placing their suffering in Christ that He may suffer for them as they in turn suffer for Him. At the same time, Christian literalism has tended to polarize the shamanic experience. It becomes either a wholly spiritual rebirth or else a literal resurrection of the body. The shaman's initiation is neither: it takes place in the daimonic 'in-between' realm, neither wholly spiritual nor wholly physical – completely concrete and real, but not literally so. It is not disembodied and angelic, but full of psychopathology – wrenching, twisting, alchemical scorching, butchering. In a sense Freud tried to bring back this kind of initiation by uncovering the discomfiting truth about the soul's perversity, by wresting it away from spirit's repression and reinstating the in-between world of 'abreaction' in which the awful moment when soul became fouled or choked can be lived again in all its intensity, releasing the sufferer into another, richer and more mythic life-story.

Actually we all intuitively understand the concrete yet metaphorical nature of shamanic initiation because whenever we suffer the loss of something or someone crucial to us, from a job to a loved one, we spontaneously use the language of dismemberment. 'I feel completely shredded,' we say. 'I'm all in pieces . . . gutted . . . my heart has been ripped out . . . it's surreal . . . like a terrible dream . . . I seem to be in another world.' These are the experiences which can transform our lives forever and for better if we can resist the temptation to sedate them and instead use the enormous energies they release to reassemble ourselves – with iron bones perhaps, for strength; new eyes for insight; and a new heart for affection.

If we want to initiate ourselves voluntarily, we are faced with a lack of understanding of the need for formal rites, as well as the rites themselves. We have to embark on our own path of ego-abnegation, perhaps ethically, through hardship and selfless service to others; or imaginatively, through patient and deep attention to, and constant celebration of, the minutiae of existence – which are not only the prerequisites of art, but of any life in touch with soul.

There is another way, too, by which we instinctively understand the reality of shamanic initiation and by which we are willy-nilly initiated – through dreams. Our nightly dip into the oceanic unconscious keeps the ego fluid and encourages it to deconstruct itself as it takes on different roles and adopts different stances in the dream world – starts to realize it is only one facet of the great glitter ball of the psyche. If, however, it clings to one facet, as the rational ego does, everything else in the unconscious seems hostile. It tries to flee, but finds itself rooted to the spot or as if running through treacle because the literal, muscular stance does not function in the Otherworld. It has to face the images it finds so frightening. They will prove harmless, or if they do not – if they inflict damage – that is precisely initiation. All initiation feels, to begin with, like breakdown and regression; but if the ego surrenders it finds that it is not plunged into madness and chaos, as Jung feared, but – as he discovered – into the clarity and precision of a myth.

A modern shaman's journey

When Jung sat at his desk and let himself plummet into the unconscious, as I recounted in Chapter Five, the myth he met with as he watched the dead blond hero float by, followed by the scarab, the red sun and the fountain of blood, was his personal myth; but its deeper meaning, as a myth of our times, was revealed to him more clearly in a dream he had six days later, and to which he attached extraordinary importance.

'I was with an unknown brown-skinned man, a savage, in a lonely rocky landscape. It was before dawn; the eastern sky was already bright, and the stars fading. Then I heard Siegfried's horn sounding over the mountains and I knew that we had to kill him. We were armed with rifles and lay in wait for him on a narrow path over the rocks . . . .

'Then Siegfried appeared high up on the crest of the mountain, in the first ray of the rising sun. On a chariot made of the bones of the dead, he drove at furious speed down the precipitous slope. When he turned a corner, we shot at him, and he plunged down, struck dead.' Jung is filled, in the dream, with unbearable guilt at having killed 'something so great and beautiful'. He wakes, turns the dream over in his mind, but is unable to understand it. He is about to fall asleep again when he hears a voice within him say: 'You *must* understand the dream, and must do so at once . . . . If you do not understand the dream, you must shoot yourself.' In fact, he has a gun by the bed. He becomes frightened. He begins to reflect more deeply on the dream, and suddenly its meaning comes to him: it is 'the problem that is being played out in the world. Siegfried, I thought, represents what the Germans want to achieve, heroically to impose their will, have their own way . . . *I had wanted to do the same.* [my italics] But now that was no longer possible. The dream showed that the attitude embodied by Siegfried, the hero, no longer suited me' – or, I might add, any of us. 'Therefore it had to be killed.'

The warning voice of what was doubtless Jung's personal daimon told him that if he failed to understand the dream – the metaphor – he might have been compelled to act it out literally; to undergo literal rather than initiatory death. In killing Siegfried he is killing the kind of ego no longer appropriate to him, or to Western culture. It is a painful moment. Jung felt 'an overpowering compassion, as though I myself had been shot: a sign of my secret identity with Siegfried, as well as of the grief a man feels when he is forced to sacrifice . . . his conscious attitudes.' But 'there are higher things than the ego's will, and to these things one must bow'.[25] Paradoxically, the alliance with these higher things is in the first place an alliance with the 'lower' – the primitive, shadow part of ourselves; the savage who initiates the killing.

Death is the last and unavoidable initiation. It is up to us how we approach it.

ELEVEN

Soul and afterlife

' . . . I was going down a long black tunnel with a tremendous alive sort of light bursting in at the far end. I shot out of the tunnel into this light. I was in the light, I was *part* of it, and I knew everything – a most strange feeling.'[1]

This could well be a description of the culmination of the Greek Mysteries in which, as Plutarch says, 'the soul has the same experience at the point of death as those who are being initiated. First one is struck by a marvellous light, then one is received into pure regions and meadows.'[2] In fact, it is the description of a modern Near-Death Experience (NDE), which may therefore be included in the kinds of experience I have been calling initiatory. In Apuleius' *Golden Ass*, Lucius describes the Mysteries of Isis in similar terms. 'As I drew near to the confines of death . . . I was borne through all the elements and returned to earth again. At the dead of night, I saw the sun shining brightly. I approached the gods above and the gods below . . . .'[3]

The spontaneous initiation of the NDE is less structured. 'It was a dynamic light, not like a spotlight. It was an incredible energy – a light you wouldn't believe . . . . It was feeding my consciousness feelings of unconditional love, complete safety, and complete, total perfection . . . . My consciousness was going out and getting larger and taking in more; I expanded and more and more came in. It was such rapture, such bliss. And then, and then, a piece of knowledge came in: it was that I was immortal, indestructible. I cannot be hurt, cannot be lost . . . .'[4]

NDEs belong to a family of religious experiences which include initiation into the Mysteries, such as those of Demeter and Isis, and the vision of God which St John of the Cross, for example, aptly describes in terms of God and the soul 'in participant transformation': 'the soul seems to be God rather than a soul, and is indeed God by participation.'[5]

The light shining like the sun at midnight and, out of the light, the Presence of divinity, irradiating them with love and a sudden torrential access of understanding of who they are, where they have come from, what it has all been about – this is what the NDE-ers bring back to us like initiates from their Otherworld journey. They come back, as St John says, *balbuciendo*, stuttering, 'I can't explain . . . there aren't the words . . . it's indescribable . . .', but convinced beyond all doubt that the ineffable experience was absolutely and awefully real. And from then on, in spite of the gainsayers who cry 'temporal-lobe epilepsy' or 'chemical changes in the brain', 'wish-fulfilment' or 'defence mechanism' – they say the same about falling in love – the lives of the NDE-ers change for the better. They no longer fear death and they live more altruistically, knowing that their greatest good comes from serving others and heeding the gods.

As I suggested in the Introduction, it is likely that more people believe the NDE-ers – believe that when they die they will be gathered into paradise by rejoicing relatives – than believe in a simplistic ideology which dismisses an afterlife out of hand. Perhaps most people do. We do not know because they do not have an organized voice in a secular society. If they see their loved ones, plain as day, at the moment of the loved one's death far away; if they go on sensing the real presence of a husband or wife after the death of these spouses; if they hear their partners speak to them, clear as a bell, after death – they tend to shut up about it. They do not want to be ridiculed for something so precious to them. They know what they saw and heard, and no amount of reductionist psychology or physiology will talk them out of it. I side with these people, just as Socrates, when asked about the learned opinion concerning a nymph of the Ilissus, said: 'the common opinion is enough for me.'

Near-Death Experiences

Thousands of Near-Death Experiences have been so well documented[6] that they have become a cliché: the initial out-of-the-body experience, floating up to the ceiling of the operating theatre and clearly hearing what the surgeons are saying; the journey through the tunnel; the bright light which does not dazzle but engulfs you with love; the sense of detachment from the world, even from loved ones; the feeling of peace and joy; the appearance of dead relatives and/or a 'being of light', a divine presence.

'I was standing next to a figure the same height as me,' said a young man who, after having his skull smashed in an accident on his bicycle, was not expected to live: '. . . he had his arm across my shoulders . . . I have since described this figure as a guide because I found it so hard to say I met God. But it was God – "my" God. As I looked at him he impressed on me that I was seeing the God I had been brought up to envisage . . . I knew that the grey-haired, white-robed, non-sexual (by that I mean he was man and woman or neither) being beside me would be everything to all "dead people" . . . .'[7]

The personal daimon, whom we at last meet face to face when we die, may look like a twin, an angel, a god, an ancestor, Jesus – we may not know its face but we will recognize it at once because we have unwittingly known it all our lives. Some will experience it as the personal aspect of an impersonal deity; others will experience it in an opposite way, as the impersonal aspect of the personal daimon.

Typically, the daimon – often just a voice coming out of the light – conducts a voluntary 'life-review'. 'For me,' writes Phyllis

Atwater, 'it was a total reliving of every thought I had ever thought, every word I had ever spoken, and every deed I had ever done; plus the effect of each thought, word and deed on everyone and anyone who had come within my . . . sphere of influence whether I knew them or not (including unknown passers-by on the street) . . . .' She surmises that we exist in a vast 'sea or soup of each other's energy residue and thought waves' where we are 'held responsible for our contributions and the quality of the "ingredients" we add.'[8] In a modern reinvention of the world-soul, David Lorimer adds his gloss to the experience. 'The only picture with which the above account makes sense is one of an interconnected web of creation, a holographic mesh in which the parts are related to the Whole and through the Whole to each other by empathetic resonance. It must be the sort of Whole in which we and the rest of creation live and move and have our being, a conscious-ness-field in which we are independent strands.'[9] Here we have another modern retelling of the Neoplatonists' belief: that our individual essence is grounded in that great consciousness they called the Soul of the World. We are drops in that supernal ocean; or, perhaps, snowflakes – each structured in the same way, yet each unique – in the blizzard of soul.

So, in the life-review, we look down on the panorama of our lives; we observe causes and effects as simultaneous rather than separated by time and space; and we experience the conse-quences of our deeds – and misdeeds. This is inevitably painful, but we are not crushed by this pain, firstly because it is balanced by the joy of all the good we have done; and, secondly, because we are now detached from the conditions that would cage us in guilt, remorse and self-recrimination. The life-review is conducted, in short, by and in an ethos of truth, justice, beauty and goodness. We have no word to describe our ecstatic partic-ipation in this ethos, this intimate yet universal divine presence, except Love. We are glad to know the depth and extent of our guilt because we want to participate as fully as possible in the Love which already bathes us; and, to do so, we have to acknowledge the truth of our transgressions in thought, word and deed. Repentance and forgiveness signify the mutual desire of us and Love to remove the obstacles which prevent our union.

Moreover, the daimon shows us that our lives are not divided into chance events and more meaningful, destined events. Rather it is a single life which should be viewed through 'double vision'. At once we see that chance and destiny are the outside and the inside of the same thing. It depends on our point of view. Events that look random in one way, look destined in another. Our lives are like a piece of embroidery: on one side, all loose ends, cut threads and knots; but, turned around at death, a marvellous coherent picture. The reconciliation of chance and destiny may be called Providence. When we marvel at the chance that brought our parents together in order that we might be conceived, we also feel that it was fate because we all feel that we are unique beings destined to be born. Thus every birth is providential, an interweaving of chance and destiny that we do not have to separate but can embrace through imagination. Some religious doctrines try to rule out chance – for example with the belief that we 'choose' our parents before birth – just as some scientistic doctrines try to rule out destiny with the belief that everything happens randomly. But the truth lies in a re-imagining of each as an aspect of the other. Analogously, free will is married to fate, whereby whatever is freely chosen is also forever ordained. Just as the absolute freedom of Love can resemble the absolute determinism of the Law, so we are both free and determined, as if (to use a Christian metaphor) the cosmos were in a constant state of creation through our collaboration with God – as if whatever we choose in time, He makes immutable in eternity.

The narrow bridge

The geography of the afterlife reported by NDE-ers is both indistinct compared with the precise landscapes of traditional peoples, and far more highly customized. This was not always so. Carol Zaleski has described the surprisingly uniform afterlife of medieval Christendom as reported by NDE-ers of those times. Their souls encounter a figure of light who leads them out of darkness and across the statutory narrow bridge, below which the souls of the damned are being tortured by demons. We see here how the dismembering daimons of traditional initiation have been converted by the Christian imagination into demons of punishment.

Over the bridge, there is a boundary such as a river or wall which they cannot traverse without remaining permanently in the Otherworld – that is, dying. But the guide explains that the ideal country full of blessed souls they can just glimpse is not Heaven but the Earthly paradise. In other words, there is an attempt to reconcile the soul's idea of an immanent paradise – this world transfigured – with the spirit vision of a Heaven beyond this world.

And so they return to their bodies, repentant and converted and ready to convert others, much like the secular NDE-ers of today, but without the Christian terminology. The latter, too, report similar borders where they are often given the choice as to whether they wish to return to Earth or to 'pass over'. All are amazed at how little they find themselves tied to Earth and even to their loved ones, and how reluctant they are to come back, so great is the sense of peace and happiness; but they do so out of a sense either of duty or of 'the time not being right' – of having still to accomplish the daimonic plan. Their ability to be so dispassionate stems from the fact that the daimon not only conducts our 'life-review' but is also, as carrier of our fate, indistinguishable from it. We see our past lives through its eyes. We see how our spouses and children, for instance, have destinies quite independent of the Earthly affection and attachment we have invested in them and so we can let them go.

Re-entry into the body can be terrible. 'I had left without the slightest struggle,' writes Leslie Grant Scott, who nearly died during an illness in Ceylon in 1931. 'I returned by an almost superhuman effort of will.' She had realized she was dying, yet felt comfortable and happy, her mind 'unusually active and clear', her consciousness increasingly acute – '[I] was aware of things that I had never contacted. My vision also was extended so that I could see what was going on behind my back, in the next room, even distant places.'[10] Her anger at having to return to her body – 'compressed, caged, in a small stupid prison' – echoes down the ages: the simile of the flesh as prison or tomb is used by Plato and, bitterly, by the even more dualistic Gnostics. Yet, from William Blake's point of view – that spokesman for soul – it is not our physical condition which is the problem, for 'Man has no Body distinct from his Soul; for that call'd Body is a portion of Soul discern'd by the five Senses, the chief inlets of Soul in this age.'[11] It is we who have betrayed the body. 'For man has closed himself up, till he sees all things thro' narrow chinks of his cavern'.[12]

When we die, few of us go straight to Heaven. We may have a taste of it, as Near-Death Experiencers report, when the full and interconnected meaning of the universe sweeps through us on a tide of love. But, as the NDE-ers also say, we are in a place of transition which can, just about, be described – that is, put in literal terms – because something of the literal world still adheres to us. It is a place which some Christians call purgatory, where the life-review with its remorse and rewards is initiatory. Some traditional cultures, such as the Native American – as we shall see – are explicit about this. They not only have to cross the narrow bridge but they also endure such ordeals as brain-removal. Modern NDEs seem smooth and unproblematic by comparison. Yet it may be that the 'brain-removal' stage of the transitional journey is taking place on the operating table, which is where most NDE-ers have their Otherworldly experiences. Perhaps medical procedures are literal enactments of initiatory processes: what from the doctors', and our body's, point of view is an effort of curing, is from the soul's point of view an initiatory wounding. Indeed, it may be that long illness prior to expiration is initiation – illness may even be brought on the body by the needs of the soul, especially if we have neglected the soul during life. Certainly we have learnt that ease of entry into the Otherworld depends on our degree of initiation. No doubt the great mystics slip easily into that permanent union with the Godhead they achieved on Earth. Socrates and the Buddha seemed to have had no trouble dying. Poets who have seen through the illusion of the literal world will step smartly into Paradise. For the sick and lonely, death will be a release, a flood of well-being and communal joy. But those who die suddenly or unexpectedly may find themselves bewildered and lost at first, even unaware that they are dead. They have only to ask for help, however, or even merely to desire it, for help to be at hand. More serious, of course, is the state of those who do not ask for help, or do not desire it, because it would mean admitting that the afterlife they did not believe in, existed.

NDE-ers confirm rather than contradict what the dead allegedly tell us directly through, say, Spiritualist mediums or modern-day 'channellers', the echo of their voices growing fainter and more inarticulate as they approach the border of what can be described. Until that point is reached, however, the Spiritualists do provide us with longer, more detailed narratives about the afterlife than the brief nature of NDEs allow.

The afterlife of T. E. Lawrence

Some of the most famous spirit messages were those given to Emanuel Swedenborg. In 1745 he had a vision of Christ in a

London café, after which he was able to converse freely with 'spirits'. They were quite Neoplatonic in their ideas, telling him for instance that there is an underlying unity of life emanating from the one infinite source they called Love. Everyone is connected to everyone else and eternally united with the Source. But each person has a 'proprium' – what we call an ego – which tries to live as if it were independent of the source, or God. Our task is the more or less Christian one: to recognize the illusions and selfishness of our proprium and to repent, that is, to 'turn around' and so re-orient ourselves towards God and thus be worthy of redemption – the Divine retrieval of the soul from the proprium's hellish world. It is a combative view of psychic life, in which reality contends with illusion, Heaven with Hell, good spirits with bad. It is the proprium which separates us from the higher levels of Divine emanation which are experienced within us, at a celestial level and a spiritual level. In the afterlife this inner world manifests itself outwardly, mirroring the conditions of Heaven, Hell or the intermediate state of spirits, according to whichever of these states the dead person inhabited while alive – albeit unaware of his or her state because it was screened by bodily existence.[13]

There are two main sorts of Spiritualist message. The first is personal and intimate; and while it cannot provide absolute scientific proof of an afterlife, it can be extremely convincing. Even a stalwart materialist such as the American psychologist William James was persuaded of the authenticity of some mediums at least when he met Leonore Piper. Although he was repelled by the triviality of many of her communications from the spirit world – a common complaint against Spiritualism – he could not in the end deny the accuracy of the details Mrs Piper relayed concerning his private life and that of his friends. He became a Spiritualist, but showed his grasp of the daimonic nature of the Otherworld when he concluded that God must have intended the spirits to remain baffling, 'to prompt our curiosities and hopes and suspicions all in equal measure,' so that, 'although they can never be fully explained away, they can also never be susceptible of full corroboration.'[14]

The second kind of message from the Beyond is of the Swedenborgian sort, describing the afterlife and its philosophical precepts. Both of these can be banal: the 'spirits' often describe the same landscape of flowery meadows, lovely weather, colours we do not have on Earth, and so on; while the unexceptional philosophy – usually of a generalized 'theosophical' kind – tends towards the wearisome sermon, complete with warnings not to cultivate atom bombs or to despoil the environment. Even Swedenborg's description of the spiritual world is leaden. It resembles nothing so much as a vast bureaucracy of spirits, appropriate, I suppose, to the civil servant (an assessor of mines) Swedenborg had been prior to his vision of Christ. He influenced Blake; but it is a telling fact that whereas Swedenborg saw spirits that he took literally, as revelations out of which a religion was formed, Blake saw daimons that he understood metaphorically, as insights out of which he made art. The Spiritualists are as literal-minded as the materialists they mirror. Just as soul does not like to be trapped by the body, equally it does not like to be trapped by the spirit. Neither body nor spirit are actual traps, of course – the trap is the actual. The Spiritualists like to see the spirit as casting off the body at death like an old overcoat; but, from soul's point of view, it is the overcoat of literalism we have to cast off, to reveal the body as it always was: the subtle and immortal form of the soul.

Nevertheless I am as disinclined to write off Spiritualistic communications as delusional or false as I am to take them as gospel. One should be in two minds about them, in concert with the perennial ambiguity of the daimonic. They are revelations of a sort. Their very literalism makes them straightforward and appealing to many people. They constitute a kind of 'folk religion' which, as with all religions labelled 'folk' or disparaged as 'superstition', we do well to stand up for, because all beliefs are true, or, as Blake said, 'an image of truth', even if none are literally so. Besides, there are many interesting Spiritualist writings. Stainton Moses' *Spirit Teachings* are all the more impressive for having been communicated through the medium of a conventional clergyman, who was by no means happy with the unchristian teachings his spirits dictated to him via 'automatic writing' (i.e. when the spirit takes control of the medium's inert hand while he or she is entranced). Stewart Edward White's *The Unobstructed Universe*[15] anticipates the physicist David Bohm's celebrated distinction between the implicate and explicate order of the world. One of the founders of the Society for Psychical Research, Frederic W. H. Myers, was sceptical about life after death, and thought that psychic phenomena came from the 'subliminal mind' – the unconscious – until he was forced to concede that many spirit communications displayed a knowledge that the medium could not possibly have, even unconsciously. Colin Wilson is surely right when he says that no one can read Myers' classic of psychical research, *Human Personality and its Survival of Bodily Death*, with an open mind and not be convinced of the reality of an afterlife. The trouble is, as he also remarks, almost no one does read with an open mind – we are all confined to our own viewpoints. Worse still, Myers' book is difficult to read at all: a little under fourteen hundred pages in two volumes of dense argument and evidence couched in turgid scientistic language tends to numb the mind more than illumine it.[16]

To get a better idea of the Spiritualists' afterlife, I would like to summarize the narrative, published as *Post-Mortem Journal*, given to the medium Jane Sherwood through 'automatic writing' between 1938 and 1959. It is worth a longish look, firstly because it expounds many of the Spiritualist axioms, but is more interesting than most communications because the spirit in question is far from being a happy soul in Heaven. In fact he purports to be the troubled spirit of T. E. Lawrence ('Lawrence of Arabia'), who died in a motorcycle crash. Secondly, the account gives me the opportunity to comment more fully on such questions as the 'laws' of the afterlife and the nature of reincarnation.

Through the hand of Jane Sherwood, then, Lawrence (as I will call him) writes that his sudden death left him in a kind of stupor. He sets off through a shadowy world, surprised that his existence is continuing and that his body feels like flesh. He finds that he is being drawn to wherever his thoughts stray – to a town, for example, where mean-looking, vaguely menacing people live in murk. Alarmed, he flees from the town with a new realization: 'my own desire could lead me towards its fulfilment if I knew clearly what I wanted.'

At once he hears a voice, asking him if he needs help. Lawrence replies that he does; and the voice then manifests as a light which leads him to a brighter landscape. This presence introduces himself as . . . 'Mitchell'. He explains how the hateful town was created by the emotions of those who live there; how, in fact, emotions cannot be hidden as they can on Earth, but show up immediately in your body and so have a direct effect on whoever you are with. This is painful for Lawrence, who has always repressed his volcanic emotions – but even more painful for Mitchell, who is on the receiving end of his resentment and despair. Seeing the instant effect his emotions have on others helps Lawrence to deal with them.

Mitchell takes him to a sort of 'sanatorium', where he is encouraged to release some of his forbidden desires. He embarks on a sexual relationship with a woman whose condition exactly complements his own. Each supplies the other with the kind of sexual experience they need. It is more satisfactory than Earthly sex because their bodies can be interfused in a bliss unavailable to physical bodies.

Lawrence continues to be drawn as if automatically to those who are at the same level of 'development' as himself, and who complement his needs, such as his need to overcome distrust and resentment of others and to cease feeling superior to everyone. He sees the damage this does to himself as well as others, and learns humility, especially when he sees the suffering of the lovely clear soul of Mitchell as it absorbs and transforms the bursts of hatred and anger his 'patients' are prey to. If this sounds a bit like psychotherapy, we might remember that psychotherapy was born out of the demands of the unconscious, the soul itself; and it can therefore be read as an Earthly attempt to replicate an archetypal – an Otherworldly – pattern of purgation.

Almost since his first moments in this new world, Lawrence has been aware of his past life unfurling before him. It is like the 'life-review' but in his case it is extended over a long period. It is not until he is much 'stronger', for example, that he begins as if physically to feel the injuries he has done to others and to accept them in all their fullness. He likes the way that Mitchell offers no palliative measures: he has to suffer the consequences of his actions and, as a result, over time, his own pain decreases.

In the afterlife, 'like attracts like'. There are many who cannot face the consequences of their actions at first and they live in diminished circumstances. But nothing is rigid, everything is based on affinity and sympathy, so that a single pang of remorse or a single selfless thought brings immediate relief and 'higher' conditions. Lawrence is aware of other spheres both 'below' and 'above' his state. Both are painful to approach as if they have 'natural' barriers – the first because it has a dark and damaging atmosphere; the second, because its light is too dazzling and intense. Life is 'indestructible'. Each soul goes to its own place and 'no one is damned however he may be warped by evil but that by effort and suffering he can free himself from it.'[17]

Now Lawrence joins a sort of 'university', which is very

congenial to him, having been a scholar as well as a man of action on Earth. He participates in lively and humorous debates – about reincarnation, for example. He finds that when he thinks, he is not alone but part of a conference which includes one soul still on Earth, two on his own 'plane' and one on a higher plane – all communicating through mental affinity.

Lawrence begins to realize that he has been 'trying to complete my Earth experience; to fill in the gaps and make good some of its deficiencies . . . I am now very alive to the defensive egoism which spoilt and wasted my years on Earth . . . But nothing can compensate fully for what I have missed; nothing here can parallel the all-and-everything condition of close human relationships on Earth.'[18] As we sow, so shall we reap – this law obtains in the Hereafter, as it does, if we did but know it, on Earth. The importance of incarnation is that it is 'the formative stage when alone any real growth in essence takes place.' In the afterlife the law of affinity ensures that conflict is removed and so 'there is no struggle for existence. Our work here is a kind of mopping up operation.' (A characteristic military turn of phrase). However high we ascend through the planes, however much we purify ourselves, there is still no actual growth in the 'essential spirit'. What we bring from Earth remains our all, so our fate is bound up with our Earthly experiences; only in the struggle and turmoil of life are we able to make any real difference to our spiritual stature.[19]

The post-mortem story of 'T. E. Lawrence' cannot of course be taken too literally, but it is a worthy attempt to translate the foreign conditions of the afterlife into Earthly language. It does not contradict other accounts of the afterlife, nor what we know about the soul, imagination and the Otherworld. Yet we notice how strongly Lawrence brings a 'spirit' perspective to the afterlife. Everything is depicted in terms of hierarchical planes; of growth, development and progress; of strength, ethics and intellectual 'university' life. His very desire to go on communicating with this world is an indication of the way he is interested in making a 'study' of the afterlife. He can describe it in more or less literal terms because he is still existing in those terms. At the same time, all the anomalies of his situation work on him from the outset as if in a long process of deliteralizing. All his learning experiences can be read as attempts by soul to reflect and thereby dissolve the dominant spirit perspective, acclimatizing Lawrence to the Otherworld of imagination. Already he has begun to see that we not only occupy the same space as those for whom we have an affinity, but that space itself is defined by the imaginative state of our souls. He sees that what was inside is now outside. He is still poor at self-reflection, so he sees his own emotions grossly reflected by another. He faces the consequences of his Earthly misdemeanours only gradually because they are too grievous to confront all at once. But increasingly he suffers the results of his transgressions or omissions as if we were punished, not *for* our sins, but *by* our sins. He understands that the oppositional conditions of Earthly life are essential for soul-making because desire is immediately gratified for better or worse in the Otherworld, where there are no barriers of matter, space, time or causality against which the soul can be abraded and honed.

Living other lives

While we exist on Earth, we are also living in the Otherworld. It is just that we are not usually – or, at least, continuously – aware of this fact until we die. Incarnation is a 'forgetting' of our eternal origins and anamnesis is the recollection of them – a recollection which is for most of us at best shadowy, fleeting and vague as a dream. The life-review given to us by the personal daimon is a full remembrance, both of our divine origins and of our temporal existence.

Reincarnation makes literal and successive what is really metaphorical and simultaneous. It is often envisaged as the return to Earth of some part of ourselves rather than the whole personality. For instance, Oriental beliefs tend to maintain that it is not our 'essence' that is reincarnated but only our wrong attitudes and desires – our karma – which cross lifetimes until they are extinguished in nirvana. Plotinus thought something similar: that our 'higher soul', our original and sinless essence, is separable from our 'lower soul', which is drawn down after death towards a state dictated by its desires; and which reincarnates at a level of existence appropriate to that state. Alternatively, the soul has been pictured as a fragment of a larger, collective soul – a fragment which has to reincarnate in order to become fully itself before re-joining the whole. All such ideas are attempts to reconcile the image of the soul as indivisible and eternally complete, with the need to see it as capable of transformation. They are attempts, that is, to smooth over the paradox that, as microcosms, our souls are individual wholes – yet parts of the collective macrocosm of the world-soul. They are both divisible and indivisible, mutable and immutable. Their contradictions cannot be resolved by thought but only by imaginative vision, something that will present itself to even the most unimaginative of us when we pass over into Imagination itself.

Perhaps we can try to re-imagine reincarnation. Its succession of lives might be a literal interpretation of the way soul circulates through a succession of perspectives; or, rather, holds different perspectives simultaneously as if in the retinue of all the gods, while highlighting now one, now another. We know how easily the deity who is presiding over our lives can be suddenly usurped by another whenever we are seized by a new idea, a religious conversion, a craze for art or fly-fishing, or a passion for someone we could never have dreamt of fancying. Even if a new deity does not storm the parapet of consciousness, it is operative in the unconscious where we live other lives or other versions of the same life, as we do in the permutations of a recurring dream: the divorced man dreams that he is reconciled with his wife, that he is killing her, that they never got divorced, that they are living happily together, that they are torturing each other, that she is pregnant by the US President and so on, perhaps over years of dreaming. Our actual life may not be our only life or even our real life. We may be living other lives in the Otherworld of the Imagination, lives of which we are hardly aware until, as it may happen, they burst forth and we find ourselves taking a completely new direction. But the new life does not have to become actual to be real, though latent, in the unconscious. So, if we portray such lives as past or future incarnations, it is more a reflection of our proclivity to turn myth into history, to make literal what was always real, but in an imaginative fashion.

Analogously, once we have passed over into the world-soul, it is not always possible to separate our lives from the lives of others, so complete is our empathy. 'Reincarnation' could be a metaphor for the way our souls participate in the experiences of other souls. For the Soul of the World is also what W. B. Yeats called the Great Memory, where all experience eternally lives on, so that we can take on the memories of others as our own. In this scheme we do not live one life after another but, as Heraclitus enigmatically said, we are 'mortal immortals' always 'dying each other's life, living each other's death'.[20] We are dissolved in the world-soul and condensed out of as if by turns, for these 'turns' are actually what the liberated soul experiences simultaneously, like circular breathing. The wheel of *samsara*, which carries us out of life and into death, and back into life again, can be read as a metaphor for soul's circular motion as it distils itself out of itself, manifesting now as spirit, now as matter, in the endless imaginative reconfiguring that constitutes soul-making.

When Lawrence discusses reincarnation with his pals in the afterlife, he concludes that we have to live again in order to 'overcome our weaknesses'. As long as we fail these tests of strength, the same pattern will recur and we will not 'progress'. We see here how the doctrine of reincarnation is viewed through Lawrence's very Protestant – even puritanical – spectacles. The emphasis is all on willpower and passing tests, as if a stronger ego were the key to success in life. Perhaps the very recurrence of 'tests of strength', as he envisages them, is precisely owing to his inability to cease treating them as tests in which the ego remains intact, and to begin treating them as caustic solvents of that same ego. Reincarnation may only be the lot of those who cannot embrace the polymorphous soul but remain wedded to spirit's single viewpoint. They have to act out – act out on Earth – what others can participate in through imagination.

Plato's cave

Yet we must not forget, too, what Lawrence reminds us of: the paradoxical importance of spirit's literalism. Without it, soul would have nothing to 'see through', nothing against which to contend in the stretching of imagination to its fullest extent. Reincarnation can also be read as a metaphor for the encasing of soul in 'single vision' and all its apparent absolutes, from the opacity of matter to the obduracy of space, time and causality. In its own imaginative realm, soul can get no purchase on itself. Only through Earthly life can it transform itself.

Nevertheless this notion does not stop Lawrence from believing that although we may not be able to transform ourselves essentially, we *are* able to change in the afterlife, by becoming fully aware of the state of our souls. If we, so to speak, unpack everything we are and all that we have become, attaining self-knowledge, we are able to progress to 'higher' planes. This is also very much part of spirit's perspective, part of its liking for hierarchical systems and ascending trajectories. Most people who imagine the afterlife think of it as some sort of system of planes ascending towards the One or God. We should take these schemes seriously because they are archetypal and therefore integral to the Otherworld. But we should also remember that systems of levels, rungs, planes etc. are only real providing we take them as images, as ways of configuring the imaginative space of the Otherworld, rather than taking them at face value.

Accordingly, if we were to imagine the afterlife in a hierarchical way, as a set of rungs on the ladder of 'development' or 'progress', we could follow J. N. Findlay's quasi-Neoplatonic map, sketched out in his book *Ascent to the Absolute*. We would expect the first rung of the ascent towards the One to be similar to our world of the senses. But sensory experience would be subject to the imagination so that perceiving and imagining would be simultaneous, our vision shared by other souls as we share theirs. On successive rungs, meaning will be more and more concentrated in the instant, as if it were music, and will not need drawn-out explanation or demonstration. We will become less embodied, yet retain a form of ourselves recognizable to anyone we are drawn to. Spatial separation will become insignificant, since we will arrive wherever we desire at the speed of thought. Our identity will coalesce with that of others so that it will become less and less important, and less possible to say exactly in whose experience something is occurring. We will be introduced by our daimon to our presiding deity, who is likely to be the daimon itself but unmasked. At any rate, we will experience the deity either spiritually and abstractly, as an impersonal Form; or bodily and concretely, as a personified image; or both at once. And we will be led via this deity to another, and another, all interrelated, until we begin to see the One who underlies them all, the unspeakable Void that is yet an absolute Plenitude where the goal of spirit is fulfilled.

The attempt here is to reconcile the many gods of soul with the One of spirit; but because it is a linear progressive model, spirit has the last word so to speak, unless either we stipulate that the One is not the end but that it fountains forth again in the multiplicity of soul, or we come up with a model of the afterlife which combines soul and spirit, the One and Many – something I will be attempting in the next chapter.

Meanwhile I will end on another hierarchical scheme of afterlife development: Plato's famous Allegory of the Cave from Book VII of *The Republic*. It is ostensibly about the path of the philosopher to enlightenment, but it might equally apply to the passage from this life into the next. It is a spiritual ascent which also takes soul into account through its emphasis on the importance of reflection and seeing. In one way, that is, it is a long journey; in another, it is a short step if we but see truly. The allegory is a clever one because, knowing that enlightenment and the afterlife are equally difficult to represent, Plato supposes that our own natural world is the heavenly one while our Earthly condition is, by comparison, to be chained up in a cave, facing a blank wall with a fire behind us. As people and objects pass to and fro in front of the fire, we see only their shadows, and the shadows of ourselves, cast upon the wall. We think these shadows are reality, just as if we were to mistake the projection of a film onto a screen for the real world. To achieve a truer perception we have to turn around – in a sense, to reflect; or take a point of view opposite to everyone else's. At once we see the fire and the things in front of it directly; and this is as near to a vision of reality as most of us ever come.

But we are only at the beginning. While we believe that the fire is the only source of illumination, the initiate or philosopher leaves the cave altogether. Suddenly to see the real world in the light of the sun is as different from the cave as sight is from blindness. It looks strange at first, even unreal, until our eyes grow accustomed to the different kind of light; but soon we begin to discern this new world truly, in all its gorgeous and various forms. (Indeed, really we are in the intelligible world of the Forms which provide the models for our shadow world.) Finally, we are able to look directly at the sun, by which all things are illuminated (a symbol, of course, for the One Form of the Good).

And what would happen if we went back to our old position in the cave? Our eyesight would be impaired by the return to darkness; we would see less of our old world. Everyone would say that our trip to a so-called upper world had ruined our vision and that only a fool would attempt the same journey . . . .

TWELVE

Soul and Otherworld

The most intense emotion felt by the Kikuyu of East Africa is reserved for the rich red soil of their homeland, which nourishes them and to which they are bound by sacred ties – each family's land has been tilled by the ancestors since time immemorial. For their neighbours, the Masai, it is the grassland which is sacred and numinous because they are not cultivators but herders, and all their love and reverence is bound up with their cattle. For them, it is sacrilege to dig up the immense pastures of swaying grass over which they love to roam.

In death, therefore, the Kikuyu ideal is to be buried in the ancestral soil and to live a happy life in the fields of the Hereafter. The Masai on the other hand are horrified at the thought of burial. They wish only to be laid out under the stars, with a pair of sandals and a cattle stick in their hands, to be disposed of by jackals and vultures while their souls join the ancestral herders who live like stars in the heavens and drive their celestial cattle across the sky.[1]

The Otherworld for traditional cultures such as the Kikuyu and the Masai is like this world. I use the word 'Otherworld' rather than afterlife because I want to indicate the ambiguity of their post-mortem state. It is like the ambiguity which attends body and soul, or shadow, as I outlined it in my first chapter. The afterlife is a separate condition as the soul is separable from the body. But, just as the soul also retains an identity with the body, the afterlife is also as it were in this world because traditional cultures believe that they already inhabit the best of all possible worlds. The idea of the Otherworld is intended to convey this ambiguity. It is like this world, only better – there is none of the pain, dearth and drought which sometimes disfigures Earthly existence. Conversely, we might imagine life for tribal peoples as already taking place in the Otherworld, so charged is their existence with richness of meaning. Even hardship, pain and physical decay have meaning since they signal relationship with daimons and gods, albeit an inharmonious relationship which has to be amended. The old age which so dismays us is for them the accumulation of mana, wisdom and respect; its proximity to death brings far-sightedness.

The Bantus of South Africa will say – much to the confusion of anthropologists – that the dead go to a great village in the earth where life is good. Or, to a country in the east; or in the north. Or else they have remained in the house of the living – or they might be wandering the bush as wild animals.[2] The apparent vagueness is really metaphysical subtlety: as we have seen, the location of the dead in a variety of places is a metaphor for the non-spatial nature of the Otherworld. We might say: there are many other worlds – but they are all in this one. In Greek myth the 'Upperworld' of the sky god Zeus and the Underworld of Hades may seem poles apart. But Zeus and Hades are brothers. Their worlds are the same, but seen from different perspectives. Zeus sees the world from above, through the light; Hades sees it from below, through darkness. Zeus gives the world its lofty spirit; Hades, like soul, supplies life's shading and depth.

Spirit imagines its afterlife as a world outside of time and elsewhere in space, over the hills and far away; soul imagines its

Otherworld as if inside time, enfolded in every moment, and always present. This is why it is available to poetic vision, like William Blake's when he saw 'eternity in a grain of sand and heaven in a wild flower.'[3] For W. B. Yeats we enter at death an 'earth-resembling life' which is 'the creation of the image-making power of the mind, plucked naked from the body'.[4] For the Otherworld is all shape-changing imagination. It configures itself according to the outlook we bring to bear on it. It is the landscape of the heart, the self's true home. It may be a cottage, a castle or a cosmos, but we are not *in* it, as we feel ourselves to be isolated entities inhabiting this world. Rather, it is the outward manifestation of our inner selves, as if we *are* our own landscape and habitation. Heavenly city or pastoral Arcadia, our Otherworld may be an ideal version of a place on Earth, not because we remember that place with love, but because the place on Earth was already a memory, a shadow, of the divine prototype. It may even be an abstract space of pure geometry rather than an Elysian Field, but whatever it is, we will not so much live in it as wear it like a heavenly robe. Like the daimon's identity, it will be exotic, amazing – yet strangely, deeply familiar.

'Paradise is a state of being', wrote the poet Kathleen Raine, 'in which outer and inner reality are at one, the world in harmony with imagination. All poetry tells of that vision . . . . And ultimately the many are sustained by those images of a lost perfection held before them by the rememberers' – a reference, this, to the poet's power of anamnesis. 'Such . . . is the whole and sole purpose of the arts and the justification of those who refuse to accept as our norm those unrealities the world calls real'.[5]

So powerful among the old European cultures was the feeling that this world was the best that – in their myths, at least – we find a reluctance to leave it. There are long and terrible lamentations in Irish mythology for the dead heroes who will no longer hear the blackbird's song or the babbling brook, no longer ride laughing to hounds or rejoice in their strength in battle. As the shade of the Greek hero Achilles remarks after he is summoned back from the dead by Odysseus: 'We who are parted from this world have the strongest desire to return to it again'.[6]

The sensuous life of the pagan heroes is wrought up to such a pitch, it seems, that deprivation of the body can only be a diminishing of life. We can all empathize with the robust heroic perspective. Death would not be death without some bitterness and regret. It is not physical death, however painful, which is bitter – it is only, after all, like slipping off the leaden diving suit we needed to breathe on Earth. Rather it is the death of the ego's fierce attachment to life which is bitter, like the tearing-off of Nessus' shirt.

The Greek and Norse heroes feared slipping insipidly out of life. Our dream of dying peacefully in our beds was anathema to them. They were desperate to die gloriously in the heightened state of mortal combat so that they would not fade away to the condition of a shade in Hades or Hel but be received among the heroic dead, rejoicing in the Elysian Fields or feasting in the mead-halls of Valhalla.

Platonic philosophy replaced the idea of the exceptional man – the hero was precisely what the rest of us could not be – with the idea of the wise man, the philosopher, who has already left Plato's cave while in this life. But such a state of illumination was for the few. Both hero and philosopher belonged to the elite. One of Christianity's attractions lay in making both the hero's sensuous paradise and the philosopher's enlightenment available to everyone. Its afterlife was determined by ethics. It was not the glorious hero or the enlightened philosopher who necessarily entered Heaven, but the good person. Or, at least, the penitent person, who took on responsibility for his or her own initiation, as it were, by abnegating egoism, overcoming

fear and attaining humility and selflessness. Even in our increasingly secular times the democratic nature of the afterlife seems
to have persisted, if the NDE-ers are to be believed; and we are
all permitted to enter bliss, providing only that we realize that
we must reap what we have sown.

In traditional cultures those who have gathered enough
mana in life, enough personal power, like the Greek heroes,
doubtless pass directly into Paradise. But for ordinary people it
is usual to enter a transitional place, like a liminal, or 'threshold',
zone which is analogous to the ones reported by Spiritualists
and NDE-ers, especially the medieval NDE-ers whose motifs of
narrow bridges and perilous fires are often found in tribal
accounts of the immediate afterlife.

Approaching the Otherworld

When the Winnebago people of Wisconsin and Nebraska die,
they find themselves on a spirit road leading to the land of the
dead. The first person they meet is 'Grandmother', to whom
they must give a pipe and tobacco. She feeds them with rice
and then breaks open their heads, taking out the brains. After
this, they forget about their people and no longer worry about
their relations on Earth. Instead, their dead relations appear
and help them across the precarious bridge which spans a great
fire raging across the Earth from one end to the other, until they
are brought safely to their new village, where they live in a great
lodge along with all the ancestors.

People of the Thompson River tribes in British Columbia
travel, after death, along a twilit road beneath the ground. It
winds down to a shallow stream they cross by means of a log.
On the other side, the trail climbs to a height heaped with the
clothes which, back on Earth, the living have brought. Three
guardians send back to Earth those souls whose time has not yet
come. The remainder are directed to a great mound-like lodge
in which they can hear talking, laughing, singing and beating

drums. When they enter the lodge, they find themselves in a wide, sweet-smelling, grassy country where it is always light and warm, and where dancers come forward to carry the newcomer on their shoulders in delight.

For the Guarayú of eastern Bolivia, the dead follow a narrow path choked with weeds, and cross two dangerous rivers: the first via the back of a ferocious alligator, the second by jumping onto a tree trunk which races between each bank. If they fall off, they are torn to pieces by palometa fish. They have to travel through a darkness lit only by the burning straw which relatives have placed in their grave. They have to shoot, but not kill, humming birds and pluck their feathers as a gift for the great mythical ancestor, Tamoi. They must undergo ordeals, such as negotiating a way through clashing rocks, and being tickled by a monkey without laughing, until they reach the paradise of Tamoi − where they are washed with magical water to restore their youth, and where they live happily, just as they lived on Earth.[7]

These descriptions of what happens to the soul immediately after death have both similarities to, and differences from, Western accounts. There is the same period of transition between the moment of death and the entry into Paradise. But for traditional cultures this transition is explicitly initiatory − it is only the final initiation in that series of deaths and rebirths which define life. A crucial part of the transition, we notice, lies with the participation of the living, whose grave-gifts of clothes, food, weapons, tobacco etc., are bits of equipment necessary to guarantee a safe passage. This suggests that we should not neglect funerary rites but support the dead, if not with literal grave-goods, then at least with prayers, wakes, vigils, sung Masses and the like, because the dead remain near to us for a while and seem to be helped in their passage if we remain mindful of them.

Whereas we do not know where we will find ourselves when we die, and even Christians do not agree on the topography of the afterlife, there are no surprises for tribal people. They find themselves in the Otherworld familiar to them from the tribe's myths, a landscape kept vital and alive by the shamans who regularly travel there and back. There is no wrench from bodily life into spiritual life: because their bodily life is already 'subtle', just as the material world is transparent to the non-material, they slip more easily than we do into the Otherworld. Nor is there any need for blinding light or supernatural revelation: they have already encountered the fullness of life and the sacred myths of the tribe in previous initiations. Hence their immediate afterlife is more likely to be twilit, symbolizing an in-between world, before they enter their bright Paradise.

The traditional Otherworld is highly concrete, but not literal, as our afterlife accounts tend to sound, as if we carried over our literalism with us. Yet the Otherworld of soul is not a different world from the afterlife of spirit. It is the same world but experienced in a metaphorical rather than a literal way. Thus there is no emphasis on spiritual ascent and development in the traditional Otherworld, nor any moral progression or growth – the soul simply goes to its proper home, as if the Otherworld were parallel to this world. If there is movement, it is not linear or ascending but circular, as we have come to expect of the soul. This circularity finds metaphorical expression in belief in reincarnation, which is common in traditional cultures. The worlds of the living and the dead are so close, almost transparent to each other, that the dead are liable to slip back into the world of the living, to circle easily between them or, as we have seen, even exist in both at the same time but in different forms.

There is no 'life-review' in tribal Otherworlds because 'judgement' is continuous in this life. Since everything in this world is held to be ensouled, every wrong action is immediately reflected in the environment as some kind of misfortune, such as bad hunting or foul weather. If the miscreants are not obvious, as people who have offended the ancestors or broken a taboo for example, they are soon rooted out by questioning or by a shaman's supernatural detection. The wrong-doers then pass the same verdict on themselves as the tribe does. There is shame, in other words, but not guilt – which presupposes the sort of inner life that we have, where what is in our hearts can remain hidden until we die, and all is revealed.

The only kind of Hell in the Otherworld is exclusion from the life of the ancestors because this is also exclusion from the life of the tribe – the tribe is always thought of as being composed of the living and the dead together; and, if anything, the dead are pre-eminent. We can see, too, why tribespeople are reluctant to convert to, say, Christianity: they fear that they will be cut off from the tribe when they die and live in the Otherworld alone.[8]

The proximity of the dead to the living makes funerary rites a delicate matter. The living revere the dead but also fear them because the dead can inflict harm, whether through jealousy or a desire for revenge, or even unwittingly, through attachment. The mutual participation of living and dead can become contagion.[9] Thus funeral rites can take weeks, months and even years, as the living ease themselves away from the dead without offending them. In some societies, such as the Dowayos of the Cameroons, the interred body will be dug up again when the flesh has had time to decompose, and the bones – identified with the immortal part of the person – will be stored in a special skull-house. There they will be revered at first, but more and more neglected until at last mud is flung at them to show that the dead are now remote enough from the living to present no threat.

Here we see how precarious 'soul' cultures can be. Their equilibrium is so finely balanced that without an element of 'spirit', they can suffocate under the weight of their own belief in the spirits of Nature, restless ghosts, malign ancestors and undetected witchcraft. In constant dread of the daimonic, which they now perceive as more harmful than helpful, they can live more in fear than in freedom. Greek polytheism may well have reached such a point of saturation when the new dualistic philosophy sprang up, and Plato's single Form of the Good provided a pure and brilliantly lit distillation of the dark, seething proliferation of gods and daimons. Analogously, the monotheism of Christianity may have been partly embraced because it offered relief from the stifling polytheism of Roman religion, with its 'almost infinite number of divine beings'[10] inhabiting virtually every grove, spring, rock and tree. Part of the attraction of the modern scientific method, too, was that it seemed to lift Reason's head above the 'clouds of demonic rumour'[11] which bedevilled sixteenth-century Europe with its medieval belief in magic, witchcraft and all manner of daimonic infestation. All these developments used the leverage of the 'spirit' perspective to achieve some traction on a 'soul' culture which had become bogged down in the cloying opulence of its own images.

The Inside-out World

'If there is one unvarying feature of the realm of the dead,' wrote Lucien Lévy-Bruhl of tribal societies, 'it is that it is the reverse of the living.'[12] For example, the Cayapa of Ecuador believe that the sun and moon in the 'lower world' of the dead travel from west to east. For the Bataks of Sumatra the dead go head-first downstairs and their markets are held by night instead of day, which is when the dead sleep. For the Pacific islanders of Aua the canoes of the dead float bottom-up above their submarine villages; for the Dyaks of Borneo the dead speak the same language as the living, but every word has an opposite meaning.[13] In parts of Indonesia, however, among the dead the words mean the same but are spoken backwards. When the Sora of northern India cut down trees to make a clearing, it annoys the dead who are cultivating the same trees.[14]

The idea of reversal, therefore, expresses the discontinuity of this world and the Otherworld but also maintains continuity – they remain connected, even interwoven. The relationship is reciprocal. Sometimes the Otherworld is seen as complementing this world; sometimes it is the inside-out version of this world; at other times it is the mirror-image of this world. However, it is not opposed to this world. It is the spirit perspective, and the monotheistic religions, which tend to take the archetypal image of reversal and turn it into opposition. The afterlife becomes a polarized and inverted version of this world, as when Christianity asserts that 'the last shall be first'. To polarize is also to literalize, so that the afterlife is depicted as equally literal as Earthly life, but in an opposite way – what was matter is now spirit, what was darkness is now light, what was suffering is now joy, and so on. It is as if the Cinderellas and Goose Girls of fairy tale were allegorical figures who invert the social order by becoming princesses, just as the country bumpkin Parzival becomes the perfect knight who wins the Holy Grail; or, for that matter, as the little carpenter becomes the Son of God. From soul's point of view, however, these characters are not 'upside-down', not inverted, but reversed, 'inside-out' – the goose girl was already the princess in the first place, and had only to be revealed as such.

To put it in psychological terms, Jung often writes as though consciousness is opposed to the unconscious. He describes how dreams are compensatory, presenting us with inverted versions of our waking lives in order to redress imbalances in the psyche. He also divides life into two halves: the first should be devoted to the development of consciousness and to forging relations with the outer world; the second should be more attentive to the unconscious – as we move towards death we should become more detached from the world, attending to soul's deeper, less personal concerns and confronting the world-soul and its daimons. We have to follow soul's promptings to orient ourselves away from this world and towards the Other. But if we are strangers to soul, such promptings threaten us. We are afraid of embracing a wider existence and cling to what we were, trying to renew the first half of life by running off with younger women and embarking on militant anti-ageing campaigns.

Conversely, we are not taught to heed the whisper of the daimon in the first half of our lives. Even those of us who do manage to discern what our soul wants and needs, do not believe strongly enough in its paramount importance because, as Jung often said, our peculiarly modern malaise is to be estranged from soul. So we are tempted, for instance, to put soul 'on hold' until we have made enough money, bought enough time, acquired enough security, to start doing 'what we should really be doing'. But our essential selves cannot be put on hold. We are changed by what we do meanwhile. And the neglected soul, like any lover, pines away so that when we wish to embrace her again, she is nowhere to be found.

We do not have to take Jung's two halves of life as gospel. They are two aspects of our single lives, one conscious and the other unconscious. Their movements can be complementary rather than antagonistic, like interlocking spirals. It is our double vision by which the one sees through the other; and their mutual abrasion which shapes the iron bones of the self. Outer events are entwined with their inner meaning so that when we die we are turned inside-out: what was inner and hidden is now outer and manifest. Earthly life is like that of a dull chrysalis which cannot imagine it will one day take rainbow flight.

Of course Jung was only describing what he observed: a culture in which the ego is so strong that it casts the soul into darkness and places itself in polar opposition to the unconscious. Attempts by the unconscious to compensate for this merely seem to the ego like demons coming out of the dark in the form of threatening images, hellish nightmares, irrational fears. The unconscious reflects back at us the face we show to it. Analogously, the Otherworld reflects whatever stance we approach it with.

So, if we were to approach Hades, say, with the humble and self-effacing attitude of one who has been initiated, we find that he is Plouton, 'the Rich One'; and his realm is one of unimaginable treasure. Whoever has died to themselves finds superabundant life. But to those who approach Hades in the blaze of their own worldliness, certainty and egoism, his realm will seem a shadowy, grey, god-forsaken place. Worse still, under the forceful Heraclean glare of the rational ego, the Otherworld will appear to lose substance altogether and become – as militant rationalists insist – non-existent. This is not an option for monotheistic religions, of course, and so they offer us either Heaven or Hell, depending on how we have lived our lives – depending, that is, on what attitude we bring to bear on the afterlife, what state of soul we carry into death.

Heaven and Hell

Since we Westerners do not have the same agreement about the geography of the Otherworld as traditional cultures, we are more at the mercy of our own imaginative capacities when it comes to entering the afterlife. This is exciting and liberating in one way, but perilous in another. How far do we trust ourselves to dream up a state of bliss?

I am pretty confident that I can imagine Heaven. I will find myself being chauffeur-driven from my Mediterranean villa, well stocked with the finest food and wine, swimming pools and compliant women, to the party at the palace where all the rich and famous and powerful are gathered to congratulate each other on having made it to Paradise. Feted and lionized by this exalted company, I am the Guest of Honour – *I* am heaped up with all the praise and admiration I was denied in life. Naturally I am modest and gracious, but pleased. We are all pleased – pleased with each other and ourselves. So pleased and self-congratulatory, in fact, that we do not hear above the chatter and chink of glasses filled with vintage champagne the singing of angels above our heads. Too busy catching the eye of other men's beautiful wives, we do not look up. We do not notice that those who wait on us are helpful daimons; we do not hear them ask us in whispers whether we would care to step outside for a moment, through the doors of the great hall flung wide, where there are interesting views . . . . We are happy where we are, comparing successes and triumphs with a noise that, to the angels, sounds like the squeaking of bats, the sound the dead are said to make in Hades.

The Heaven I have imagined is, of course, the Heaven of the egotists – which to everyone else is Hell.

We know that Hell exists because we see people every day trapped in little hells of their own making and, whether through fear, self-centredness, defiance or simply habit, unable to escape – unable, that is, whether through a lack or distortion of imagination, to walk out. For the gates of Hell are always open. It is we who do not take the single step into Heaven, despite the prompting of our daimons and the imploring of our ancestors, because to walk through would be to admit of another life outside ourselves, which, having admitted it, we would have to lead. We would have to change, and this we cannot do: however miserable my little self, it is mine, all mine, and I won't let go of it.

And so we go on partying, listening to the echo of ourselves, day after day, under a dazzling sun and a sky of uniform blue, until one day perhaps we find ourselves longing for a cloud to appear. And it does appear; and in its shadow we see for the first time the face of our pool-attendant. It is the face of an old familiar friend – we can't quite remember the name – who asks us if we might like to swap a swim in the heated pool today for a dip in the ocean, just beyond our high electrified fence, where we had never noticed it before . . . .

This fanciful scenario is to remind me that I must be suspicious of finding myself in any Heaven I can imagine. I do not mean that Heaven cannot be like this world – indeed it will, initially at least, be like this world, but unutterably transformed, just as those who have experienced in this life the great Visions of Nature or of the Beloved have reported. Hell may well be getting the Heaven we have imagined – I should say: fantasized. Since nothing is outside soul's imagining, even our egoism is a way of imagining. The trouble is, it does not give itself up to Imagination, but manipulates and coerces it for its own self-serving fantasies. It insists on its own version of Heaven, and this is why there may be no Hell – only a myriad false heavens. As Virgil remarks in *The Aeneid*, 'each one of us we suffer the afterworld we deserve'.[15]

Among the 'many mansions', therefore, which Christ attributed to his Father's Kingdom, we must suppose that there is, for example, a Valley of Shadows, peopled by souls who refuse to admit that they are dead; a Narrow Street of the timid, who cannot give up the habits and routines of their life on Earth; a Gridlocked Highway of the trapped, who cannot give up the jealousy, resentment and hatred which binds them to their former lives; and a Hall of Slumbering Atheists, who have insisted on oblivion. Even the Angelic Cloud of the Pious can seem like a false Heaven to a man of 'Genius', as William Blake calls himself. In 'A Memorable Fancy', he lampoons the unimpeachably orthodox Christians by depicting their perspective on his paradise of the Imagination: 'As I was walking among the fires of hell, delighted with the enjoyments of Genius, which to the Angels look like torment and insanity . . . .'[16] To the purely spiritual, that is, soul's imaginative bliss can look like Hell.

Consequently, we cannot logically be denied the right to

burn always. Since there is no coercion in the Otherworld – Love is the only power, but it will not use force – we can defy soul, personal daimon, God, indefinitely. Theologically, this is the sin of pride. It can be seen in those tyrants and Man-Gods, such as Hitler and Stalin, whose self-exaltation and conviction of their own divine rightness leads them to believe that everyone else is beneath them and, indeed, barely human. They secretly desire that all others should be soulless numbers or corpses. Therefore, after death, they stalk alone through a wasteland of an Otherworld, a death-camp of an afterlife, whose scent is burning flesh, whose music is the screams of the dying – their perfect Heaven. But even these satisfactions are not enough because the void left by the denial of soul is bottomless and can never be filled, no matter how many other souls it devours. And so they are gnawed by the vultures of a craving that can never be gratified and burned by a thirst that can never be slaked.

We can, and do, forget, ignore, renounce, sell or betray soul – but we cannot get rid of it. We will have to face it in the end. I take the optimistic view that most of us will tend to face it sooner rather than later. I am hopeful, for instance, that even hardened materialists who deny any Otherworld will quickly see their mistake. If the impact of death itself is not enough of an initiatory shock to wake them to the reality of the Otherworld, there will always be some fragment of imaginative life to appear before them and prise open a crack in their ideological preconceptions – something like the selfless engagement they had with their work or something overlooked like the love they had for a pet. After all, the realities of soul they denied during life will have built up a head of steam in the unconscious and can scarcely be prevented from bursting out at death, like the dazzling presence of Christ which blinded the arch-persecutor of Christians on the road to Damascus.

We all wear the shirt of Nessus because it is really the skin of the soul, which cannot be removed without tearing ourselves to pieces.

It is the gift of Love, which warms and nourishes, illumines and delights us – unless we resist it. Then, of course, it burns like Hell. But in truth the burning is only Love's attempt to fit us for bliss.

Eternity and perpetuity

It may be that Hell is nothing other than our refusal to give up our literalism. If we insist on maintaining in the Otherworld the constraints of Earthly time, for example, the timeless state of the Otherworld symbolized by the word 'eternity' becomes perpetuity. Everything goes on 'forever'. Hell may be nothing other than this continuation of time because nothing can go on forever without becoming appalling. The only things which could keep us trapped in this perpetuity are events in our lifetime which we cannot give up or assimilate. We experience them over and over again, as if they were actually happening. This notion is metaphorically embodied in the persistent folk tales of ghosts who perform the same actions or haunt the same places. Often they are said to have committed suicide or murder; or to have been heinously betrayed. We sense some sort of truth in this, as if some crimes keep the perpetrators and victims alike 'earth-bound'. W. B. Yeats believed that during its 'dreaming-back' in the afterlife, the soul's most momentous experiences 'awake again and again, all our passionate events rush up about us and not as seeming imagination, for imagination is now the world'.[17] We are easily able to assimilate good experiences, of course, but there may be traumatic experiences or crimes which we cannot come to terms with – as we cannot in life. Then we are compelled to live them over and over again until we are free of them – something psychotherapists are familiar with in their patients.

If it seems too harsh to condemn the whole soul, as it were, to this pattern, it may be that only part of us is trapped in this way, just as we are not wholly confined in, or wholly defined by, neurotic compulsions and obsessions while we are alive. It may be only some fragment of the dead person's soul – or, better, only one image of soul – which continues to act out, like a looped videotape, the original trauma.

Repetition looks like Hell. In Greek myth, Sisyphus forever pushes a rock up a hill, only to have it roll back on him before he gets it to the top; Ixion revolves forever on his burning wheel; Tantalus craves the food and drink which are forever just out of his reach. Since these figures are part of myth, they cannot be left out of psychic life. And in fact we can all empathize with the states of frustration, pain and craving they symbolize. However, they may not only be illustrating kinds of Hell, as our Judaeo-Christian outlook tends to interpret their fates. They may be illustrating the psychic necessity for repetition. They might be the base images of the soul's natural affinity with circularity, such as the endless telling of the same stories we never tire of, or the cycle of the same seasons we welcome as emblems of death and rebirth. They might reflect the soul's love of performing the same sacred rituals daily or yearly, in order to 'make the sun rise', for example. The voluntary repetition of rituals is an image of that self-renewing eternity of which the involuntary repetition of compulsions is the shadow. They may even look the same: one man's meaningless and hellish routine can be another's meaningful and delightful ritual. Everything depends on the degree to which it is invested with imagination and imbued with sacred meaning, as the whole of life is for traditional societies.

If this is so, repetition might itself be transformative, as if its desperate circuits can automatically – alchemically, perhaps – generate of themselves the imaginative loosening of the noose and the hope of salvation.

The 'Great Mysterie'
I apologize for the duplicitous title of this book (did two-faced Hermes have a hand in it? Or was it just the publishers?)

because there can be – as we can appreciate by now – no complete guide to the soul. It is fathomless and defies definition. It never appears as itself but always as something else, some image of itself. The very word 'soul' is just such an image. It is all imagination, including its own self-imagining. It is paradoxical, encompassing all contradictions. I have been concentrating on those contradictions which, I guess, cause the most confusion, namely the way soul manifests both individually and collectively, personally and impersonally. Its preferred mode of manifestation is the personified image, notably gods and daimons. It likes to appear to us *in* another person, as Beatrice appeared to Dante; or *as* another person, like the unknown Beloveds we meet in dreams. Soul is like Jung's anima: both our personal soul, conferring our sense of uniqueness; and also the impersonal face the world-soul shows to us. But soul is also the personal daimon who guides and protects us, and mediates between us and the gods – as well as that which is guided and mediated.

All ideas or statements about the soul are from soul in the first place. The variety of bodily parts where we have historically located it – head, heart, blood, 'kidney-fat', brain etc. – is a metaphor for its omnipresence. We cannot capture it head-on, but only obliquely, whenever we are opened out onto unsuspected depths, giving meaning; whenever we sense a secret, something within, giving insight; whenever we suddenly make a connection, like a metaphor, bringing new vision. By the same token we cultivate soul by seeking depth, interiority and connectedness – in short, by exercising imagination. This includes the practice of changing perspective, or 'seeing through' to another reality; the practice of looking poetically at the world, or 'seeing double' – seeing the metaphorical in the literal, the story behind the 'facts'; the practice of reflection or 'seeing back' in order to connect the present to the past, and, more especially, present experience to its archetypal background; the practice of amplifying and developing images, whether they are in dreams, works of art or even in the super-market aisle, by becoming aware of what associations and feelings the images evoke – by 'dreaming the myth onward', as Jung used to say.

Soul-making

However, since soul will always remain in itself unknown and unfathomable, what Paracelsus – arguably the first great natural scientist – called the 'Great Mysterie',[18] the other disappoint-ment is therefore that there can be no final answer to the questions with which I began: 'What is my purpose? What am I for? Where do I go when I die?' The provisional answer might be: our purpose is to fulfil the daimon's secret plan and build our selves from its blueprint. From spirit's point of view this is a Goal, like a height we have to scale; from soul's point of view it is a Way, like a mazy wandering in the course of which we are transformed. After death, the linear trajectory of spirit is reconciled with the spiral path of soul, like the impossible squaring of the circle. 'The way up and the way down', said Heraclitus, anticipating the Zen masters, 'are one and the same.'[19] The answers to the questions of life will be self-evident because to enter into the fullness of our selves is self-evidently fulfilling. As part of the Soul of the World we are part of a cosmic dance of which it is meaningless to ask the purpose and meaning – because it is all purpose and meaning.

Yet in our Earthly state we still feel incomplete – a feeling induced by spirit's standpoint, from which soul appears as all potential, as something which must be unfolded, made actual, in the self. From soul's point of view, she is complete from the start, as if she were herself the personal daimon which directs our unfolding but does not itself develop. Spirit maintains that we change – grow, develop and progress; soul refutes this, holding that we simply manifest different facets of our wholeness, as if we were cutting and polishing our diamond selves. It is as if all the changes spirit initiates and undergoes are only the adoption of different outlooks, each of which, like the gods, is already latent in the soul. Every mother looks at her child from both points of view: even as she watches him or her grow and change, she also recognizes the same personality which, often to her amazement, was complete and fully formed at a very early age, even at birth.

Our task is to heed the daimon, glean from each situation the greatest possible insight, try to acquire a larger, more meaningful context in which to view our lives; which, in turn, means asking ourselves what deity is operative in our lives and trying to connect it to other deities in order to achieve the most and the deepest perspectives. Often our presiding deity will become apparent by what we instinctively shun. If we are too rigid to let ourselves go in a bit of Dionysian madness, we can be sure we are in thrall to the prissy side of Apollo or to prim, over-chaste Artemis. If we are too earnest, banging on about social justice or political theories, we are one-sidedly gripped by Athena, who can make us dogmatic and humourless without the leavening wit of Hermes or the sense of ridiculousness provided by Pan – whose grotesque appearance at birth made the gods burst out laughing. Perhaps the most invisible wallflower among us is really under the aegis of Hestia, goddess of the hearth, of whom little mention is made and less known – telling characteristics in themselves. She seems to embody that sense of focus (in Latin, a 'hearth'), inwardness and enclosure which enables deep psychic transformation to take place, as if hermetically sealed, without dissipating itself. Simply by acquainting ourselves with myth and attending to our dreams and fantasies, we soon become aware that one story resonates with us more than another, and stays with us, providing a clue as to where our world-view is coming from and whither the deity is conducting us. We cannot know what tribulations this will involve, but we can treat them as essential elements of the long initiatory process of life.

We are all alchemists who are looking for the primordial ingredient necessary to begin the Great Work. It can be found 'in the sweepings of the street' yet it is the 'treasure hard to attain'. Once we have found it we cannot begin the work of transmutation until we have unearthed 'our mercury' – the 'secret fire' which is the chief agent of the Work. Even if we obtain these, there is no guarantee we will reach our goal, or indeed even know what that goal is, since it is called the 'Stone that is no Stone'. In short, the Work is its own beginning, process and end result. The secret ingredient is soul, with which we begin; its imagination is the secret fire by which we transmute ourselves; and the self is the transmuted soul in which we are consummated.

The more we realize our selves, the less they seem to be *our* selves, as if the world-soul merely wishes to reflect itself through our eyes. The less self-important we are, the more important we are as selves, with a unique perspective on the cosmos. The self is what spirit spends a lifetime searching for, heroically setting out by land and sea to circumnavigate the globe, to suffer hardship and slay dragons, until he comes to the remote overgrown castle. He hacks a way through, climbs to the top of the tallest tower and – there, the love of his life, Beauty, lies sleeping. He kisses her. She wakes . . . . Her waking symbolizes the soul's dormant state till spirit wakes her, and makes her real. What is less obvious in our heroic age is that the kiss also wakes spirit. He looks around him, rubbing his eyes, and sees that the castle is in fact his castle, the place he started from. Beauty always slept there, but he did not notice her, so eager was he to set out and find her elsewhere.

As soul comes to herself in spirit, so spirit returns to himself in soul – and they are joined in the holy matrimony of the self.

Dancing at the wedding-feast

When we die we return to the Soul of the World whence we came. In fact we never left it. We are still in that great Imagination but we do not see it. We cannot imagine Imagination itself. Those who have glimpsed it tell us over and over again that we are like sleepers or blind people until death wakes us and restores our sight. Most of us have sensed this, however fleetingly, in the course of our lives – perhaps in a sunrise or in an epiphanic dream, in a work of art or the joy of love; in quiet moments at midnight when eternity descends on our hushed souls like moonlight. Then, for a second, we understand that we are like the prisoners in Plato's dim and musty cave, unable to conceive of sunlight and a scented breeze; understand that our chains are Blake's 'mind-forg'd manacles'[20] we can shake off at the instant, and step out into the glory of the Earthly Paradise.

It has always been difficult to find the right metaphor or symbol for the mutual inherence of soul and spirit. I can only think of two successful ones: marriage and music.

As an example of marriage, T. S. Eliot drew on the long poetic history of the rose as a symbol of soul, and of fire as a symbol of spirit. At the end of the *Four Quartets*, he unites these incommensurables in a cry of gratitude and praise – and a mystical image of flames being knotted into the shape of a rose.

At the end of his four-volume *Mythologiques*, the French anthropologist Claude Lévi-Strauss concludes that if there is one pair of symbols which embodies our two-fold condition, it is Heaven and Earth. For nearly all mythologies speak of a time when the sky world lay with this world; and it was their separation which caused all our unhappiness and their reunion which we yearn for. The *hieros gamos*, or sacred marriage, of Heaven and Earth is a symbol of all our longed-for reunions up and down the scale of being. Emotion and intellect, matter and spirit, body and soul, One and Many, male and female, human and divine, freedom and necessity – all the contradictions of our riven existence are most marvellously ravelled up in the wedding of soul and spirit, which preserves our two-foldness right into the heart of the One. The metaphor of marriage tells us that the truism is also true: that while we are always and only ourselves, we are also only truly our selves when we find ourselves in another, like Dante and Beatrice reflected in each other's eyes as they stand before the blazing altar of Love.

Like the Hermetic definition of God, soul is 'an intelligible sphere whose centre is everywhere and whose circumference is nowhere'. It is the beating heart of the cosmos, and also the circulation of its life-blood. It contracts into the One, the abstract God, and expands into the Many, the personified gods, just as our psyches move centrifugally towards a centre and centripetally towards a circumference as if breathing in and out. Breathe in – and everything is within you; breathe out – and you are in everything. For our souls are contained in the Soul of the World, yet, through the impossible convulsion of Love, we also contain that immensity. Congruent with the cosmos, we also are One and Many as we contract and expand in harmony with the heart of soul.

Music provides a useful way of picturing how it might be possible to retain our identity while submerging ourselves in a greater whole because, whether musician or listener, the more we forget ourselves and the more transparent to the music we become, the more we are our unique selves. We can imagine that our souls participate in Paradise as an individual voice participates in a choir, or as a musician in an orchestra. However, the image of the heavenly choir sounds a bit, well, *spiritual* for my taste. Its community smacks too much of the monastery and not enough of the marriage-feast. I would mistrust an afterlife which was too pure to include fools and rogues, just as I cannot picture a literature without Falstaff and Bottom, Sam Weller and the Artful Dodger, Sancho Panza and Bertie Wooster.

Thus I cannot help hoping that the music of the Otherworld will be more like tribal music, especially the tribal music that is close by: the old music of Ireland which can still be chanced upon in unexpected pubs and rural kitchens, where fiddles, wooden flutes, goat-skin drums, tin whistles and uillean pipes continue to celebrate centuries-old reels, jigs, hornpipes, polkas and slides. In the Platonic Form of the Pub, of course, I trust I will find myself in an Otherworldly session where the music is inseparable from dance, like all traditional music; where the same ancient tunes, like myths, are recreated afresh with every playing; where each musician has a chance to call the tune and no one is left out – the audience is as important as the players; where pauses in between the tunes – for jokes and laughter, talk and drink – are as crucial as the music; where beneath the apparent informality there are, like courtesy, exacting, unspoken and voluntary rules which allow each person the most freedom, as in a ritual, to play their part to the full, whether it is singing or fiddling, dancing or making merry, or even not listening at all. Where all are woven together in the music, it is suddenly possible to see what is meant by agape, communal love, as, in the midst of a heart-stopping reel, one by one – Dionysus arm-in-arm with Hades – the gods begin to slip in by the back door.

Marriage and music are only symbols. Once we cross the border from the transitional realm into the Otherworld proper, we run out of images and language, as the ecstatic stutterings of the mystics attest. We only know that to enter the Soul of the World is to consummate that lifelong desire which, no matter how we dress it up, is the longing for the Paradise we lost at birth; the longing for the Beloved who waits with open arms to whirl us, both dancer and dance, into that kingdom where, as wise Heraclitus (with whose definition of a soul we can never know, so deep is its measure, we began) says: 'there awaits us what we neither expect nor even imagine'.[21]

REFERENCES

Abbreviation Frg.: Fragment

INTRODUCTION

[1] Quoted in Wilson (1987) p. 267

[2] Letter to George and Georgiana Keats 14 Feb. – 3 May 1819, in Keats pp. 335f

[3] Review of Roth's *Everyman* in *The Times* (London), 22 April 2006

ONE: Soul and body

[1] Eliade (1977) p. 177

[2] in *Primitive Culture* (London, 1871)

[3] Eliade (1977) pp. 177–8; Lévy-Bruhl p. 128

[4] Eliade p. 179

[5] Lévy-Bruhl p. 164

[6] Ibid. p. 160

[7] Quoted in Robbines, Rossell and Hope, *The Encyclopedia of Witchcraft and Demonology* (New York, 1981) p. 346

[8] Lévy-Bruhl pp. 160–1

[9] Ibid. pp. 167f

[10] Personal communication from Nigel Barley, April 1979. See Barley (1983, 1986)

[11] Lévy-Bruhl p. 203

[12] Ibid. pp. 167f

[13] Ibid. p. 174

[14] Lady Gregory (1976A) p. 10

[15] Littlewood, R. and Douyon, C., 'Clinical findings in three cases of zombification', the *Lancet*, 11 October 1997

[16] Quoted by Merrily Harpur, album notes to Matt Molloy's *Shadows on Stone* (RCA Records, 1996)

[17] Léévy-Bruhl p. 301

18 Ibid. pp. 265–6
19 Ibid. p. 267

TWO: Soul and psyche

1   Dodds (1952) p. 150; p. 210
2   Onians p. 100
3   Snell p. 8
4   Onians p. 168
5   Ibid.
6   Dodds (1952) p. 153
7   Onians p. 94
8   Ibid. p. 100
9   Quoted in Onians. Note to p. 197
10 Frg. 45
11 Dodds (1952) pp. 140f
12 See, for example, Godwin p. 2
13 See, for example, Plato's *Phaedo* (62B) and *Cratylus* (400C)
14 Naydler (2006) p. 75
15 Ibid. pp. 75–6
16 Ibid. p. 77
17 Ibid. p. 78
18 Ibid. p. 79
19 *Phaedo* (67E)
20 Naydler (2006) p. 80
21 Ibid. p. 79
22 Naydler (1996) pp. 203–4
23 Ibid. p. 209
24 Naydler (2006) pp. 83–4
25 *Phaedo* (66E)
26 *Phaedrus* (246E–247E)
27 Hillman (1983). Note to p. 141
28 Copleston p. 153

THREE: Soul and world-soul

1 Henry, P., Introduction to the *Enneads* in Plotinus p. civ
2 Ibid. IV, 4, 33; III, 2,16
3 Quoted in O'Meara p. 17
4 Harpur, Patrick (2002) pp. 5–7
5 Ibid. pp. 5f
6 Lines 8–18
7 Quoted in Dodds (1965) p. 37
8 Quoted in Raine and Harper pp. 460–1
9 *De Defectu Oraculorum*, 13
10 Plotinus IV, 3, 9
11 This sketch of the Imagination is based on my long discussion of it in Harpur, Patrick (2002) chaps. 5, 23, 24
12 Coleridge p. 167
13 Hillman (1975) p. x
14 O'Meara p. 21
15 Ibid. pp. 26–7
16 Quoted in Hillman (1986) p. 155
17 O'Meara pp. 15–16
18 Ibid. p. 113
19 This view is discussed at length in Lewis (1964)
20 O'Meara pp. 30–1
21 Wallis pp. 157–8
22 Wallis p. 131

FOUR: Soul and mana

1 Wordsworth, III, lines 127–32
2 Vitebsky (2005) pp. 259–61
3 Ibid. pp. 268–9
4 Ibid. p. 269
5 Ibid. p. 265
6 Ibid. p. 264
7 Harpur (1995) *passim*

8   'On the Gods and the World', IV, quoted in Murray, Gilbert, *Five Stages of Greek Religion* (London, 1925)

9   Vitebsky (2005) p. 269

10 Ibid. p. 296

11 Barfield p. 78

12 Ibid. pp. 94–5

13 Turnbull (1963) p. 28

14 *My Goat's Eyes*. Channel 4, 3 June 1996

15 Letter to Thomas Butts, 22 November 1802, lines 27–8, in Blake p. 817

16 'The Everlasting Gospel' ('d' version), lines 103–6 in Blake p. 753

17 Op. cit. lines 29–30, in Blake p. 817

18 Op. cit. lines 27–8 in Blake p. 817

19 Letter to Dr Trusler, 23 August 1799 in Blake p. 793

20 Quoted in Hillman (1975) p. 149

21 Ibid. p. 150

22 Turnbull (1963) pp. 74–5

FIVE: Soul and the unconscious

1   Jung (1967A) p. 199

2   Ibid. p. 201

3   Ibid. p. 202

4   Ibid. p. 203

5   Freud p. 20f

6   Jung (1967A) pp. 203–4

7   Jung (1968A) §105

8   Jung (1967B) §388

9   Proclus' Commentary on Plato's *Republic* quoted in Raine and Harper p. 376

10 Hillman (1979) p. 23

11 Wallis p. 60

12 Much of this section is indebted to Hillman (1985). For our inhuman depths, see for example pp. 88–9

13   Ibid. p. 81
14   Hillman (1985) pp. 58–9
15   Ibid. pp. 173–5
16   See Jung (1981)
17   Jung (1967A) p. 231
18   A thoroughgoing account of the alchemical Great Work can be found in Harpur, Patrick (1990). This section is largely drawn from my sketch of alchemy in Harpur, Patrick (2002) chapters 7 and 8
19   Jung (1967A) p. 222

SIX: Soul and myth

1   'The Hollow Men' II, line 2 in Eliot p. 89
2   Popper, Karl, 'The Rationality of Scientific Revolutions' in Haking, I. (ed.), *Scientific Revolution* (London, 1981) p. 87
3   Cf. Raine and Harper pp. 460–1
4   Yeats (1961) p. 107
5   Cf. Hillman (1975) pp. 168–9
6   Quoted ibid. p. 151
7   Cf. Hillman (1979) p. 69
8   Ibid. pp. 35–6
9   Tarnas (1991) p. 110
10   Snell pp. 40–1
11   I, 6,9
12   Kingsley pp. 102–3
13   Ibid. pp. 110–11
14   Hillman (1979) p. 92
15   Hillman (1975) p. 71

SEVEN: Soul and daimon

1   Bloom p. 42
2   Macdonald p. 39
3   Briggs p. 132

Bloom pp. 202–3

[5] Ibid. p. 202

[6] Ibid. p. 47

[7] 11: 10

[8] Quoted in Dodds (1965) p. 37

[9] Ibid.

[10] Jung (1967A) pp. 208–9

[11] Jaffé p. 108

[12] Iamblichus III, iii–iv

[13] Onians pp. 137–8; 161–2

[14] Lévy-Bruhl p. 234

[15] Ibid. pp. 190–1

[16] Ibid. p. 192

[17] Stephens p. 192

[18] Lévy-Bruhl pp. 193–4

[19] Ibid. p. 195

[20] Cited in Auden (1971) p. 164

[21] Lévy-Bruhl p. 200

[22] Lévy-Bruhl pp. 198f

[23] Naydler (1996) pp. 193–5

[24] Ibid. p. 198

[25] Ibid. p. 200

[26] Porphyry, 'On the Life of Plotinus', trans. Stephen MacKenna, in Plotinus p. cx

[27] Wallis p. 71

[28] Iamblichus IX, vi

[29] X, 620E

[30] Quoted in Peake pp. 231–2

[31] Lewontin p. 100

[32] Dawkins p. 8

[33] Hillman (1996) pp. 39–40

[34] Quoted in Avens, Roberts. *The New Gnosis* (Dallas, 1984) pp. 79–80

35   Hillman (1997) pp. 14–17

36   Weil (1972) p. 73

37   Jung (1967) p. 356

38   Hillman (1997) pp .4–7; 251–3

39   Ibid. p. 193f

40   Ibid. p. 41f

41   Quoted ibid. p. 7

42   Quoted in Auden (1964) pp. 144–5

43   Hughes p. 268

44   Ibid p. 275

45   Yeats (1959) p. 335

46   Quoted in Raine (1986) p. 163

47   Hughes, p. 9

48   *The Pavement Doctor of Calcutta, An On-line E-book About the
     Extraordinary Life and Work of Dr. Jack Preger, MBE – Founder of the
     Charity 'Calcutta Rescue'*, 'Based on many hours of private
     interviews', at http://basilicum122.googlepages.com/chapter11

49   Yeats (1959) p. 336

EIGHT: Soul and spirit

1   Quoted in Wilson (1989) p. 24

2   Ibid.

3   Berenson p. 18

4   From 'As kingfishers catch fire . . . ' in Hopkins p. 51

5   'Lines composed a few miles above Tintern Abbey . . . ' in
    Wordsworth pp. 47–9

6   See Hardy's *The Spiritual Nature of Man* (Oxford, 1979)

7   Quoted in Wilson (1989) p. 43. For a fuller version, see Coxhead,
    Nona. *The Relevance of Bliss* (London, 1985)

8   This discussion is indebted to W.H. Auden's essay 'The Protestant
    Mystics' in Auden (1973)

9   See the discussion of Dante's *La Vita Nuova* in Williams (1943)

10 Auden (1973) p. 24

11 Ibid. p. 102

Williams (1963) pp. 212f

13   Galatians 2: 20

14   Weil (1972) p. 21

15   Anon. (1967) pp. 53–4; 135

16   12: 2–4

17   Dionysius the Areopagite pp. 194; 200

18   Ibid. p. 201

19   Quoted in Auden (1973) pp. 73–4

20   'Upon a Gloomy Night . . . ' ('En una noche oscura . . . ') in St
     John of the Cross pp. 26–9

21   Quoted in Wilson (1989) pp. 44–5

22   Pascal p. 309

23   Henry, P. Introduction to the *Enneads* in Plotinus p.lxxxvi

24   Plotinus IV, 9, 7

25   Ibid. IV, 8, 1

26   Dodds (1965) p. 88

27   Some of the following distinctions between soul and spirit are
     indebted to Hillman (1975) pp. 67–70 and Hillman (1989) pp.
     57–69

28   Hopkins p. 31

29   Quoted in 'A Consciousness of Reality' in Auden (1973) p. 415

30   Yeats (1967) p. 533

31   For the distinction between Arcadia and Utopia, Eden and the
     New Jerusalem, see 'Dingley Dell and the Fleet' in Auden (1964)
     pp. 409f

32   Raine (1991) pp. 105–6

33   Quoted in Wind pp. 63–4

34   Murdoch (1993) p. 318

35   Tillich pp. 180–3

36   See Miller pp. 27–8

37   Hillman (1989) pp. 67–8

38   Hillman (1975) p.69

NINE: Soul and ego

1 Dodds, E. R. 'Tradition and Personal Achievement in the Philosophy of Plotinus' in *The Ancient Concept of Progress and Other Essays* (Oxford, 1973) p. 135

2 Hillman (1979) pp. 110–17

3 Picard p. viii

4 Ibid. pp. 214f

5 Midgley p. 77

6 Lévy-Bruhl pp. 115–21

7 Letter to Richard Woodhouse, 27 October 1818, in Keats pp. 227–8

8 Tarnas (2006) p. 25

TEN: Soul and initiation

1 Eliade (1995) pp. 24; 31

2 Lévy-Bruhl p. 215

3 Review in the London *Times*, 10 August 2008

4 Lady Gregory (1976A) pp. 9–10

5 'Swedenborg, Mediums and the Desolate Places' in Lady Gregory (1976A) note 39 on p. 364

6 Lady Gregory (1976A) pp. 9–10

7 Ibid.

8 Halifax (1991) p. 161

9 Hillman (1985) pp. 105–7

10 Quoted in Barratt p. 8

11 Levi (1988) p. 37

12 Bettelheim p. 140

13 Ibid. pp. 140–2

14 Levi (1987) p. 96

15 Vitebsky (1995) pp. 146–7

16 Ibid. p. 46

17 Ibid. p. 60–1

18 Quoted in Halifax (1991) p. 14

Vitebsky (1995) p. 59

[20] Ibid. p. 59

[21] Eliade (1989) pp. 137–8

[22] Halifax (1991) p. 16

[23] Ibid. pp. 82–5

[24] James p. 344

[25] Jung (1967A) pp. 204–5

ELEVEN: Soul and afterlife

[1] Zaleski p. 124

[2] Plutarch, *On the Soul* quoted in Eliade (1977) p. 302

[3] XI, 1–26

[4] Zaleski p. 125

[5] Quoted in Lorimer p. 93

[6] By, for example, Kübler-Ross, Ring, Lorimer, Fenwick and Parnia – see Bibliography for details

[7] Parnia p. 78

[8] Atwater, P. M. H. *Coming Back to Life* (New York, 1988) p. 36, quoted in Lorimer p. 22

[9] Lorimer p. 22

[10] Quoted ibid. pp. 11–13

[11] 'The Marriage of Heaven and Hell' in Blake p. 149

[12] Ibid. p. 154

[13] Swedenborg pp. 27–9

[14] Quoted in Wilson (1987) p. 176

[15] London, 1949

[16] Ibid. pp. 146f

[17] Sherwood p. 60

[18] Ibid. p. 81

[19] Ibid. p. 91

[20] Frg. 60

TWELVE: Soul and Otherworld

1   Turnbull (1978) pp. 82–3
2   Lévy-Bruhl p. 300
3   'Auguries of Innocence' lines 1–2 in Blake p. 43
4   Quoted in Parkin pp. 4–5
5   Raine (1991) p.48
6   *The Odyssey*, XI
7   Eliade (1977) pp. 366–9
8   Lévy-Bruhl p. 306
9   Ibid. pp. 220–1
10 Hutton, Ronald p. 202
11 Yates pp. 92–3
12 Lévy-Bruhl p. 303
13 Ibid. p. 304
14 Vitebsky (1995) p. 18
15 Vergil, *The Aeneid*, VI, 743, trans. Patric Dickinson (New York, 1961)
16 Blake p. 150
17 Yeats in Lady Gregory (1976A) p. 314
18 Cf. Paracelsus p. 15
19 Frg. 60
20 'London' line 8 in Blake p. 216
21 Frg. 27

BIBLIOGRAPHY

Abbreviation *CW*: Collected Works

Anon., *The Cloud of Unknowing* (London, 1967)

Apuleius, *The Golden Ass*, trans. Robert Graves (London, 1950)

Auden, W. H., *The Dyer's Hand* (London, 1964)

— *A Certain World* (London, 1971)

— *Forewords and Afterwords* (London, 1973)

Barfield, Owen, *Saving the Appearances: A Study in Idolatry* (London, 1957; Middletown, Conn., 1988)

Barley, Nigel, *Symbolic Structures: An Exploration of the Culture of the Dowayos* (Cambridge, 1983)

— *A Plague of Caterpillars* (London, 1986)

Barratt, William, *The Death of the Soul* (Oxford, 1986)

Berenson, Bernard, *Sketch for a Self-Portrait* (New York, 1949)

Bettelheim, Bruno, *The Informed Heart* (London, 1970)

Blake, William, *Complete Writings*, ed. Geoffrey Keynes (Oxford, 1966)

Bloom, Harold, *Omens of Millennium* (London, 1996)

Briggs, Katharine, *The Fairies in Tradition and Literature* (London, 1967)

Coleridge, Samuel Taylor, *Biographia Literaria* (1817; London, 1965)

Copleston, F. C., *Aquinas* (London, 1963)

Corbin, Henri, *Creative Imagination in the Sufism of Ibn Arabi* (Princeton, NJ, 1969)

Dawkins, Richard, *The Selfish Gene* (London, 1978)

Dionysius the Areopagite, *The Divine Names* and *The Mystical Theology*, trans. C. E. Rolt (London, 1979)

Dodds, E. R., *The Greeks and the Irrational* (Berkeley, 1952)
— *Pagan and Christian in an Age of Anxiety* (Cambridge, 1965)
Eliade, Mircea, *From Primitives to Zen* (London, 1977)
— *Shamanism: Archaic Techniques of Ecstasy*, trans. Willard R. Trask (London, 1989)
— *Rites and Symbols of Initiation* (Woodstock, Conn., 1995)
Eliot, T. S., *Collected Poems 1909–1962* (London, 1963)
Fenwick, P. and Fenwick, E., *The Truth in the Light* (London, 1995)
Findlay, J. N., *Ascent to the Absolute* (London, 1970)
Freud, Sigmund, *An Autobiographical Study* (The International Psycho-analytical Library, ed. Ernest Jones, M.D., No. 26) (London, 1950)
Godwin, Joscelyn, *The Golden Thread: The Ageless Wisdom of the Western Mystery Traditions* (Wheaton, Ill., 2007)
Graves, Robert, *The Greek Myths*, 2 vols. (London, 1960)
Gregory, Lady Augusta, *Visions and Beliefs in the West of Ireland* (Gerrards Cross, Bucks., 1976A)
— *Gods and Fighting Men* (Gerrards Cross, Bucks., 1976B)
Guthrie, W. K. C., *Orpheus and Greek Religion* (Princeton, NJ, 1993)
Halifax, Joan, *Shaman; The Wounded Healer* (London, 1982)
— *Shamanic Voices* (London, 1991)
Harpur, James, *Love Burning in the Soul* (Boston, 2005)
Harpur, Patrick, ed., *Mercurius: or, the Marriage of Heaven and Earth* (London, 1990; Glastonbury, 2008)
— *Daimonic Reality: A Field Guide to the Otherworld* (London & New York, 1994; Ravensdale, WA, 2003)
— *The Philosophers' Secret Fire* (London, 2002; Glastonbury, 2009)
Hillman, James, *Re-Visioning Psychology* (New York, 1975)
— *The Dream and the Underworld* (New York, 1979)
— 'The Pandaemonium of Images' in *Healing Fiction* (Barrytown, New York, 1983)

Anima: An Anatomy of a Personified Notion (Dallas, 1985)
— 'Plotino, Ficino and Vico as Precursors of Archetypal
 Psychology' (1973) in *Loose Ends* (Dallas, 1986)
— *Puer Papers* (Dallas, 1989)
— *The Soul's Code* (London, 1996)
Homer, *The Odyssey*, trans. E. V. Rieu (London, 1971)
Hopkins, Gerard Manley, *Poems and Prose* (London, 1971)
Hughes, Ted, *Winter Pollen; occasional prose*, ed. William
 Scammell (London, 1994)
Hutton, J. H., *The Sema Nagas* (London, 1921)
Hutton, Ronald, *The Pagan Religions of the Ancient British Isles,
 Their Nature and Legacy* (Oxford, 1995)
Iamblichus, *On the Mysteries of the Egyptians, Chaldeans and
 Assyrians . . .* , trans. Thomas Taylor (London, 1821)
Jaffé, Aniela, *Apparitions* (Dallas, 1979)
James, William, *The Varieties of Religious Experience* (London,
 1985)
Jung, C. G., *Memories, Dreams, Reflections* (London, 1967A)
— *Symbols of Transformation CW5* (London, 1967B)
— *The Archetypes of the Collective Unconscious, CW9, I*
 (London, 1968A)
— *Psychology and Alchemy, CW12,* (London, 1968B)
— *The Structure and Dynamics of the Psyche, CW8* (London, 1969)
— *Mysterium Coniunctionis, CW14* (London, 1970)
— *Aion, CW9, II* (London, 1981)
Keats, John, *The Letters of John Keats*, ed. M. B. Forman
 (London, 1935)
Kerenyi, C., *The Heroes of the Greeks* (London, 1974)
— *The Gods of the Greeks* (London, 1992)
Kingsley, Peter, *In the Dark Places of Wisdom* (London, 1999)
Kirk, G. S. and Raven, J. E., *The Presocratic Philosophers*
 (Cambridge, 1957)
Kübler-Ross, Elizabeth, *On Death and Dying* (New York,
 1969)

Levi, Primo, *If This is a Man* (London, 1987)

— *The Drowned and the Saved* (London, 1988)

Lévy-Bruhl, Lucien, *The 'Soul' of the Primitive* (London, 1965)

Lewis, C. S., *The Discarded Image* (Cambridge, 1964)

Lewontin, R. C., *The Doctrine of DNA: Biology as Ideology* (London, 1993)

López-Pedraza, Rafael, *Hermes and his Children* (Einsideln, Switzerland, 1989)

Lorimer, David, *Whole in One* (London, 1990)

Macdonald, Hope, *When Angels Appear* (Grand Rapids, Michigan, 1982)

Midgley, Mary, *Science and Salvation: a Modern Myth and its Meaning* (London and New York, 1992)

Miller, David, *The New Polytheism* (Dallas, 1981)

Moody Jr., Raymond A., *Life after Life* (New York, 1976)

Murdoch, Iris, *The Fire and the Sun* (Oxford, 1978)

— *Metaphysics as a Guide to Morals* (London, 1993)

Myers, F. W. H., *Human Personality and Its Survival of Bodily Death* (New York, 1961)

Naydler, Jeremy, *Temple of the Cosmos: the Ancient Egyptian Experience of the Sacred* (Rochester, Vt., 1996)

— 'Plato, Shamanism and Ancient Egypt' in *Temenos Review* (London, 2006)

O'Meara, Dominic J., *Plotinus: An Introduction to the Enneads* (Oxford, 1995)

Onians, R. B., *The Origins of European Thought about the Body, the Mind, the Soul, the World, Time and Fate* (Cambridge, 1981)

Paracelsus, *Selected Writings*, ed. Jolande Jacobi (Princeton, NJ, 1958)

Parkin, Andrew, *The Dramatic Imagination of W.B. Yeats* (Dublin, 1978)

Parnia, Sam, *What Happens When We Die?* (London, 2008)

Pascal, Blaise, *Pensées* (London, 1966)

...ke, Anthony, *Is there Life after Death?* (London, 2006)

Picard, Barbara Leonie, *Tales of the Norse Gods and Heroes* (Oxford, 1953)

Plato, *The Republic*, trans. H. D. P. Lee (London, 1970)

— *Timaeus* and *Critias*, trans. H. D. P. Lee (London, 1971)

— *Phaedrus* and *Letter VII and VIII*, trans. Walter Hamilton (London, 1973)

Plotinus, *The Enneads*, trans. Stephen MacKenna (London, 1991)

Raine, Kathleen, *Blake and Tradition*, vol. I (London, 1969)

— *Yeats the Initiate: Essays on certain themes in the work of W.B. Yeats* (London, 1986)

— *Autobiographies* (London, 1991)

Raine, Kathleen and Harper, George Mills, eds., *Thomas Taylor the Platonist: Selected Writings* (London, 1969)

Ring, Kenneth, *Life at Death: A scientific investigation of the near-death experience* (New York, 1980)

Rougemont, Denis, de *Passion and Society* (London, 1940)St John of the Cross, *Poems*, trans. Roy Campbell (London, 1968)

Sherwood, Jane, *Post-Mortem Journal* (London, 1964)

Snell, Bruno, *The Discovery of Mind: The Greek Origins of European Thought*, trans. T. G. Rosenmeyer (New York, 1960)

Stephens, Anthony, *Private Myths* (Harvard, Mass., 1995)

Swedenborg, Emanuel, *Essential Readings*, ed. Michael Stanley (Wellingborough, 1988)

Tarnas, Richard, *The Passion of the Western Mind* (New York, 1991)

— *Cosmos and Psyche* (New York, 2006)

Tillich, Paul, *The Courage to Be* (London, 1962)

Tillyard, E. M. W., *The Elizabethan World Picture* (London, 1963)

Turnbull, Colin, *The Forest People* (London, 1963)

— *Man in Africa* (London, 1978)

Vitebsky, Piers, *The Shaman* (London, 1995)

— *The Reindeer People* (London, 2005)

Wallis, R. T., *Neoplatonism* (London, 1972)

Weil, Simone, *Gravity and Grace* (London, 1972)

— *Notebooks*, 2 vols., trans. Arthur Wills (London, 1976)

Williams, Charles, *The Figure of Beatrice: A Study in Dante* (London, 1943)

— *The Descent of the Dove* (London, 1963)

Wilson, Colin, *Afterlife* (London, 1987)

— *Beyond the Occult* (London, 1989)

Wind, Edgar, *Pagan Mysteries in the Renaissance* (London, 1967)

Wordsworth, William, *Poetical Works* (Oxford, 1971)

Yates, Frances, *Giordano Bruno and the Hermetic Tradition* (London, 1964)

Yeats, W. B., *Mythologies* (London, 1959)

— *Essays and Introductions* (London, 1961)

— *Collected Poems* (London, 1967)

Zaleski, Carol, *Otherworld Journeys* (London, 1988)

Index